CW01082016

Childhood's Domain

Childhood's Domain

Play and place in child development

Robin C. Moore

CROOM HELM
London • Sydney
• Dover, New Hampshire

Croom Helm Ltd, Provident House, Burrell Row,
Beckenham, Kent BR3 1AT
Croom Helm Australia Pty Ltd, Suite 4, 6th Floor,
64–76 Kippax Street, Surry Hills, NSW 2010, Australia

British Library Cataloguing in Publication Data

Moore, Robin C.
    Childhood's domain: play and place in child
    development
    1. Child development   2. Man—influence
    of environment
    I. Title
    155.4   BF721
    ISBN 0-85664-936-8

Croom Helm, 51 Washington Street,
Dover, New Hampshire 03820, USA

Library of Congress Cataloging in Publication Data

Moore, Robin C.
    Childhood's domain.

    Bibliography: p.
    Includes index.
    1. Play.   2. Recreation areas.   3. City children.
4. Environmental psychology.   I. Title. (DNLM:
1. Child development.   2. Environment design.
3. Play and playthings. WS 105.5.P5 M823C)
HQ782.M65   1986   305.2'3   86-8226
ISBN 0-85664-936-8

Composed by the author at the
School of Design, North Carolina
State University, on a Compugraphic
MCS 10-8400, with Garamond (ITC)
and Univers, set nine on twelve.

Printed and bound in Great Britain by
Biddles Ltd, Guildford and King's Lynn

Robin Moore was educated at Sevenoaks School, Kent; in the Boy Scouts; at the Bartlett School of Architecture, University College, London; and at Massachusetts Institute of Technology, Department of City and Regional Planning. He is past Chair of the Environmental Design Research Association and a Vice President of the International Association for the Child's Right to Play. He has taught at the University of California, Berkeley, and at Stanford University; and currently teaches at the School of Design, North Carolina State University, Raleigh. He is a partner in the firm of Moore Iacofano Goltsman.

*In memory of Donald Appleyard and Kevin Lynch—
urban designers with empathy and professional
concern for urban childhood—who believed
that policy should be based on field research.
And in memory of the "Uneducated Lady"
of Hurtwood, whose urgings spawned this book
and whose passionate advocacy still nurtures
the field of childhood and environment.*

CONTENTS

FIGURES

Acknowledgements

Figure 2, p.7, adapted from an original version in *Plants and the Ecosystem,* Third Edition, by W.D. Billings. © 1978 by Wadsworth Publishing Company, Belmont, California 94002. Reprinted by permission of publisher and author.

Excerpt, p.8, from *The Ecology of Imagination in Childhood,* by Edith Cobb. Copyright © 1977 by Columbia University Press. Reprinted by permission.

Excerpts, pp.8 and 9, from *Magical Child,* by Joseph Chilton Pearce. Copyright © 1977 by Joseph Chilton Pearce. Reprinted by permission of the publisher, E.P. Dutton, New York, a division of New American Library; and Grafton Books, London, a division of Collins Publishing Group.

Excerpt, pp.9 and 10, from "To Catch the Wind: Kites, Kids and the Environment in Barranquitas, Puerto Rico," by Denis Wood. Copyright © 1981 by Denis Wood. Reprinted by permission of the author.

Excerpt, p.10, from "Some Aspects of Operations," by Jean Piaget. Copyright © 1972 by W.W. Norton, New York. Reprinted by permission of the publisher.

Excerpts, pp.11 and 19, from "The Ecology of Imagination in Childhood," by Edith Cobb. Reprinted by permission of publisher, *Daedalus,* 88(3): 537-548, Summer 1959, Boston, MA.

Figure 3, p.13, adapted from an original version in *Born Curious: New Perspectives in Educational Theory,* by R.A. Hodgkin. Copyright © 1976 by Robin Hodgkin. Reprinted by permission of author, and publisher, John Wiley & Sons, Ltd, London.

Excerpts, pp.231 and 233, from *Between Past and Future,* by Hannah Arendt. Copyright © 1958 Hannah Arendt. Reprinted by permission of the publisher, Viking Penguin, Inc., New York.

Photographs throughout the book are by the author, except the aerial photographs appearing on pp.26 and 27 by permission of Aerofilms, and p.28 by permission of Meridian Airmaps.

Introduction

Twenty years ago I began work, from the perspective of urban design, on the idea that urban environments could be managed to support human development—like an evolving ecosystem. In pursuit of this purpose, the most obvious point of intervention seemed to be the environment of childhood.

The first step was to review the child development literature, hoping to find research results that would offer guidance to a designer interested in the support of human needs. The search was almost fruitless. Most of the research did not reach beyond five-year-olds; nearly all came from work conducted with special problem groups under isolated conditions, in laboratories, clinics, or psychologists' offices. Hardly any related to ordinary children in settings of everyday life. A surprising number of conclusions were derived, not from research with children at all, but from experiments with animals. I concluded that either the effects of living environments on children's development was not considered to be important, or it was not considered to be researchable. Either assumption, or both together, explained why most research covered only preschool relationships between mother, child, and siblings, and why the physical attributes of the environment were so drastically discounted.

I moved along more shelves, scanned more bibliographies, now on the lookout for educational research relating to children's environments. As before, I found almost no indication that investigation of children's everyday surroundings was an important or valid topic. Geography covered just about everything—except life down the street. History likewise. Nature study came closest; yet it was isolated as a special subject, with fieldwork conducted in nature reserves away from school and community—an approach that tended to put nature on a pedestal and ignore or, worse still, denigrate the rest of the urban environment.

At that point I set out to conduct my own investigations. Initial efforts were focused on the design and evaluation of designated places for children, such as playgrounds and schoolyards. This continues as an important area of related work; but I realised, early on, that children themselves do not discriminate strongly, and sometimes not at all, between such areas and a multitude of other places in the environment that they find attractive—or places that they are obliged to use simply because there are no other options available. Neighbourhood streets are the most obvious example. Then the thought arose, well, maybe some streets and other anonymous everyday spaces actually function perfectly well as ecological niches for children; and maybe, if the reasons for their success were understood more clearly, other places could be improved to the same or better standards. In 1974 I began studying the everyday landscapes of childhood in the San Francsico Bay Area, where the groundwork was laid, and the methods refined, for the British work conducted the following year and reported here.

Childhood's Domain should be viewed as a close relative of Colin Ward's marvellously expansive and erudite *The Child in the City*[1]—a book which set a new intellectual tone for investigating children-environment relations. My own effort represents a modest investigation with children in their 'middle years' (eight-to-twelve-year-olds), across a range of present-day neighbourhood conditions. The study grew out of a desire to feel more secure about local community environmental planning and design decisions—to see how the configuration and content of urban settings could support or enhance (or at the very least not suppress) children's devlopmental potential.

Even more than when my own studies started, there is a need to take a more critical look at the use of public space and physical resources in our towns and cities, to find ways to improve their social utility. Above all, children themselves need to collaborate in this activity through formal educational channels, as well as through nonformal community education and action. The growth of environmental education during the last decade—especially in Britain—provides an excellent vehicle for the integration of childhood environment research with the participation of young people, in the planning, design and management of local community settings. In this way, experience in documentation, debate, negotiation, and other crucial decision-making skills, can be acquired. They are essential for political effectiveness. It is imperative that young people learn how to assert more influence over their local living conditions; they are so much more vulnerable than even a decade ago, given the rise in biologically toxic substances in the environment—not to mention the psychologically-warping threat of nuclearcide. In the space of a few years, the world has become a small and alarmingly vulnerable biosphere, facing global issues beyond the ability of national governments to resolve on their own.

This study is concerned with relations between child, other people and physical habitat, and with environment-behaviour phenomena that can be translated into policy or that have policy implications. The value of policy in dealing with the anarchy of children's environmental play is, I would be the first to admit, open to debate. But what other choice exists? If play is considered a developmentally crucial mode of learning, and therefore part of a child's broad education, it must inevitably become the business of government, acting in partnership with nongovernment community interests.

It was the work of Iona and Peter Opie[2] that encouraged me to accept what years of informal observation had taught: that there was a wonderfully rich childhood culture lurking in the interstices of every neighbourhood—what the Opies refer to as the "child-to-child complex...[of] people going about their own business within their own society...fully capable of occupying themselves under the jurisdiction of their own code."[3]

As a professional planner, I had experienced many instances where, because this hidden life of children was not understood, acknowledged, or taken seriously, the places necessary for its support were 'tidied-up' or destroyed or were not replicated in urban redevelopment. The Opies did not investigate this issue. Their purpose was to document the "simple games for which, as one child put it, 'nothing is needed but the players themselves.'"[4] The extraordinary richness and cultural significance of their findings—there are almost 3000 entries in the book's Index of Games and Game-Rhymes

—wholly vindicates their intention. Indeed, after reading the Opies' account one must wonder if there is, indeed, an issue at hand. The butt of their sparse critical comments is laid on adult attempts to "provide for" children's play. The Opies see it as wasted effort.

The fact remains, however, that serious issues exist regarding the state and status of children in those communities where there is a paucity of opportunities for the creative use of their leisure time. There are viable and important roles and responsibilities for adults to assume in their relationships with children—not as play 'supervisors,' but as guides, facilitators and teachers in the broadest sense; and as policy makers, too—recognizing that it is adults who hold political and economic power, not children.

Observations about the physical environment are seldom expressed by the Opies—not even comments about urban traffic, which, beyond a few cars per hour, renders many street games impossible or highly dangerous undertakings. It is only in the book's introduction that a few editorial remarks and quotes from children slip in that indicate recognition of issues such as "the cult amongst elders to trim, to pave, to smooth out, to clean-up, to prettify, to convert to economic advantage...wastelands [and] wild corners of parks ...the secret places 'where no one else goes' [where] peaks of a child's experience [occur]...when he escapes into places that are disused and overgrown and silent."[5]

The Opie's work is so utterly fascinating and carried out with such scholarly thoroughness, one is relieved to find it unsullied by editorializing about the obvious fact that many settings are not supportive of children's play. The Opies convince us that, countrywide, children's traditional games still flourish as vigorously as they have in the past. But, self-evidently, this is not uniformly true at the level of individual neighbourhoods, housing estates and streets. Some are obviously much more supportive than others. There are many types of play (including some traditional games) that require specific physical conditions, that have specific environmental dependences (in contrast to the 'environmentally independent' games collected by the Opies).

In point of fact, the Opies deal only with one type of play: traditional games with rules, for the most part played in indigenous close-to-home spaces (steps, driveways, pavements, streets, carparks, schoolyards, playgrounds and so on). Traditional games of this type cropped up from time to time in the present study, often identical to or variations on games recorded by the Opies. But many of my recordings were of more spontaneous, free-flowing activity and environmental interactions, which did indeed occur in "disused, overgrown and silent" places.

Research that is used as a basis for changing the circumstances of people's lives must, for me, satisfy two conditions in order to be effective. First, it has to be conducted within an ideological framework—a system of values and assumptions concerning the nature and prognosis of society. Second, the subjects of investigation must be involved as much as possible as collaborators in the research itself and in the formulation and implementation of policy arising therefrom.

The forging of connections between the way things *are* and the way they *ought* to be—the present to the future, the descriptive to the prescriptive—is a complex, multilevel, cyclical and cumulative process. This complexity makes it imperative that long-term purposes be explicitly embodied in the conduct of research activity. Assessments of current conditions must cycle into on-going processes of decision making and change—where 'researcher' and 'community' are distinguished on the basis of role, rather than by power and position. Knowledge must be given back to the people it came from so they can use it to improve their own circumstances.

In the tradition of the Opies, I investigated the reality of children's everyday, anywhere life—documented as much as possible in children's own terms, as they themselves experienced it. Without this grounding of reality, policy development becomes a foolish, if not dangerous, wasted effort. We have no business making policy and spending money on facilities for children until we have at least a modest empirical understanding about what parts of the environment children actually use, and why. How can suggestions be made about what ought to be changed, before we know what exists as social reality? But what may be true for one group is not necessarily true for another. For this reason three different communities were included in the study, to reduce the risk of cultural bias as well as for obvious comparative purposes.

Recognition that the user, rather than the outsider, is the expert in matters of user-environment relationships, has been professionally liberating for me. Far from reducing the challenge of professional work, it has added an entirely new dimension of meaning and commitment. To discover that users can be an ally against lethargy and ignorance is a far cry from the meaningless comparison of one over-worked design cliché versus another.

Immersion in another person's reality, coming to it without preconception, accepting it for what it is, was such a simple act; the main difficulty was one of getting into the act, of being able to drop roles, titles, and mutual expectations, and find a neutral meeting ground. It is perhaps not difficult to imagine the great advantage of being accepted into a school as a nonteacher. When children realised they were not being 'tested,' that the results were not going to be 'marked,' they became greatly interested in sharing all they knew.

Designers, like myself, need to take the simple step of going out and meeting people in their own habitat; not 'community leaders,' or anyone else speaking on behalf of others, but people who can speak and act for themselves. For there is a fundamental difference bet-ween working with someone directly in their own physical setting, and working at any other level of communication—away from the actual stuff of a person's life.

I was interested in investigating children's *specific* interactions with their surroundings—something that few authors deal with. My starting point in understanding the relationship between play, place, and child development, was to find out what children actually did, where, when, with what, with whom—when not in class or at home engaged in routine chores.

The results are structured and conveyed in ways which I hope will engage the attention of sympathetic childhood-and-environment professionals (educators, play workers, recreation specialists, en-vironmental planners and designers). It has been a carefully trodden path, since some of the conclusions fly in the face of conventional wisdom; or they extend the notion of socially significant environ-ments beyond the normal limits of professional concerns and policy-making initiatives. Jane Brown's *The Everywhere Landscape*[6] cour-ageously raises the broader professional issues that connect to the specific interest pursued here (to see how systematic people-environ-ment research can be used to inform professional decision making).

My research agenda includes the assumed connections—via children's play—between childhood competence, environmental quality, education, and politics. Unavoidable issues are raised when one observes the vast difference in self-motivation exhibited by some children in their outdoor play behaviour, compared to their classroom behaviour. Surely more integration can be made between these two domains of childhood, so they might reinforce each other more effectively. My hope is that the book presents a case for regarding the quality of the physical environment as a significant factor in child development—for the benefit of both children and biosphere.

My purpose is not to present a set of precisely defined cause-effect relationships. Quantitative documentation is introduced where appropriate; but at the same time, in order to properly convey the idiosyncracies of individual behavior, I have chosen to present a large measure of qualitative illustration. At the same time I have tried not to admit conclusions, or to state them too forcefully, unwarranted by the evidence. Occasionally, however, I have stepped beyond the limits of sometimes skimpy data into the realm of unsubstantiated assertion; for there are some issues that cannot wait to be verified *a priori*. They must be set up for debate.

The bias of my own 'environmental biography' should be borne in mind at this point. I grew up on the fringe of a town in Kent, in the South of England, surrounded by an easily accessible landscape of woods, streams, fields and half-built houses (abandoned at the outbreak of World War II). Interpretation of my research material has been undoubtedly and unavoidably coloured by my own childhood experience—and its recollection. I, too, grieve for a landscape now covered with suburban houses, where once we dug, climbed trees, played cops-and-robbers, went bird-nesting, rolled in the bracken, built camps, dammed streams and caught 'tiddlers.'

Apart from my own childhood grounding, a number of sources affected both my attitude in approaching the research task and my orientation towards interpreting the results. They include Robert Cole's *Children of Crisis*,[7] Paulo Friere's *Pedagogy of the Oppressed*[8] and Frederick Perls, Ralph Hefferline and Paul Goodman's *Gestalt Therapy.*[9] I am grateful to Lars Lerup and Donald Young, who, with uncanny timing, in the space of a memorable few days, introduced me to Merleau-Ponty's *Phenomenology of Perception*[10] and the work of other phenomenologists, and to Robert Pirsig's *Zen and the Art of Motorcycle Maintenance* (very illuminating on the concept of quality).[11] During later drafts, Peter Marris' *Loss and Change*,[12] Geoffrey Vickers' *Freedom in a Rocking Boat*,[13] E. F. Schumacher's *Small is Beautiful*[14] and Colin Ward's *Anarchy in Action*[15] clarified and directed my thinking in particular ways. All of the above helped me sharpen my own values and cast the light of understanding on particular parts of the tangled heap of empirical material.

I would be remiss not to mention an intellectual debt to the Department of Urban Studies and Planning at MIT—to the late Kevin Lynch in particular—for enthusiasically supporting my interest in children's environments and helping me acquire sufficient professional self-confidence to adopt field-oriented, action-research methods of investigation. I should also record my appreciation of intellectual support, over the years, from Clare Cooper Marcus and the late Donald Appleyard, at the College of Environmental Design, University of California, Berkeley. Encouraging words from Urie Bronfenbrenner, Susan Goltsman, Daniel Iacofano, Jane Knight, Brian Little and Mary Jo Porter were also welcomed.

Four professional organizations must be mentioned: the Environmental Design Research Association (EDRA); the International Association for the Child's Right to Play (IPA); Childhood City (publishers of *Children's Environments Quarterly)*; and Streetwork (publishers of BEE, *The Bulletin of Environmental Education*).[16] Over the years, they have become invaluable sources of information and peer support in this and other endeavors.

The general approach and methods used owe much to Roger Hart's pioneering fieldwork and his generous advice during the early days of the study. Pia Björklid's work shares an equal debt. Together they provided a crucial ecological framework of child development theory, within which I could integrate my concern for the quality of children's relationships with the physical world. I must also note the influence of Herb Wong, who, over many years, also helped me develop an ecological orientation for investigating children-environment relations. Special acknowledgements go to Donald Young, who helped formulate the original research design with Lucia Kittredge and Marlene Lustick, and to Maureen Simmons who gave freely of her time to help organize the data and converse with the computer. I am especially indebted to Louise Chawla, Roger Hart and Denis Wood for their perceptive, provocative and helpful critical reviews of the draft manuscript. Their comments, together with later ones by Pia Björklid, have added much to the quality of the final result.

Support for the fieldwork came from the Beatrix Farrand Endowment Fund of the Department of Landscape Architecture, University of California, Berkeley. I should also acknowledge the U. S. National Endowment for the Arts, Design Arts Program, for their support of the first phase of research conducted in the San Francisco Bay Area (where field methods were developed that were used in the British study reported here).

To make grass roots connections, footloose action researchers, like myself, rely heavily on the goodwill of personal contacts. In this regard I must acknowledge the assistance of Colin Ward and Anthony Fyson, both formerly of the Town and Country Planning Association Education Unit; Chris Webb at the Notting Dale Urban Studies Centre; Inga Jackson in the Public Relations Department, Stevenage Development Corporation; Mark Lintell of Land UseConsultants, London; and Trevor Siggers at Brownhills School, Stoke-on-Trent. Very special thanks go to Louis and Maria Hellman for the warm hospitality offered to a researcher away from home.

My grateful thanks go to the staff and children at St. Clements Primary School, Notting Dale; Bedwell Junior School, Stevenage; and Mill Hill Middle School, Tunstall, for the enthusiastic interest and cooperation that made this venture possible. Additional thanks go to the children who took me on field trips around their favourite places —from whom I learnt so much—and to their parents for taking time to answer my questions.

Lastly, my sincere thanks to Peggy Harrison for her enduring good humour during the typing and retyping of numerous drafts; to Cindy Crawford who did the final word-processing; to Sandy Lowrance and Ann Seymour who designed the book; to Rod Cockshutt and Jo Stipe who helped with copy editing; and to Bill Bayley, Martha Lange, Claude McKinney, Ken Pittman and Greg Prygrocki, at North Carolina State University, School of Design, who contributed in various ways to the final production; and to David Croom—the most patient and understanding of publishers—for his constructive criticism and unfaltering encouragement.

* * * * * *

The book is presented in three parts. In the first, two contrasting field experiences are introduced, illustrating, in essence, the positive and negative relationships that exist between children and their surroundings. A conceptual framework is laid out, drawing on the work of those child development theorists who include play and interaction with the environment as critical components. The framework is used for interpreting the qualitative material gathered on field trips, in combination with the more quantitative information gleaned systematically from drawings and interviews, concerning favourite places and activities.

The second part of the book, containing the bulk of the field material, is organized around chapter topics describing how principal territories, types of space, and particular facilities, were actually used by children. As much as possible, interpretations are made which highlight childhood policy issues in environmental planning, design and management.

The third part of the book focuses on issues of conservation and change in relation to children's environments. Material is introduced to illustrate some of the underlying social, psychological and cultural factors, that help explain why things are the way they are—factors which must be recognised and taken into account in any move to change the status quo. A chapter is devoted to how children themselves perceived change to their environment (compared to their parents) and what they wanted to see happen in the future. In the final chapter, policy directions are developed. Different realms of action are proposed and discussed in the light of existing initiatives by local, national, and international organizations.

Ham Street, Kent.

Raleigh, North Carolina.

Playing, learning and place

Quality is not a **thing,** it is an **event**!
—*Phaedrus*

The rudiments of knowledge imbibed through play are an essential part of education.
—*Mahatma Gandhi*

1 *Questions of quality*

We wandered around a piece of undulating, weedy wasteland, partway through a trip around twelve-year-old Heather's favourite places in Notting Dale—a central London neighbourhood. Fireweed (rosebay willowherb) puffed messages of urban decay around erstwhile middle-class homes. A corrugated iron fence kept out the noise of the surrounding streets, and provided shelter from sharp October winds and prying adult eyes. As we talked, Heather knelt to pick wild flowers and grasses, adding them one by one to a posy to take home to her mother.

This was no wasteland, I began to realise, but a peaceful haven, moments from the cramped and dingy basement where Heather lived. The more she talked about this fertile land, the more it began to acquire a rich significance invisible to me moments before. She told me about the games she and her friends played, how they dug for "buried treasure," their archeological search for "lost civilizations." She described the myths of her playscape—pointing to a blackened hole in the ground where a man had been "blown up by electricity." She showed me a "wasp's nest" and a place where she and her best friend made "little fires for picnics," and a tree (remaining from a former garden) where they sat "to share secrets." There was a real sense of childhood possession there, in a place temporarily abandoned by the adult world.

Making a posy of wasteland wildflowers and grasses to take home.

Later, Heather took me home to talk with her mum (who worked for the borough council as a road sweeper). Heather gave her the posy: a simple gesture of wasteland flora, accepted with obvious affection and understanding. Heather's mum said her daughter was doing well at school, and that she had a special interest in biology. "We bought her a biology book last Christmas. It was a bit unusual," she commented, almost apologetically, "but that's what she wanted."

For the next several hours after the visit, I mused upon the future potential of Heather's creative intelligence, her understanding and supportive parents, and her fertile outdoor play environment. Child, parents, and physical environment seemed to form a close-knit trinity. At the same time, I wondered if Heather's potential would ever fully flourish, given the severe limiting conditions of low-income, inner-city, working-class life.

The next day I found myself in a very different situation, just a few streets away in the same neighbourhood, on a field trip with eleven-year-old Gill. We were walking home from school accompanied by her mother, who was too suspicious to allow her daughter to go with me alone. In the ensuing, strained conversation, I tried to identify the limits of Gill's territory. "She can play down on the play equipment," her mother said, "as long as I can see her from the kitchen window" (they lived on the sixth floor of a tower block on the Edward Woods Estate). Gill nodded in agreement. By then we had arrived at the play equipment: a pair of swings, a set of climbing bars and a merry-go-round, all surrounded by a large expanse of lawn. The place was overshadowed on three sides by tall blocks of flats—the nearest one being where Gill's family lived.

We all began to shiver as the wind gusted around. Gill consented to have her photograph taken on the play equipment, half-heartedly rocking back and forth on one of the swings, her mother keeping a watchful eye from behind. Picture taken, they hurriedly disappeared into the building, without smiles or friendly goodbyes.

The poor microclimate of Gill's play area was greatly exacerbated by the wind-tunnel effect—caused by the tall buildings that had replaced the sheltering Victorian terraces formerly occupying the site. The place had none of the playful ambiance of Heather's wasteland haven. The positive aspects of Heather's situation seemed completely absent in Gill's case. Living sixty or seventy feet above an unresponsive ill-defined playscape had helped breed apprehension

1 *The social ecology of childhood. The development of each child can be supported or inhibited by different levels of social and cultural influence: the everyday circumstances of family life, the quality of community institutions, the ideology and effectiveness of national policy, and the general state of the world. The ecological approach emphasises the importance of recognising the local-global connections in policy formulation and raises the issue of whether child development is seen as a consequence of these systems, or whether the systems themselves are designed to implement a consciously adopted child development policy.*

Based on a drawing by Reuben Hill, adapted from principles contained in Bronfenbrenner: The Ecology of Human Development, *1979.*

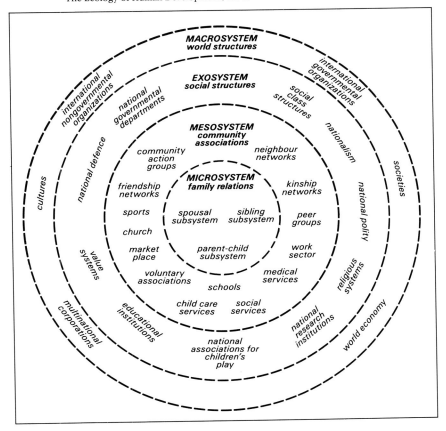

and ignorance, instead of trust and understanding. Other factors had certainly helped foster alienation in Gill's situation; but the insurmountable barrier of living in a high building, with nowhere decent to play, seemed significant. The difference between Gill's repressive, negative environment and Heather's supportive, positive environment was vast. It was impossible to imagine that Gill's development would ever receive the high quality of environmental stimulation and support that Heather's had.

Before we start jumping to conclusions, a framework for analysis and interpretation is required so that these and other cases can be considered within a broader social-environmental context.

AN ECOLOGICAL APPROACH

Environmental experience is a function of diversity and access—itself limited or controlled by a variety of social, cultural and physical factors. These factors coact with each other and the child's personality in a complex ecological process of growth and development. Urie Bronfenbrenner has outlined a unified, multilevel, ecological approach to human development (Figure 1) that allows all the social forces impinging on the quality of a child's life to be reckoned with, in research *and* policy formulation.[1] Although physical environment factors are absent from the model, Bronfenbrenner agrees (personal correspondence) that they are significant.

Admission of the physical environment (Figure 2) recognises that children live on the Earth—more precisely, they live *in* the biosphere. They also live in an era when, for the first time in history, the healthy future of the biosphere has become a serious political issue —given the awesome powers for its destruction now possessed by adult humans.

The ultimate framework for thinking about the role of the physical environment in child development is the interdependence between childhood and biosphere—the *thrival*[2] of the human species on planet Earth. This may seem lofty and presumptuous, but not if we heed Rene Dubos' exhortation to "think globally, act locally." What other choice is there but the local-global connection? We live in an ecologically interdependent world—more so than ever before in human history.

2   *The child's potential interactions with the world of objects, natural phenomena and people. All are ecologically controlled by institutions. The most influential are those with direct influence over the quality of children-environment interactions: family, school, housing industry, local government, planning and design professions...*
Adapted from Billings: Plants and the Ecosystem, *3rd. ed., 1970, p.12*

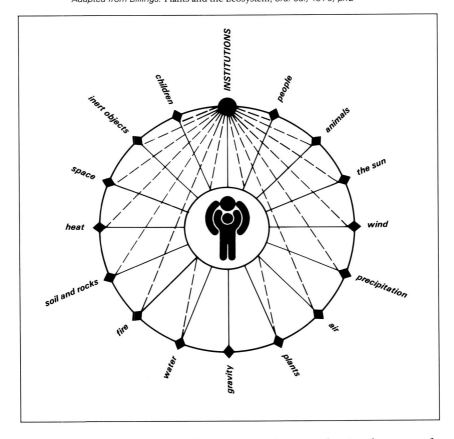

Two writers have, for me, come closest to charting the scope of child development in the context of evolutionary history: Edith Cobb and Joseph Chilton Pearce. In the *Ecology of Imagination in Childhood*,[3] Cobb discusses the "evolutionary biocultural process" that begins with the "natural genius of childhood and the spirit of place." This she interprets as the "*genius loci*: a living, ecological relationship between an observer and an environment, a person and a place."[4] Cobb sees play as "a sort of fingering over of the environment in sensory terms, a questioning of the power of materials as a preliminary to the creation of a higher organization of meaning."[5] She uses the key terms, "map" and "mapping" to express:

> ...an immediacy of experience of organism and environment that has been extended, extrapolated, and transformed into speech as well as into systems of behavior...an image that mobilizes and fuses the spatiotemporal experience of the perceiving nervous system into a form that has in turn become a symbolic abstraction, a condensation of level upon level of experience and information fused into symbol and code.[6]

Cobb's book, based on an exhaustive collection of autobiographic works of "creative thinkers," was thirty years in the making. In just over a hundred pages, it presents an extraordinarily powerful explication of the purpose of childhoods' middle years, in the context of humanity's place on Earth.

In *Magical Child*,[7] Joseph Chilton Pearce casts a similar literary spell, using the brilliantly conceived metaphor of the hologram. His work relates explicitly to that of Piaget and other developmental theorists, but he pushes the vision of human competence much farther than conventional scientific investigation alone can take us:

> Through interaction, intelligence grows in its ability to interact. We are designed to grow and be strengthened by every event, no matter how mundane or awesome. The flow of nature and seasons, people, extreme contrasts, apparent catastrophes, pleasantries—all are...opportunities for learning, leading to greater ability to interact...with anything and everything possible. If there is anything intelligence cannot interact with, intelligence is to that extent crippled... The first ten years or so are designed for acquiring a full-dimensional knowledge of *the world as it is* (emphasis added)... Intellectual growth is an increase in ability to interact, which means a coordinated flow of the mind-brain-body with the experience at hand.... Development can take place only on the foundation given by the child's actual body movements, making sensory contact with the world of things and processes... Without a full-dimensional world view structured in the formative years, no earth matrix can form, no knowledge of physical survival can develop, and no basis for abstraction and creativity can arise.[8]

A term is needed that could stand for the special quality of children's relations with living environments and the particular knowledge and developmental support that can be acquired through playful interaction with natural materials and phenomena. *Terra ludens*—a companion concept of Johann Huizinga's *Homo Ludens*[9] —is one possible term. Whether rich or impoverished, free or fenced in, fragmented or flowing, concentrated or spread out, *terra ludens* is the basis upon which the child can acquire creative intelligence by interacting with the inherited world. Pearce captures the essence of this process of progressive interaction:

> To interact with the living earth according to [its] principles and natural laws...to interact with the earth according to the principles of creative logic...and to interact with the processes and products of the thoughts and creations of our own mind, the minds of others and the whole thought system underlying our reality.[10]

Two exquisitely detailed studies by Denis Wood, *To Catch the Wind* and *Early Mound Building*, dealing with "kite time" in Puerto Rico and kid's dirt play,[11] bring Pearce's general statement literally down to earth and give a wonderful sense of the rich complexity of interactions related to just two of the phenomenal components in Figure 2—and their *secondary* interactions (too many crisscrossing lines to show diagramatically). The cultural quilting of play and environment through *time* (a crucial, hard-to-convey dimension) is eloquently conveyed in this passage from *Wind:*

> As the child coordinated the many experiences mediated by air to discover the air that mediated them, so we must coordinate the many experiences that kiting mediates to discover kiting. We must be able to see kiting in the kids skulking along the road toward a bamboo stand, in the coterie beneath the *flamboyan* [royal poinciana tree], rubbing sticks on the concrete curb, in the group assaying its wealth before the hardware store, in the kid begging a little flour at the door, in the kids rifling the trash for old beer cans, and the kids gone home to search for rags. We must be able to see kiting in the *chiringa* [tiny sledlike kite, built by novice five- to nine-year-old flyers], as well as the *torito* [large dihedral kite, built by flyers over twelve or so], in the littlest kids as well as the older ones, in the group as well as the individual, across the weeks of kite time as well as this afternoon, over the years of of a child's life as well as this

season, through the ages as well as in our own epoch. Kiting is not a sport or...a science curriculum idea or a field far from the fetch of power lines. In the *caserio* [Puerto Rican public housing project on the outskirts of town], at least, it's an integral process in the unfolding of life.[12]

DEVELOPMENT AND ENVIRONMENT

In *Children's Outdoor Environment*,[13] Pia Björklid discusses child development from the "interactional" perspective of environmental and ecological psychology, which assumes (as distinct from developmental psychology) that "the environment itself develops, and can be modified, changed and moulded by the individual." She emphasises "the reciprocal nature of the adaptation process [whereby] the individual is not only influenced by but also influences his environment, and has an *inner need* (emphasis added) to do so."[14]

Based on the work of George Herbert Mead,[15] Björklid stresses the importance of children and adults taking responsibility for their environment *together*. She suggests that as a result of this interaction of people with each other and their surroundings, "individuals learn to behave in socially meaningful ways and to develop, through language, a social consciousness."[16] Mead, she observes, pays special attention to the individual's *experience* of the physical environment and the developmental function it performs. "For children," she declares, "objects derive significance from their use [a tree that can be *climbed*]. The environment is not an objective phenomenon but is interpreted...reconstructed, never a copy."[17] She notes Jean Piaget's insistence that:

> Children should be able to do their own experimenting, their own research... In order for a child to understand something he must construct it for himself, he must reinvent it...if in the future individuals are to be formed who are capable of creativity and not simply repetition.[18]

In *Children's Experience of Place*, Roger Hart articulates the developmental significance of the physical environment.[19] He cites psychiatrist Harold Searles' notion that it is easier for a child to effect the physical environment than the social environment because (quoting Searles) "the nonhuman environment is relatively simple and stable, rather than overwhelmingly complex and ever shifting...and generally available rather than walled off by parental injunctions."[20]

Hart and other researchers acknowledge the substantial and fascinating research literature on children's play; they also note how little of it, with few exceptions,[21] pays attention to the relationship between play and the places actually used by children. Most child development research has been conducted at preschool level within the fixed and geographically limited boundaries of adult-managed, domestic and institutional settings, with the children's attention focused on small toys and educational materials.

But child development does not cease at five years old. As direct dependence on adults begins to fade, children continue to assert their urge to engage with the environment, to investigate and test its possibilities and to try things they haven't tried before. Relationships with the physical world grow and develop until the apex of childhood, around eight-to-twelve years of age, which Edith Cobb describes as:

> ...a special period, the little-understood, prepubertal, halcyon, middle age of childhood, approximately from five or six to eleven or twelve—between the strivings of animal infancy and the storms of adolescence—when the natural world is experienced in some highly evocative way, producing in the child a sense of some profound continuity with natural processes and presenting overt evidence of a biological basis of intuition.[22]

This is Cobb's "middle age of childhood," when children have the greatest chance to strike out, alone or with peers, to explore an ever-expanding repertoire of reachable places, in search of new experiences and adventure.

"You cannot educate mind *in vacuo*," wrote mathematician and philosopher Alfred North Whitehead. He, too, identified stages in the educational process and laid particular emphasis on the "stage of romance," (preceeding stages of "precision" and "generalization") that provides "the vividness of novelty...unexplored connections...[like] the sudden perception of the half-disclosed and half-hidden possibilities relating Crusoe and the sand and the footprint and the lonely island."[23]

In *Born Curious*,[24] Robin Hodgkin weaves a theory of child development and education around the core of Piaget's developmental stages and his dialectic of *assimilation/accommodation*. A child assimilates—fits new experience into her/his image of the world, to the point where it will no longer fit and (quoting Hodgkin), "we reach the point on our journey when we stop trying to cram souvenirs into our old luggage and buy a new suitcase."[25] Children must modify their ideas about the world to accommodate the results of new experience.

The "interactionists" discussed by Björklid (Piaget, George Herbert Mead and Erik H. Erikson) all agree, along with their interpreters (Pearce, Cobb and Hodgkin), that development occurs according to a genetically predetermined sequence of stages (although the age variations are much greater than some Piagetians believe, and there is still much debate about the relations between the stages and the degree to which they are affected by the physical environment).[26]

In Hodgkin's scheme (Figure 3), four developmental stages are combined with four modes of acquiring and representing experience (echoing the earlier quote from Pearce). The latter are based substantially on the formulations of Jerome Bruner, who uses the example of *enactive* play on a seesaw.[27] This precedes the child's *iconic* investigation of a balance beam in model form or as represented diagrammatically. Eventually the phenomenon can be described verbally, and/or its physical properties can be represented mathematically in the *symbolic* mode. Hodgkin terms this the *semiotic* mode, to emphasise the linguistic content. He also emphasises the all-important *interpersonal* mode, which, in the seesaw/balance beam example, signifies the child's interactions with parent, play leader or teacher, in the course of playing with/learning about the people-and-seesaw system.

In *Childhood's Domain* we are concerned primarily with Piaget's *concrete operational* period—approximately between ages seven and twelve—when, to quote Hart, "a child is now capable of logical thought...to make full use of reversible cognitive operations, [but] these operations are still limited to *real objects*" (emphasis added).[28]

ENVIRONMENTAL COMPETENCE

Playing is learning. The above-mentioned (to whom we might add names such as Friedrich Froebel, Margaret Mead, and D.W. Winnicott) all consider children's play to be a developmental phenomenon. Over the course of time, the child's playful interaction with the environment and her/his assimilation of wordly experience, produces a feeling of competence: a sense of mastery and control over the environment, utilizing it to "achieve one's goals and enrich one's experience."[29]

3   *The dimensions of development and growth of competence. Core
skills develop, guided by genetically-controlled developmental stages.
Playing and learning are advanced through appropriate modes of
experience and representation.* **Depending on its quality**, *the environment engages the child in exploration and discovery; it is a source of
knowledge; it promotes the growth of environmental competence,
stimulates the practice of skills and enhances performance.*
Adapted from Hodgkin: Born Curious, *1976, p.96*

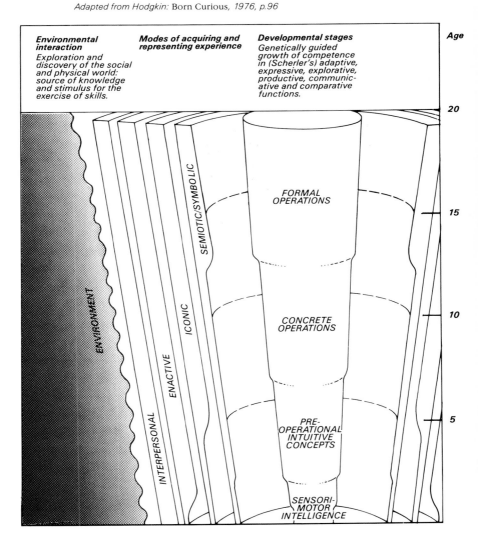

**Environmental
interaction**
*Exploration and
discovery of the social
and physical world:
source of knowledge
and stimulus for the
exercise of skills.*

**Modes of acquiring and
representing experience**

Developmental stages
*Genetically guided
growth of competence
in (Scherler's) adaptive,
expressive, explorative,
productive, communic-
ative and comparative
functions.*

Age

ENVIRONMENT

INTERPERSONAL

ENACTIVE

ICONIC

SEMIOTIC/SYMBOLIC

FORMAL
OPERATIONS

CONCRETE
OPERATIONS

PRE-
OPERATIONAL
INTUITIVE
CONCEPTS

SENSORI-
MOTOR
INTELLIGENCE

20

15

10

5

The wellspring of competence may be seen as a natural striving by the young child to acquire knowledge and skills, which can be further enhanced through practice and performance (in traditional games, for instance). As the child develops biologically, new play opportunities must become available to support the growth of competence. If too many barriers (parental restrictions, heavily trafficked streets, narrow minded teachers, impoverished surroundings, social deprivation) are encountered, motivation towards competence will begin to waver. Especially for school-aged children, it will become replaced by a sense of inferiority and inadequacy (unless compensated for by extracurricular sports, music, guiding/scouting, etc.).

Low self-esteem and lack of motivation are so common in school classrooms and so difficult for teachers to surmount. They demand so much attention that, ironically, little time is left to deal with the ethics of environmental interaction, except at the most authoritarian level of do's and don'ts. This low level of intervention teaches nothing of what Geoffrey Vickers (*Freedom in a Rocking Boat*[30]) calls *appreciation*: to value an environment that is constantly changing, where a sense of responsibility must develop from each individual's own experience and understanding, instead of teachers' or parents' behavioural prescriptions.

Different ethical issues are raised, depending on whether competence is exercised "over," "under" or "with" the environment. To feel master or mistress of one's natural surroundings may be good for self-esteem, but it is not good for the environment and in the long run will not be good for *homo sapiens* on planet Earth. On the other hand, to feel controlled "under" big-city, people-made environments is equally unhealthy. The notion of *terra ludens* suggests an ethic based on the mutuality of ecological psychology, its concern for interaction, its sense of responsibility for both people and environments and their coevolution. Christopher Stone's *Should Trees Have Standing?* [31] presents a case with forceful clarity with regard to natural objects. Similar arguments could be applied to cultural objects.

Björklid notes Erikson and Piaget's view that "play has a healing or cathartic value...[through which] the child is able to relive and possibly resolve earlier [social] conflicts."[32] Play is the child's way of dealing with her/his social and physical surroundings. Given appropriate guidance and instruction, the *symbolic/semiotic* mode begins to dominate. At this point, learning is transformed through formal language, is integrated with other strands of similarly transformed learning, evolves into an intellectual realm, and is now transferable to any context, independent of the physical world. Yet many adults avoid becoming dependent solely on this realm of abstraction. They continue to engage all representational modes in creative work,[33] and employ Edward de Bono's "lateral thought,"[34] what Robert Pirsig calls "lateral drift,"[35] to escape the trap of "functional fixedness" that Bruner warns us of.[36]

The fragments from Heather's trip and similar anecdotal reports used in later chapters, provide many examples of how particular qualities, elements and characteristics of live environments stimulated and supported the aquisition of manual dexterity and sensori-psycho-motor, social-emotive, perceptive, imaginative, affective, cognitive and verbal skills. Mary Reilly suggests that these competence skills are both cause and effect of the child's engagement with the physical world and the means for differentiating it.[37] Skills motivate interaction. Interaction stimulates the learning of skills. Thus the number and type of skill-related behaviours supported by a given setting, would be a reasonable measure of its *childhood environmental quality*.

J.A. Hadfield emphasises the critical role of environmental play in stimulating innate skill potentials (in *anticipation* of eventual need) and the on-going *repetition* of action and practice of skills.[38] In other words, for Hadfield (as for White[39]), childhood opportunities to interact playfully with the environment are a critical factor in the development of human competence.

German educator, Karl Scherler, presents a concise description of competence-through-play, by defining six development functions: 1) The *adaptive* function—the biological adjustment of the child, development of strength, stamina, speed and pliancy; 2) the *expressive* function—evoking such emotions as tension, inquisitiveness, fury, hate, pleasure, joy and annoyance; 3) the *explorative* function—learning how to distinguish high, low, small, large, before, behind, soft and hard; to distinguish social roles and to learn how the adult world works; 4) the *productive* function—learning how to make things and how to alter them; 5) the *communicative* function—learning how to behave in relation to other people, to cooperate, to accept rules, to protect the weak, to empathise and relate to the points of view of other people; and 6) the *comparative* function—learning to measure one's strength against others and to win and lose.[40]

For Hodgkin, the task of teachers (and, we should add, all adults who directly or indirectly affect the quality of children's lives) is to join with children in creating, judging, enriching and understanding the role of play episodes in the development of competence. He suggests—referring to D. W. Winnicott's notion of the 'potential space' that exists between adults and children[41]—that play episodes are likely to have the greatest impact in "halcyon moments of 'slack' time and space, when causal winds blow gently and we are not driven."[42] Our concern is with both the timing and location of such moments.

PEOPLE

The *interpersonal* mode is the backbone of child development, beginning with the relationship between child and mother. Björklid stresses Piaget's view of socialization, whereby the child proceeds from "childish" egocentrism ("me" as the centre of the world) towards reciprocity and social competence (Scherler's *communicative* function).[43] Socialization is the hazardous road that all must travel, through the twists and turns of R. D. Laing's psychological landscape (*Politics of Experience*). Here we see how interpersonal relations can enrich experience or stifle it; how a person can validate, encourage, support and enhance the experience of another, or invalidate, discourage, undermine and constrict it.[44] The physical environment, Laing suggests, can offer similar possibilities for enriched experience, or curtail them. In other words, experience is neither subjective nor objective, but a consequence of the coaction between people and their surroundings—or people-with-people as portrayed by the Newsons (child-with-child, child-with-parents, child-with-relations, child-with-teachers and child-with- 'significant others' such as baby sitter, music teacher and play leader).[45]

For the age group under consideration, other children (siblings, friends and relations) assume a crucial role as play partners, cooperating protagonists and co-investigators. Margaret Mead reminds us that "'The Child' does not exist. Only *children* exist; children in a particular context; children who are different from each other."[46] Neighbourhood friends, classmates and cousins provide a social ingredient as important as any physical resource; and yet, if children also have access to a diversity of physical settings—both natural and people-made—positive social interaction can be greatly enhanced, deepened and extended.

4   *Territorial range development: a sociospatial system that evolves, with age, from the coaction of children's personalities, parents, cultural circumstances, and the play opportunities and access barriers of the physical environment.*

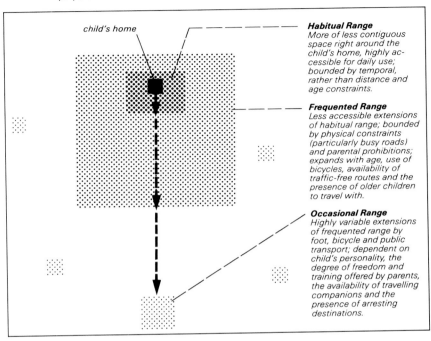

child's home

Habitual Range
More of less contiguous space right around the child's home, highly accessible for daily use; bounded by temporal, rather than distance and age constraints.

Frequented Range
Less accessible extensions of habitual range; bounded by physical constraints (particularly busy roads) and parental prohibitions; expands with age, use of bicycles, availability of traffic-free routes and the presence of older children to travel with.

Occasional Range
Highly variable extensions of frequented range by foot, bicycle and public transport; dependent on child's personality, the degree of freedom and training offered by parents, the availability of travelling companions and the presence of arresting destinations.

DIFFERENTIATION OF SPACE AND TIME

When children are beyond the four walls of home and school, where do they go and what do they do? What are the factors that limit their experience? How do these factors relate to age? A useful concept is *territorial range*. Familiar to investigators of animal behaviour in the wild, the concept is especially suited to describing the urban geography of children (Figure 4).

In an earlier review,[47] *territorial range* was described as encompassing a child's play and leisure places and the pathways connecting them. It is a procrustean, fluctuating phenomenon. Every child has several overlapping ranges that reflect variable social and psychological constraints in space and time. There is the *habitual range* of places right around the home, accessible on a daily basis for short periods of time—the use of streets for instance, wedged between homework and suppertime. There is the *frequented range* of less accessible places, more likely to be used on weekends and holidays, especially during the summer. And there is the *occasional range* of more distant places, visited once in a while, perhaps as part of a special expedition. Although it expands with age, at any point in time occasional range defines the child's ultimate territorial frontier. As the child grows older, moves around more rapidly, and develops a more adequate and elaborate mental image of the environment (cognitive map), former occasional places become frequented, and some are eventually absorbed into the everyday habitual range.

Range evolution involves two interlocking processes. The first is *range growth*, which occurs in spurts as new lumps of territory are discovered for the first time (assimilated) and mark new range boundaries. The second is *range development*. With every visit to the same place, with every repeated 'play episode,' new possibilities are discovered, tested and verified, and provide an accumulation of experience, knowledge and understanding of the environment (accommodation) that builds with time. The developmental potential of different ranges varies enormously, depending on the motivational 'pull' of the places they contain. Some places are discovered, never revisited and soon forgotten. Others are visited time and time again because there is always something new to discover. They are places of lifetime rememberance. Others may still be strongly remembered—even though visited just once or twice—because of their particularly evocative character.

Range growth is likely to receive its biggest boost when children start kindergarten and primary school. Thereafter gradual growth and development occurs, conditioned initially by a foundation of environmental experience gained in the company of parents or other adults and older children—via trips to local shops or parks, for example. The extent of range exploration varies from one child to another, depending on home address, parents, sex and personality. In Western societies, certainly, parents exert strong social control over their children's territorial range, even extending into adolescent years. The process of negotiating 'permission,' that goes on continuously between parents and offspring, has been carefully documented by Hart.[48]

In the study sites, children's territories usually overlapped. Both Heather and Lesley used the same park (one went alone, the other had just stopped having to go with her mother). Both traversed some of the same streets leading to and from the park. Both spoke the conventional language of play—of ball games and play equipment (as nearly all the children did). But whereas Lesley's communication stopped there, Heather's expanded into a realm of verbal description far beyond that of other girls in Notting Dale. She was a 'play expert,' who explored the full potential of her accessible surroundings by using all four experiential modes. The key question is whether Heather's territory was in some way 'better' than Lesley's and, if so, how?

REMEMBERANCE

As the full potential of newly discovered places is explored in depth, a sense of attachment and meaning arises. In some special places the process can go on for years with the layering of successive 'play episodes.' In territories where experientially-layered places are thick on the ground, range development is correspondingly substantial and can create a feeling of affiliation which Yi Fu Tuan calls "topophilia,"[49] which Kevin Lynch called "rootedness,"[50] which Edward Relph calls "placeness."[51] A purpose of this book is to understand the characteristics of such persistently memorable places and to cast light on their role in human development.

Besides Edith Cobb, other investigators of 'environmental autobiographies'[52] have uncovered persistent childhood recollections crowded with memorable objects, smells, colors, textures, sunlit glades and shadowy corners; places that evoke a sense of wonder about life, stirring deep feelings beyond any capacity for rational understanding—a state of intuitive oneness with the world, well-appreciated by writers such as A. A. Milne, Coleridge, Wordsworth, Goethe, Blake, Rousseau, Lewis Carroll, Rachel Carson, Gaston Bachelard and Robert Paul Smith.[53]

Is it important that adults remember the places they knew as a child?[54] For Edith Cobb:

> It is significant that adult memories of childhood, even when nostalgic and romantic, seldom suggest the need to be a child but refer to a deep desire to renew the ability to perceive as a child and to participate with the whole bodily self in the forms, colors, and motions, the sights and sounds of the external world of nature and artifact.[55]

What is the difference between an adult who is able to recall rich and memorable images, and someone who cannot? What are the implications for the health of the respective individuals *and* their surroundings? To what extent do such images provide play-guidance to a new generation of parents, now rearing their own children?

POLITICS OF CHILDHOOD AND PLACE

Town planners often cite "sense of place" as a desirable objective. At the same time, the critics of contemporary urban development often speak as if historic towns and well-preserved country villages are the sole purveyors of "sense of place" and that much contemporary urban development lacks it. Why? Is it simply a matter of adult taste, or a function of time; or do substantial differences in quality exist between old and new—as the result of economic and technological forces that have guided urban development since World War II? Clearly something more than adult 'expert judgement' must enter the picture. Young people, too, must use places for the most part designed by adults for adult purposes—making do with whatever they can find and accepting the consequences. By working directly with children in places of their own choosing, factors tending to either support or undermine and block child development were investigated in this study.

Children grow up under such a wide range of circumstances. Are we to assume that developmental effects are equal? Obviously not. The fact is that little is known about the comparative effects of different types of environments on development. Thus the participation of children themselves seemed the most reliable method of assessing environmental equity.[56] Let them speak for themselves, I thought, as in the opening examples, where one set of interactions apparently supported creative, highly motivated behaviour, and another set apparently repressed it. "Erikson paid great attention in his clinical studies to 'play disruption,'" Björklid notes. "Being unable to play peacefully because of interruption...may result in such insecuity that playfulness decreases and the child finally feels an aversion or inability to play."[57]

Writing about the origins of alienation, Bronfenbrenner has offered a factual picture of children being born into a profoundly political situation, facing forces of alienation, community breakdown and family fragmentation;[58] and yet each new birth brings forth a potential for rediscovering a marvellous planetary inheritance. How can this potential be made to flower, rather than wither at an early age?

Edward Relph's *Place and Placelessness*, John Berger's *Ways of Seeing* and architect Martin Pawley's *Private Futures*[59] all raise the issue of centrally controlled, mass media, publicity-consumption systems that substitute homogenized vicarious images for the flesh and blood of live experience. There is a danger that children in the West are becoming the passive receivers of predigested messages from secondary sources, instead of being agents for self-initiated interaction with the living world around them. To the degree that they remove personal control, all centralized systems (urban renewal, mass housing, T.V. networks, franchised services) tend towards alienation and what Richard Sennett calls "purification" of the urban environment.[60] Children who live exclusively in a secondary media environment—where the present always consists of effortless images of past and future states—inevitably pose a threat to the future of the planet because such images substitute vague dreams for those intuitive values that can only be acquired by live experience of the biosphere.

It will be interesting to see how microcomputors—which potentially offer a high degree of user-control—will effect this complex issue, since they have the capacity for introducing an entirely new type of *iconic* learning. Their cultural value, however, will still depend on the child's *enactive* grounding. Primary and secondary sources of experience should complement and support each other. The task of education is to recognise the power of primary experience and help children use secondary media and materials to extend their culture and development.

My assumption is that stimulating and memorable environments advance children's development significantly; and conversely that dull, easily forgotten environments can delay or block development. With this in mind, elements and qualities of place have been highlighted in the narrative for the benefit of those who directly or indirectly guide children's playing and learning: parents, teachers, school administrators, city planners, architects, interior designers, landscape architects, community workers and playleaders. It is these professions that must involve our children and take responsibility for protecting, conserving and creating places of special childhood significance. They must also face inevitable real-world politics and value judgements: support for playleaders or playspaces? For ponds or football pitches? For wasteland or traffic-free streets?

Social and technological changes in society (mothers in the workforce, single-parent families, unemployment, out-of-family childcare, traffic dangers) have brought us to a point where children's play must be increasingly regarded as a policy imperative. The establishment of a Minister for Children's Play by the British Government and the setting up of Play Board (1983) were great steps forward at national level.[61] At the same time, an even more energetic, responsible and imaginative effort is required at the local level, where the quality of children's lives must be directly affected.

Suzanne de Monchaux's *Planning with Children in Mind* (A Notebook for Local Planners and Policy Makers), published by the New South Wales government,[62] presents a model guide to political intervention—including direct consultation and participation of the children themselves. Incidently, de Monchaux makes the important point that the word "play," is sometimes used by adults to belittle children's activity: "Oh, they're just playing." For her, play means "all those independent activities that children adopt by choice as an enjoyable and interesting way of behaving, beyond the adult imposed demands of home, family and school."[63]

ENVIRONMENTAL EDUCATION

For play and its environmental dependencies to be considered essential partners in child development, an environmental education framework is needed. All sectors of of the child's environment—at all ecological levels—need to become the content and process of learning, instead of being viewed as a taken-for-granted backdrop. This of course is not a new idea, but it becomes more and more relevant in addressing contemporary social-technological issues. Colin Ward and Anthony Fyson's *Streetwork* and the pages of the *Bulletin for Environmental Education* (BEE)[64] portray environmental education as a cultural foundation, binding children, school, and community. This book attempts to investigate some of the bindings and their policy implications.

Family life, social class, genetic inheritance, culture and material surroundings are all-important factors. The scope must be ecologically inclusive. Yet our analysis needs purpose and direction. A framework of values is required that reflects enhancement of life on the planet. As children acquire environmental competence, they must also achieve ethical responsibility towards their environments and learn to apply technology in wiser and more healthful ways for planetary thrival.[65]

The uniquely human skills of tool making, problem solving and decision making are learned competences. In order to develop in the right ethical direction, they must be rooted in childhood opportunities for fully experiencing the Earth and for understanding the influence of humankind upon it. How will we learn to live collaboratively with the planet, otherwise? E. F. Schumacher considered education to be "our greatest resource."[66] But how big is "great"? Nothing less than the total people-planet system—our inheritance of wisdom—can provide the scope of a proper education; one that emphasises ethics and competence for guiding the future. Such a system of education would link past and future, people and planet, experience and learning, recreation and education.

2 *Investigation*

Three contrasting types of urban neighbourhood were chosen as study sites (Figures 5-8):

NOTTING DALE a 'big city' neighbourhood, west of central London.

BEDWELL a 'new city' neighbourhood in Stevenage New Town, thirty miles north of London.

MILL HILL an 'old city' neighbourhood in Tunstall, one of the six "pottery towns" that comprise present-day Stoke-on-Trent: an industrial city founded on coal and clay, midway between Birmingham and Manchester.

Children in the three neighbourhoods were asked to make a map or drawing of all their favourite places—where they went after school or on weekends, including the summer—around their homes and neighbourhoods. Each child used an 18" by 24" sheet of white paper, a finely-tipped black marker and coloured wax crayons. The exercise was introduced by saying I was interested in learning from *them* about how they used their environment and how they would like to see it improved (see Appendix A for further details of the research procedure.)

Follow-up interviews with the children were used to gather further information: the location of their homes; their family back-

24

ground; time spent watching T.V. and doing chores; where they went and what they did, how often, after school and at weekends; how they got around; where they went to be alone or with their friends; places they were not allowed to go, and why; things they liked and disliked about their environment, and what they would like to see added or changed in it.

Ninety-six girls and boys (in equal numbers), aged nine to twelve, participated in the study, and were divided almost evenly among the three sites. About a quarter of the children led me on field trips around their territories. They were chosen on the basis of drawings and interviews as being the most 'expert'—that is, they had the most extensive and diversified territories, and were the most articulate in describing and explaining them.

5 *Location of study sites.*

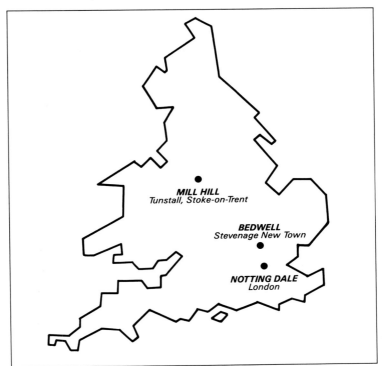

6   *The Notting Dale study site, showing locations of homes of children participating in the study and major landmarks.*

St. Mark's Park

Westway

Powis Square

Thomas Jones School

Ladbroke Grove

St. Clements School

Avondale Park

West Cross Route A41

Edward Woods Estate

Holland Park Avenue

roundabout

Holland Park

Shepherd's Bush

The 'Venture

★ Locations of children's homes.

0   500
N ↑ ⊢──┴──┴──┴──┴──┤
metres

Drawn September, 1985

Commonwealth Institute

Photo: Aerofilms, 1982.

7   *The Bedwell study site, showing locations of homes of children participating in the study and major landmarks.*

The Sewer Pipes

Marat Farm

St. Georges Field

Fairlands Way

Bedwell School

The Dip

little lake

Bedwell Crescent

playground

Downtown

Bedwell Shops

The 'real' forest

big lake

Six Hills Way

Fairlands Park

Locations of children's homes.

0   500

N↑

metres

Drawn September, 1985

Canyon Adventure Playground

Photo: Aerofilms, 1980.

The Mill Hill study site, showing locations of homes of children participating in the study and major landmarks.

Bomb Holes

Greenway

Sausage Tunnel

Brickers

Greenway

Catholic School

Clanway

Greenway

Little Chell Lane

The Banks

The Little Park

Greenway

Victoria Park Road

Greenway

Greenway

Grogs

High Lane

Tunstall Park

Mill Hill School

playground

Greenbank Road

Greenway

Tracy's marlhole

Locations of children's homes.

Glenn's marlhole

0   500

N ↑

metres

Greenway to Westport Lake

Drawn September, 1985

Photo: Meridian Airmaps, 1981.

9   *The multilevel 'wedge' methodology—expresses the need for quantitative and qualitative modes of investigation to be combined, so that the uniqueness of each individual can be recognised within each social and cultural grouping.*

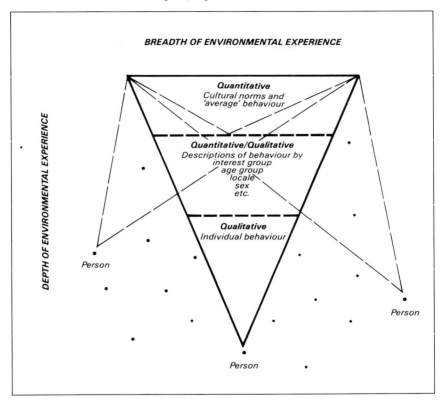

METHODOLOGY

In order to reflect a local-global/individual-and-society research perspective, a 'wedge' approach (Figure 5) was used so that both the breadth and depth of children's relationships with their surroundings could be taken into account. Each set of person-environment relationships was conceptually represented as a wedge—an "ego-world unity," to use Edith Cobb's words.[1] The broad tops of the wedges overlap, to the extent they represent a common ground of experience. The thinner ends of the wedges diverge, until the separate tips represent each child's own unique relationship with her or his surroundings. In the middle area, wedges overlap, more or less, depending on the density of relations between children and their degree of shared territory. Some kids covered a lot of ground, but did not get deeply involved; others became intimately involved with fewer places. Some kids did everything together. Others were loners.

The 'wedge' methodology allowed a range of results to be interpreted, extending from detailed design implications to urban planning policy. The results of a standardised, *systematic* procedure were combined with a more open-ended, *phenomenological* approach. This allowed aggregated, numerical data to be mixed with anecdotal, idiosyncratic material, in progressively more general levels of interpretation. For instance, Heather provided the only example of a child making a posy for her mother. More generally, her case was one of several where kids harvested natural resources as a play material. More generally still, it was one of many illustrations showing how children interacted with the natural world.

David's favourite places in Notting Dale—an unusually competent, rare, plan-view drawing, complete with key (colour-coded on the original); note the last item in the key, "Places I Play."

Analysis of the systematic data, and the archive of field trip accounts, generated the midstratum of material used to develop the structure of the book. The archive also reads like a storybook (like the examples opening Chapter 1), illustrating and supporting the principal lines of argument.

OUTDOORS VERSUS INDOORS

During the introduction of the drawing exercise, no direct references were made to "play" or to "outdoors"—in fact it was made clear that both inside and outside spaces could be drawn. Nonetheless, the overwhelming majority of places drawn were outdoors. Only four of the ninety-six drawings mentioned building interiors and only one drawing was devoted exclusively to interior space.[2]

The drawings indicated that, when time was available, outdoors was an ideal place to be. This conclusion was somewhat tempered by

David "mountain climbing" up a flank wall in one of his favourite places—a Notting Dale Street.

the interview results, where a fifth of the mentions related to the child's room at home as a favourite place to go after school. This suggests that although nearly all the children who drew their houses portrayed an exterior view, some obviously intended their drawings to also represent the interior. Also note that one-in-five interview mentions of favourite weekend places were related to indoor community facilities such as swimming pools and cinemas (Table 3, Appendix C).

TURF MAPS

'Turf maps'[3] (Figures 10-12) were constructed by plotting items from the drawings on topographic overlays, so that the configurations of favourite places could be compared across sites. A strong impression of increasing territorial diversity is conveyed as one moves from the Notting Dale to Bedwell turf maps; and again, even more strongly, as one moves from Bedwell to Mill Hill. These impressions are borne out numerically. The average number of items mentioned per drawing increases from six for Notting Dale, to seven for Bedwell, to nine for Mill Hill. In other words, Mill Hill children put a third more items into their drawings than the Notting Dale children did. What is the explanation—that the Mill Hill kids had a greater aptitude for graphic communication? Surely not. A more convincing answer is that their territory was in some way richer, experientially.

The Notting Dale turf map (Figure 10) has a few principal nuclei: two housing estate play areas and three parks. Avondale Park—and particularly its playground—was drawn by a large number of children, showing it to be a place of special significance and also indicating a lack of 'official' play opportunities elsewhere in Notting Dale. (Nearly all the Georgian squares and gardens in the area were locked —the privilege of use vested in adjacent residents' keys—a long-standing bone of contention in the community.) Some of the more adventurous Notting Dale children satisfied their play needs by using a variety of 'unofficial' open spaces, like Heather's building site.

Also note the attraction of Royal Holland Park. Even though many minutes walk away from the neighbourhood and separated by a heavily trafficked arterial street, Holland Park's size and diversity exerted a considerable 'pull' over Notting Dale children.

The Bedwell turf map (Figure 11) also has a pronounced central focus: a small playground set within the large expanse of Fairlands

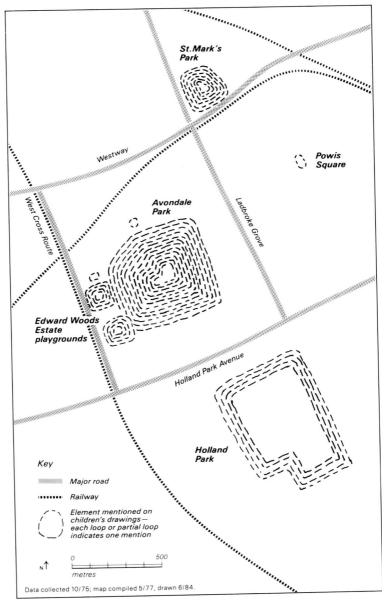

St.Mark's
Park

Westway

Powis
Square

West Cross Route

Avondale
Park

Ladbroke Grove

Edward Woods
Estate
playgrounds

Holland Park Avenue

Holland
Park

Key

Major road

Railway

Element mentioned on
children's drawings —
each loop or partial loop
indicates one mention

N↑

0   500

metres

Data collected 10/75; map compiled 5/77, drawn 6/84.

Park. Subsidiary attractions in the park (a boating lake, a stream and an area of natural woodland) were also drawn. The acres of mown lawn, taking up most of the space in the park, were not mentioned.

An interesting aspect of the Bedwell map is that it included several mentions of both a local shopping area and a school site. The attractiveness of the school was perhaps a genuine reflection of a sense of belonging on the part of children, attributable to the educational programmme and/or the special qualities of the physical setting. The grounds were well used by children after school hours. A sizable grass area, behind the building, was laid out for ball play and surrounded by a tall hedge—giving a sense of privacy and enclosure (in contrast to the expanse of lawn in the adjacent park).

The Bedwell shopping area was typical of a New Town neighbourhood commercial development: a sizable, traffic-free, paved precinct, surrounded by shops, easily accessible by pedestrian paths

Brian's favourite places in Bedwell—a bridge over the stream feeding the Fairlands Park lakes (visible beyond the bridge), and part of Marat Farm (described in Chapter 7, "Rough ground and abandoned places"). (opposite) Brian on the bridge.

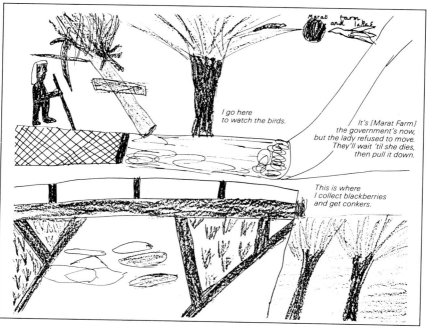

11   *Bedwell turf map.*

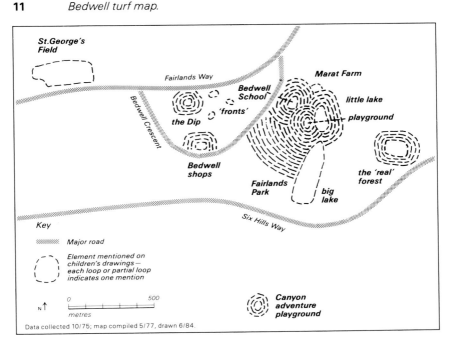

St.George's
Field

Fairlands Way

Bedwell
School

Marat Farm

little lake

'fronts'

playground

the Dip

Bedwell Crescent

Bedwell
shops

Fairlands
Park

the 'real'
forest

big
lake

Six Hills Way

Key

▒▒▒ Major road

Element mentioned on
children's drawings —
each loop or partial loop
indicates one mention

0 ——————— 500
N↑
metres

Canyon
adventure
playground

Data collected 10/75; map compiled 5/77, drawn 6/84.

from the children's homes. The precinct was used as a bike-riding circuit and as somewhere to play games by using the raised planting beds, telephone kiosk, letterbox, and advertising hoardings.

Other hot spots on the Bedwell map included the Dip (a sunken, grassy area) and the Canyon Adventure Playground (located in a former quarry some distance from the neighbourhood). Both spaces had the same form: a deep bowl-like depression in the ground.

The Bedwell neighbourhood was a model of pedestrian layout, with many cul-de-sacs and ancillary open spaces. A large open grassy space occupied the centre of the housing area. However, the turf map shows that in spite of the substantial open space resources located so close to home, many Bedwell children preferred to cross the busy peripheral distributor road to use the school grounds or the playground and other facilities in the park. What is the implication? The somewhat bland close-to-home spaces could have been more attractively developed perhaps—especially for children whose territorial limits were constrained by parents.

The Mill Hill turf map (Figure 12) obviously looks different to the other two. A similarity, however, is that the principal favourite place is again a playground, this time located in a corner of Tunstall Park. Other significant places are scattered throughout the neighbourhood, many of them 'fronts,' 'backs,' greens or rough ground. The Mill Hill map indicates a level of choice and diversity of play places above the other sites. From a policy standpoint this is especially noteworthy since many of these Mill Hill places, so popular with children, went unnoticed or were called "eyesores" by adults.

A WOVEN METAPHOR

Children were discriminating about their use of local resources. Each child wove a pattern of personal playtraces through the neighbourhood, laced together with the traces of other known and unknown players. As each child responded to newly discovered opportunities the pattern extended geographically, guided by the developing capacity of the child, whose environmental competence, in turn, was enhanced by the continuing interaction with his/her surroundings.

Metaphorically, the result looks like a cloth of varied solids and voids, arranged in an irregular geometric pattern. Some threads terminate in line with each other where a major road, a railway line, or some other uncrossable barrier blocks territorial extension. Else-

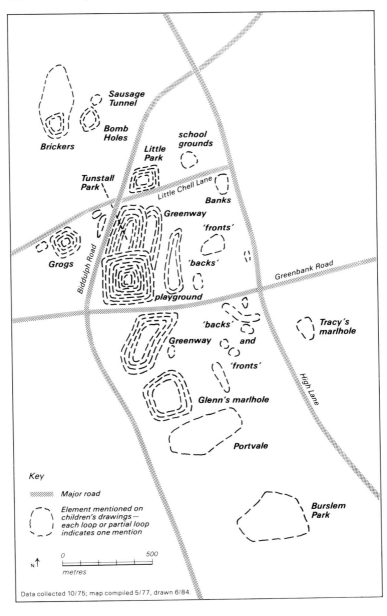

Key

▦   Major road

Element mentioned on
children's drawings —
each loop or partial loop
indicates one mention

N ↑   0   500

metres

Data collected 10/75; map compiled 5/77, drawn 6/84.

Labels within figure:

Sausage Tunnel

Bomb Holes

Brickers

Little Park

school grounds

Tunstall Park

Little Chell Lane

Banks

Greenway

'fronts'

'backs'

Grogs

Biddulph Road

Greenbank Road

playground

'backs'

Greenway   and

'fronts'

Tracy's marlhole

Glenn's marlhole

High Lane

Portvale

Burslem Park

where some of the strongest threads extend by different amounts to form a ragged edge. Sometimes they form a subsidiary piece of cloth tenuously connected to the larger whole.

Checkered areas, echoing street alignments, stand out at regular intervals. The longest threads combine to form a number of heavier ribs crisscrossing between the main solids. Other threads are so short they can be easily pulled out.

These are no ordinary weavings hanging immobile on museum walls. They vibrate with life as new threads weave in while others dwindle away. Some parts of the cloth have a regular pulse; others, out toward the edges, have sporadic and unpredictable rhythms.

The background environment also changes as the brightly coloured playtraces weave through it. Hues shimmer and change periodically, chameleonlike, in lockstep with the playtrace patterns.

The Notting Dale cloth is predominantly grey, with two fair-sized patches of green. A third, larger patch, hangs by a few threads, off to one side. The Bedwell cloth has a large green section, surroun-

Dawne's favourite places in Mill Hill.

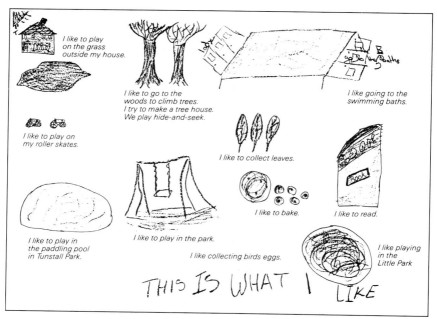

ding an elongated blue area firmly attached to one edge, plus a scatter of smaller green patches throughout. The Mill Hill cloth has a motley mix of colours: gray areas, lines and patches of green and blue, and blobs of pink and black.

As the seasons pass, the cloth colours change, more or less in unison, particularly the greens. At one point they seem to disintegrate into many shades of red and gold, before disappearing entirely for a while...only to reappear as a vivid scatter of bright greens, slowly deepening and coalescing together to reform the patterns of the previous season (a few of the darkest green spots having remained unchanged throughout the cycle).

Occasional convulsions occur, sending shock waves reverberating discordantly through the weave, gradually subsiding, modifying the ongoing rhythm with colour changes around the epicentre. Each cloth has a different shock pattern. The Notting Dale cloth suffers intense, frequent jolts at scattered points. The Bedwell cloth appears serene, almost dull, by comparison, with only the vaguest

Dawne and her friend doing cartwheels on a carpet of leaves in the dry autumn paddling pool (shown on the left side of her drawing, opposite), in Tunstall Park.

reverberations around the edges—from sources beyond the extremities; the Mill Hill cloth appears in a constant state of flux. Scattered heavy shocks occur from time to time, mixed with many smaller changes in several places simultaneously. The overall impression is of increasing greenness, with more and more threads filling in the larger voids.

FAVOURITE PLACES

Assuming that the children's drawings represented individually significant and memorable experiences, it is 'lawns,' 'playgrounds/ schoolyards' and the 'child's own home'—the only items mentioned in more than half the drawings—that come across as the most important places (Figure 13). A further eight items were mentioned in just under a quarter of the drawings: 'local parks,' 'single trees,' ' streets,' 'pavements,' 'other dwellings' (i.e., homes other than the child's or those of friends, relatives and baby-sitters), 'fences,' 'friends' homes' and 'footpaths.' A picture of habitual range emerges, with day-to-day leisure time revolving around the children's homes (and those of their friends and other people), local parks and playgrounds, streets and pavements—and trees (wherever they could be found). Other types of places diminish in significance, without pronounced breaks, across the children's assumed frequented and occasional ranges.

By collapsing the results (Figure 14), a more general comparison between place categories and sites can be made. Now we see that 'homesites,' 'open space,' 'vegetation,' 'natural ground surfaces' and 'pathways' (streets, pavements and footpaths) account for almost two-thirds of all mentions.

It is difficult to know what the high ranking of 'fences' means. On the one hand they function as an enclosing element, affording privacy and a sense of security; on the other hand, they restrict access. This negative aspect is much less likely to be perceived by children, however, as they sometimes have difficulty projecting the consequences of a world they take for granted. Thus, the majority of fence mentions can be assumed to be positive enclosing elements rather than negative restrictive elements.

The impressive score for 'pathways' in Mill Hill most likely reflects the ad hoc network of informal routes that traversed the local landscape—apparently making a greater impact than Bedwell's evenly laid out system of planned routes.

LAWNS .71
PLAYGROUNDS
PLAY EQUIPMENT
SCHOOLYARDS .65
CHILD'S OWN HOME .51
LOCAL PARKS .40
SINGLE TREES .36
THROUGH STREETS .34
PAVEMENTS .30
OTHER DWELLINGS .29
FENCES .28
FRIEND'S HOMES .25
FOOTPATHS .24
SWIMMING POOLS .19
SPORTS FIELDS .18
FLOWERS/MISC. STRUCTURES .17
PONDS & LAKES .16
SHRUBS .15

CHILD'S SCHOOL/CHILD'S FRIENDS .13
TRAFFIC/BRIDGES .11
SELF PORTRAIT/TOPOGRAPHY/DIRT & SAND .10

★ ★ ★ ★ ★ ★

TREE CLUSTERS/YARDS & GARDENS .09
HILLS/ASPHALT & CONCRETE/CLIMATIC CONDITIONS .08
CAR PARKS/CLIMBING TREES/WOODLAND/ABANDONED BUILDINGS .06
WILD BIRDS & INSECTS/CUL DE SACS/CULVERTED STREAMS/*LOCAL* SHOPS/TALL
GRASS, LEAVES & WEEDS/CATS & DOGS/BUILDING INTERIORS/SHOPPING CENTRES/COMMUNITY
BUILDINGS/VEGETABLE GARDENS/ROCKS/STREAMS/WILD ANIMALS/CHILD'S RELATIVES & OTHER
ADULTS/RAILWAY LINES/BUS STOPS/FORTS, CLUBHOUSES & CAMPS/SPORTS COURTS/VACANT BUILDING
SITES/FRUITING TREES/NEIGHBOUR'S & BABYSITTER'S HOUSES/SECRET, HIDING PLACES/TREE
HOUSES/TREE SWINGS/FISH & AQUATIC LIFE/CHILD'S SIBLINGS/CHURCHES —.05 and less.

Mill Hill children also expressed a stronger interest in 'home-sites,' perhaps reflecting the stable home-based working-class culture of the Potteries, compared to the more plural, social character of the other two sites.

Two Notting Dale scores reflect a more intense level of urban development. The high score for 'open space' mirrors the appearance of the Notting Dale turf map and reemphasises the dependency of Notting Dale children on local parks and playgrounds. Further reinforcement is given by the low mention of 'macro-landscape features' long since obliterated by urban development (except the wooded crest of Holland Park recorded as 'open space').

To sharpen a comparison of *natural* environment elements across sites, 'vegetation,' 'natural ground surfaces,' 'macro-landscape features,' 'aquatic elements' and 'animals' were combined (Figure 14). Both Bedwell and Mill Hill have two-thirds more mentions than Notting Dale—a clear indication that natural elements were less widespread in highly developed Notting Dale. The almost identical score for Bedwell and Mill Hill, however, is suprising when one considers the great contrast between Bedwell's tidy swards and Mill Hill's unkempt acres. Even though the perceptual impacts, as expressed on paper, show little difference between the two sites, the contrasting impacts on children's overt behavior during the field trips was quite apparent—as we shall see in later chapters.

Since the similarities across sites are stronger than the differences, the scores for remaining categories indicate a common core of childhood-environment experience. This raises a note of caution concerning cross-cultural differences. Suppose additional sites in continental Europe, Africa, Asia or Latin America had been included, then surely the variations would have been much greater—as indicated by the UNESCO study of young people's environments.[4]

The interview results (Figure 15), although more sparse and less rich than the drawing results, reinforce the above conclusions. The full list of responses (Table 3, Appendix C) has been reduced to seven categories. Note that local open space has been divided into 'formal/official' (mostly parks and playgrounds) and 'informal/unofficial.' This useful subdivision was not feasible with the more finely-grained drawing results. (See Appendix A for a discussion of differences between interviewing and drawing methods.) The 'informal/unofficial' category included 'fields,' various types of 'rough ground,' and 'greens' (a category of open space falling between formal park and rough ground).

14   *Favourite place types by study site, in rank order of mention rates.*
Based on children' drawings, Table 2, Appendix B.

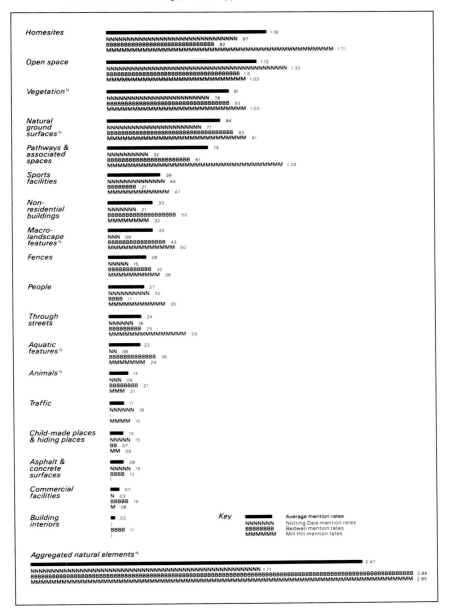

Homesites
NNNNNNNNNNNNNNNNNNNNNNNNNNNNNNNNN 97
BBBBBBBBBBBBBBBBBBBBBBBBBBBBB 82
MMMMMMMMMMMMMMMMMMMMMMMMMMMMMMMMMMMMMMMMMMMMMMMMMM 1.71   1.19

Open space
NNNNNNNNNNNNNNNNNNNNNNNNNNNNNNNNNNNNNNNNNNNNNNNN 1.32
BBBBBBBBBBBBBBBBBBBBBBBBBBBBBBBBBB 1.0
MMMMMMMMMMMMMMMMMMMMMMMM 1.03   1.12

Vegetation[N]
NNNNNNNNNNNNNNNNNNNNNNNNN 76
BBBBBBBBBBBBBBBBBBBBBBBBBBB 93
MMMMMMMMMMMMMMMMMMMMMMMMM 1.03   91

Natural ground surfaces[N]
NNNNNNNNNNNNNNNNNNNNNNN 71
BBBBBBBBBBBBBBBBBBBBBBBBBBBBB 93
MMMMMMMMMMMMMMMMMMMMMMMM 91   84

Pathways & associated spaces
NNNNNNNNN 32
BBBBBBBBBBBBBBBBBB 61
MMMMMMMMMMMMMMMMMMMMMMMMMMMMMMMMM 1.29   75

Sports facilities
NNNNNNNNNNNNN 44
BBBBBBB 21
MMMMMMMMMMMMM 47   39

Non-residential buildings
NNNNNN 21
BBBBBBBBBBBBBBB 50
MMMMMMMM 32   33

Macro-landscape features[N]
NNN 09
BBBBBBBBBBBBB 43
MMMMMMMMMMMMM 50   33

Fences
NNNNN 15
BBBBBBBBBB 32
MMMMMMMMMM 38   28

People
NNNNNNNNN 32
BBBB 11
MMMMMMMMMM 35   27

Through streets
NNNNN 18
BBBBBBBB 25
MMMMMMMMMMMMMMMMM 59   24

Aquatic features[N]
NN 06
BBBBBBBBBBB 36
MMMMMMMM 29   23

Animals[N]
NNN 09
BBBBBBBB 21
MMM 21   14

Traffic
NNNNNN 18
|
MMMM 15   11

Child-made places & hiding places
NNNNN 15
BB 07
MM 09   10

Asphalt & concrete surfaces
NNNNN 15
BBBB 12
| 08

Commercial facilities
N 03
BBBBB 14
M 06   07

Building interiors
| 03
BBBB 11
| 03

Key
Average mention rates
NNNNNNN Notting Dale mention rates
BBBBBBBB Bedwell mention rates
MMMMMM Mill Hill mention rates

Aggregated natural elements[N]

NNNNNNNNNNNNNNNNNNNNNNNNNNNNNNNNNNNNNNNNNNNNNNNNNNNNNNNNNNNNNNNNNNNN 1.71
BBBBBBBBBBBBBBBBBBBBBBBBBBBBBBBBBBBBBBBBBBBBBBBBBBBBBBBBBBBBBBBBBBBBBBBBBBBBBBBBBBBBBBBB 2.86
MMMMMMMMMMMMMMMMMMMMMMMMMMMMMMMMMMMMMMMMMMMMMMMMMMMMMMMMMMMMMMMMMMMMMMMMMMMMMMMMMMMMMMM 2.85   2.47

The first three items in Figure 15—'formal/official open space,' 'homesites,' and 'streets and associated spaces'—account for just over three-fourths of the total after-school mentions. This result dramatically emphasises the experiential investment that children make, by necessity, in their homesites and immediate surroundings. The ranking of 'streets and associated space' has been boosted in Figure 15 by the inclusion of alleyways, small lawns, 'fronts' and garage courts that the interviews showed (reinforced during field trips) were 'associated' with street play..

The interview results also point to some interesting weekday/weekend differences. There is an indication that streets were much more frequently used after school than at weekends, most likely because there was not enough time after school for anything else but street play—on the way home, or before and after mealtimes and homework. Larger blocks of time, available at weekends, were more frequently invested in the use of community facilities, including trips to Saturday morning pictures, visits to swimming pools and outings to football matches.

MISSING ITEMS

In reviewing the results, it is important to remember that a wide range of individual differences are masked—that what may have been 'habitual' for one child may only have been 'occasional' for another.

The popularity of some items can be explained in terms of proximity, intrinsic attractiveness, and social or cultural significance. For other, less popular, items explanations are not so easy. Was it because they did not exist on the ground? Were there access difficulties? Parental restraints? Variations in taste amongst children? For all places there are value judgements to be made regarding their contribution towards, or hinderance of, child development. Just because something was well-used does not make it automatically more desirable for human development—and vice versa.

Considering the normal attraction of children to water, the low rate of mention of 'aquatic features' in all three sites (Figure 14) indicates a lack of water-play opportunities close to home. None of the major parks or playgrounds in Notting Dale offered features suitable for water play. Nearly all the mentions related only to the lakes in

15 *Favourite places to go after school and on weekends.*
Based on childrens' interviews, Table 3, Appendix C.

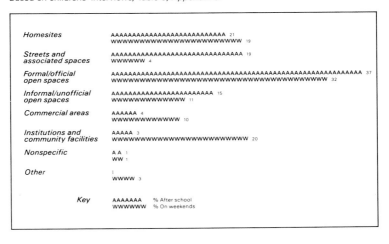

Homesites	AAAAAAAAAAAAAAAAAAAAAAAAAAA 21 WWWWWWWWWWWWWWWWWWWWW 19
Streets and *associated spaces*	AAAAAAAAAAAAAAAAAAAAAAAAAAA 19 WWWWWW 4
Formal/official *open spaces*	AAAAAAAAAAAAAAAAAAAAAAAAAAAAAAAAAAAAAAAAAAAAAAAAAAAAAAA 37 WWWWWWWWWWWWWWWWWWWWWWWWWWWWWWWWWWWWWWWWWWWWWW 32
Informal/unofficial *open spaces*	AAAAAAAAAAAAAAAAAAAAAAA 15 WWWWWWWWWWWWWW 11
Commercial areas	AAAAAA 4 WWWWWWWWWWWW 10
Institutions and *community facilities*	AAAAA 3 WWWWWWWWWWWWWWWWWWWWWWWWWWWW 20
Nonspecific	AA 1 WW 1
Other	I WWWW 3

Key	AAAAAAA	% After school
	WWWWWW	% On weekends

Fairlands and Tunstall Parks. Additional aquatic resources were available, but were too far away and appeared only in the occasional ranges of a small minority of the most mobile children.

Very few mentions of 'animals' were made (Figure 14), except for pet cats and dogs and an occasional bird. One reason is that children's relationships with urban wildlife are hard to document. The scale of organism is usually too small to draw on paper. Neither are they often mentioned verbally. Perhaps it is because of the ephemeral quality of interaction. Animals are not place-specific. They migrate and hibernate and constantly move around in search of food and shelter. Children move around a lot too, so that although the paths of children and wildlife may cross frequently, they are the briefest moments...a butterfly fluttering out of reach...a beetle disappearing down a crack in the pavement. Yet some children were extremely aware of the presence of wildlife and knew very well where and when to find it.

Mentions of *local* shops were surprisingly low (Figure 13, bottom) and inconsistent with field observations. Small shopping areas and corner stores were present in all three study areas, so the results were not biased because of non-availability. One reason for the low score was that children associated local shops with running domestic errands—with chores, rather than play. Nonetheless, local shops were a source of important childhood items and some of the children were highly discriminating about the quality of shops they patronised. For instance Heather mentioned a nearby corner shop that was her favourite place for "ice cream and sweets." Her second favourite was "the post office down the street...for toys, cards, comics, and things." One boy described the detailed pros and cons of seven toy-and-hobby shops where he hung out in Stevenage town centre.

The low incidence of 'child-made places' (Figure 14)—forts, clubhouses, secret places, hiding places and tree houses—was most surprising, since such places are often portrayed by adults as ideal childhood environments. Perhaps they were difficult for children to recall; for, as with wildlife, they also bore aspects of impermanence and transitory experience. They could quickly fall apart, were "bashed" by other kids or were worked on only during the summer. Also, in communicating the existence of such places, children were sometimes confused or concerned about the legality of the situation; or if not, they were simply unwilling (understandably) to share their private knowledge.

In spite of these difficulties, powerful examples were recorded in the field. Chapter 1 stressed the need for children to manipulate their surroundings with imagination and competence, to create their own personal world. Because of its developmental importance, the topic will be given more space in later chapters than merited strictly by its rate of mention in the drawings and interviews.

'Traffic,' 'asphalt,' 'commercial facilities' (including local shops and shopping centres) and 'interiors' all received such low scores (Figure 14), that one may assume they represent items of such ubiquity and mundaneness that they were either under-illuminated in most minds, or children saw no point in mentioning them. The complete lack of traffic mentions in Bedwell, however, may perhaps be taken as an indication of the effect of the traffic-free conditions within the neighbourhood

A final note. The low mention of 'people' in Figure 14 is surprising, but it may reflect a bias of the procedure. Children were only asked for the whereabouts of their favourite *places* and not their favourite *persons*. Even so, nearly all the mentions of people (other than the child her/himself), were of a 'best friend'—indicating the im-

Favourite activities after school and on weekends.
Based on children's interviews, Table4, Appendix C.

General outdoor play and games	AAAAAAAAAAAAAAAAAAAAAAAAAAAAAAAAAAAAAAAAAAAAAAAAAAAAAA 36 WWWWWWWWWWWWWWWWWWWWWWWWWWWWWW 22
Play on equipment	AAAAAAAAAAAAAAAAAAAAAAAA 14 WWWWWWWWWWWWW 10
Ball play and ball games	AAAAAAAAAAAAAAAA 10 WWWWWWWWW 7
Adventure play	AAAAAAAAAAAAAAAAAAAAAAAAAAAAAAAAAAAAAAAAAAAA 26 WWWWWWWWWWWWWWWWWWWWWWWWWWWWWWWWWWWWWWWWWWWWWW 31
Mobile play	AAAAAAAAAAA 7 WWWWWWWWWWW 8
Spectator and formal events	AAA 2 WWWWWWWWWWWWWWWWWWW 13
Activities inside the home	AAAAAAAA 5 WWWWWWWWWWWW 9

Key   AAAAAAA   % After school
      WWWWWW   % On weekends

portance of close peer relationships. Parents, other adults and siblings (except best friends) were hardly mentioned. This result parallels what happens, in my experience, when adults are asked to recall favourite childhood places. Intense memories are recounted of small, private, 'best friend' spots. Heavily populated places rarely feature.

FAVOURITE ACTIVITIES

Interviews indicated that what I have called 'general play and games' was the most common category of activites, both after school and on weekends (Figure 16). Responses included nonspecific activities like "play in the grass" and traditional games such as "skipping," "hopscotch" and "hide-and-seek." Children did not differentiate their outdoor activity in much detail verbally—hence my insistence on child-led field trips to observe place-specific activity first hand. 'General play and games' was a challenging category to document since it consisted, largely, of children wandering or running about, or hanging around talking—perched on walls, sitting on balustrades and benches, propping up trees and lampposts, lounging on lawns or scratching in the dirt.

'Equipment play' included any activity on traditional or contemporary play apparatus. 'Ball games' included all mentions of ball-related activity—from organised competitive sports to informal pickups around the home—including traditional games such as 'catch.' Taken together, 'equipment play' and 'ball games' accounted for barely a quarter of the activites mentioned, yet they are frequently considered by recreation providers to be a majority interest of children.

Activites within the home were not mentioned as frequently as one might expect, given the high score of 'homesites' as favourite places. Watching television, even, was not mentioned very often. The implication seems to be that children preferred playing outdoors—often immediately around the home—although poor weather, darkness, and domestic obligations frequently prevented it.

Within the 'formal/spectator' category, "shopping" and "eating out with parents" were the most commonly mentioned weekend activities, along with other activities like "visiting the Institute," "Guy Fawking," "going to the pictures," "watching football" and "going to dances."

'Mobile play,' which included mentions of "walking," "rollerskating," "go-carting," "biking," "horse riding" and "cross-country running," received a surprisingly low score, considering how often footpaths, pavements and streets—where mobile activities occur—were mentioned (Figure 13). Indeed, the low interview score was so strongly counteracted by many marvellous experiences in the field that the whole of the next chapter will be devoted to descriptions of mobile activity.

One reason why "walking" was not mentioned more often in the interviews is that it is such a matter-of-fact daily occurrence that children are unlikely to make note of it—except under special circumstances such as "going for a hike." One reason for the low mention of bike riding was the lack of safe, functionally adequate places to ride. The danger posed by street traffic meant that many parents restricted bike riding to streets immediately around the home. Also, bikes were not owned by all children; and, of those that were, some were out of commission because of flat tyres and other malfunctions (Table 7, Appendix C).

ADVENTURE PLAY

'Adventure play' is the term I will use to describe activities where the environment is manipulated or acted on in some way by children—activities generally regarded as having a high developmental value. Some readers may consider this a narrow and specialized interpreta-

David in one of his favourite places—up one of the few climbing trees in Notting Dale—an ancient weeping willow in Avondale Park.

Childhood's Domain/*Investigation*

tion of "adventure," which it undoubtedly is; however, the English language term is well-established and originated with the adventure playgrounds developed in Britain during the last several decades. Other terms, such as "building playgrounds" (Scandinavia) and "Robinson Crusoe playgrounds" (Switzerland and Germany) are used elsewhere. Also note that in much of the English-speaking world the term "adventure playgrounds" has been so misused that it is almost meaningless. Genuine adventure playgrounds provide children with an opportunity to work with all manner of loose materials, to invent their own games and artifacts, and to plan and construct their own environments under the guidance of trained leaders or "animators."

Between a quarter and a third of all activities (Figure 16) were defined as 'adventure play,' with the larger proportion happening on weekends. The largest number of replies (a quarter) mentioned "climbing" ("climbing trees," "climbing fences" and "climbing about"). Other adventure play activities included "playing on a Tarzan swing," "making camps," "playing in the sand," "making fires," "setting off fireworks" (it was the Guy Fawkes season), "throwing stones" ("at trees," "at birds" and "into ponds"), and "collecting things" ("bird's eggs," "newts," "wood for a bonfire" and "conkers"[5]).

Over a third of the adventure play activities related to 'found objects' like those above. Further examples were documented during field trips of children on the lookout for missiles to throw, tools to do things with, and objects to delight in for their own sake—a further indication of how free time at weekends was used for exploration in depth, farther away from home. Twice as many water-related play activities happened on weekends, especially "swimming" and "paddling," which were grouped together with other adventuresome aquatic activities such as "canoeing," "going in boats" and "watching boats."

A number of adventure playgrounds were located in or near the study sites. It was particularly interesting to record their use (in addition to adventure play in the environment at-large) and to discover that even though both Notting Dale and Bedwell children had reasonable access to adventure playgrounds, only eight of the total of fifty recorded instances of adventure play actually occurred on them—suggesting that the broader environment should be made even more adventuresome, rather than concentrating effort solely on a few specialised sites.

The chapters that follow provide detailed evidence to show how children's use of the outdoors went beyond specialised facilities such as playgrounds, and how play activities could be extended or limited by social and physical factors. The major policy themes that emerge, discussed fully in Chapter 10, can be summarised as follows.

ACCESS TO DIVERSITY This is a crucial limiting factor on children's experience of the environment. More than half the place elements listed in Figure 13 appeared in less than one-in-ten drawings. This suggests that the outdoor experience of many children is severely constrained. Every child needs equal access to opportunities for asserting her or his individuality, through interactions with the environment. The potential for interaction exists at all levels of range experience, depending on the availability of adequate resources, the absence of physical constraints, and the degree of freedom accorded by parents.

ADAPTATION TO CHILDREN'S RIGHTS The right to a stimulating, developmentally-appropriate environment and the right to play are part of the United Nations Declaration of the Rights of the Child. Environments must be adapted to meet these needs. To do so will require the assimilation of knowledge, by adults, about the complex ecological relationships and varied contexts of children's lives; and this must go hand-in-hand with adults' accommodation to images of children as primary users of local environments physically adapted to meet their needs.

Implementation of children's rights raises many issues related to basic health, and the social and economic conditions that enhance or dimimish children's status in society—that lie beyond the scope of this book. However, there is a highly germane issue regarding what genuine, developmentally stimulating play looks like, where it actually happens—what it really is. An understanding of this issue is essential for effective policy formulation.

MAKING STREETS LIVABLE This is the topmost action that would advance both children's access to diversity and the child's right to play.

CONSERVATION OF SPECIAL CHILDHOOD PLACES Important childhood resources are not recognised, nor valued, nor protected by the community. The identification and conservation of such places, especially in areas of redevelopment and restoration, is crucial.

ROUGHING-UP URBAN PARKS AND GREENS Landscapes used by

children are often overdesigned and too highly manicured. "Roughing-up" would increase diversity by allowing ecological forces to invade more easily. Low-maintenance vegetation can be manipulated more freely by children without creating negative visual impacts. Diverse landscapes are more resilient to damage and are able to recover more easily.

URBAN WILDLIFE MANAGEMENT Enhancement of the shelter and nutrition needs of animals and micro-organisms would increase the number of species and size of populations, so that children can benefit more from their presence. Roughing-up sections of the urban landscape is the most obvious first step.

ADVENTURE PLAYGROUNDS Evaluations need to be made and issues examined in relation to these important community facilities.

COMMUNITY ANIMATION New educational functions, revised professional roles and institutional initiatives need to be fostered. Children are an integral part of the community. Their environment cannot be arbitrarily partitioned-off to create childhood ghettos. Effective use and continued improvement requires creative, cooperative work by children and adults together. Practical examples of 'animation' in Britain and elsewhere are noted in Chapter 10, together with a discussion of the related roles of play leadership, and environmental education.

CHILDREN'S PARTICIPATION in the planning, design and management of their surroundings. The work of participatory community groups, in Britain and elsewhere, demonstrates the feasibility of collaborative work between people, to evaluate their own environments, to involve them in genuine decision making and to help them make improvements to their surroundings. Yet despite the attention paid to public participation on both sides of the Atlantic since the early 1960's, children and youth are still rarely involved in an appropriate, authentic manner. To be effective, participation needs to begin early in life, at home and at school. Government authorities, community organisations and professional bodies need to collaborate and commit themselves to institutional change so that the participation of young people can reach a significant level of influence.

Exploring childhood territories

The near landscape is valuable and lovable because of its nearness, not something to be disregarded and shrugged off; it is where children are reared and what they take away in their minds to their long future. What ground could be more hallowed?
— Frank Fraser Darling

We have, from the beginning , a kind of freedom, not to do what we like, but to work on the materials — stones, plants, secretions, languages, cultures — which come our way. This freedom is sometimes recognizable as play.
— R.A. Hodgkin

3 *The flowing terrain*

On a number of the field trips I was struck by the continuity and
diversity of interaction between children and their surroundings.
The content of these trips was much too rich and subtle to have
been clearly expressed in the drawings and interviews alone; besides,
I had only asked for "favourite places," rather than asking for
"pathways" as well. As a result, it seemed probable that children's
answers had emphasized spaces with well-defined boundaries.

Two aspects of children's continuity of behaviour impressed me
in the field. The first was what one pair of children called "gymnast."
This was an apt description for the way in which they hopped,
climbed, balanced, skipped, rolled, swivelled and squeezed through,
on, over, around and inside their surroundings—using ledges, posts,
walls, curbs, banks, bollards, doorways, steps and paving stones—
their movement choreographed by the landscape, as their bodies
responded to its every opportunity.

The second aspect of continuity was a less visible reflection of
the merging of pathway and place. It applied to a number of children, who, like *Zazie dans le Metro*, made so many digressions from
their original goal that it became lost in a wealth of substituted activity. Some of the trips were rather like starting out driving down a
motorway and then allowing oneself to be progressively diverted by

narrower and narrower country lanes, stopping at every point of interest along the way, until the original purpose and destination of the trip become completely forgotten.

WANDERING

Although we tend to think of children as always being "on the go," the truth is that at all ages they engage in quiet social interaction, introspection, and sensous contemplation of their surroundings. Such a state cannot be classified (as recreation specialists might) as "passive," since it implies being "done to" rather than "doing." Many field trips indicated a great deal going on—not highly energetic, nor clearly observable, but developmentally significant. For it is at such times that children make their most intimate and prolonged contact with the social and physical phenomena around them. Research has shown that in some residential areas, pathways are the most heavily used spaces.[1] Given the opportunity, children spend more time wandering around outdoors than most adults, and their patterns of interactions are more intimate, fluid and intense. For this reason, it is important that they have spaces where they can wander at their own pace and not have to keep up with adults or be chastised for dawdling.

To wander through a diverse terrain is to feel the surroundings pass through one's body as the body passes through the surroundings—at one with each other. Like the rambler, one experiences a floating state of mind, drugged by a wealth of sounds, of smells, of sights and textures. Indeed, opportunities to 'ramble' should be built into every urban neighbourhood.

A prime characteristic of wandering, strolling or rambling is solitude. *Solivagant* is the closest term I have found, meaning "to wander alone." However, in conducting field trips I discovered that the most common social group was the 'best friends duet,' embodying social relationships different from an individual alone or a group of friends. Sharing the world outdoors with a best friend carries special significance. When children are engaged in primary exploration, they get to know themselves and their surroundings more thoroughly when sharing experiences with a trusted friend. Such relationships can develop more fully outdoors because of the greater indeterminacy of unfolding experience. Everchanging constellations of interactions stimulate a higher level of communication—both verbal and nonverbal—which is much harder, if not impossible, to replicate inside buildings.

PEDESTRIAN NETWORKS

To facilitate the child's right to wander, pedestrian networks must be extensive and continuous so that access to diversity can be maintained with each extension of territory.

In Notting Dale, traffic dominated the streets and overshadowed the possibility of extensive wandering. Movement around the neighbourhood was severely limited for many children by the frequent occurrence of busy streets. Hence local parks and playgrounds were heavily used.

Whereas Notting Dale streets were so dominated by traffic that their play potential was severely restricted, Bedwell streets seemed almost too free of traffic—to the point where the stimulation provided by modest comings and goings of vehicles (and their passengers)

A Bedwell pedestrian path running past Brian's house.

was removed. Mill Hill streets represented a happy medium, with enough local traffic to generate human interest, but not so much that the impact of vehicles dominated the scene.

Tunstall was permeated by a network of residential alleyways and dirt paths that crisscrossed unused industrial land. Intimate close-to-home networks occurred wherever pedestrian routes were connected to sections of the adjacent street system. Carole, for example, took me to the cul-de-sac in front of her house, where many games were played, then down a narrow path alongside the house (the last one on the terrace) to a junction of paths at the back (Figure 17). To the right was a straight asphalt route to the main road, used by people travelling to and from work. The path we were on carried us to the next cul-de-sac serving the "new houses" that had been recently completed behind Carole's terrace. To the left, the path broadened out into a larger red shale[1] area that Carole called "the backs." She went to school that way she said. "There's a gap between the garages you can get through...then you can get on the Greenway and go under the bridge...and the school is straight ahead."

Bedwell, like Stevenage as a whole, had been laid out deliberately to serve the needs of pedestrians; as a result, several examples of close-to-home networks were documented. Undoubtedly they provided excellent access; yet, on the other hand, they lacked the surprise of Mill Hill's ad hoc pathways and the sensory interest of the graceful curves, bulbous cul-de-sacs and thickly vegetated traffic islands of its 1940s housing layout.

The nearest Notting Dale equivalent to the close-to-home pathway networks of Bedwell and Mill Hill, were the asphalt paths of housing estates. Located between fenced-off lawns, they usually didn't lead anywhere worthwhile, and in anycase were controlled by the personnel of an apparently oppressive housing authority (discussed later).

When asked where they went to be alone, several Bedwell children mentioned "going for a walk" or "walking the dog." Such responses were unheard of among Notting Dale children and were not often mentioned in Mill Hill. Stevenage residents seemed conscious and proud that they lived in a town where a successful balance had been achieved between the needs of pedestrians and cars. The town was truly walkable from end to end. The town centre was a relaxed and bustling pedestrian paradise—a joy to experience. A walking tradition clearly had evolved among the inhabitants, who used the neighbourhood pedestrian networks and the major paths and cycleways to provide safe passage between neighbourhoods and the town centre (Figure 18).

Tunstall's Greenways (Figure 18) had not been planned comprehensively like the Stevenage system, but had been reclaimed from old railway rights-of-way that had formerly connected mineheads and town centres. Although the Greenways tended to run alongside rather than through the residential areas, they offered considerable potential as crosstown, traffic-separated, routes connecting principal open spaces.

The major pathways in both Stevenage and Tunstall were not exploited by most children as a means of extending their territorial range. The distances seemed too large for most nine-to-twelve-year-olds, who preferred to travel on the more intimate network of neighbourhood paths, back alleys and side streets. Also, the major path-

17 *Carole's close-to-home territory in Mill Hill.*

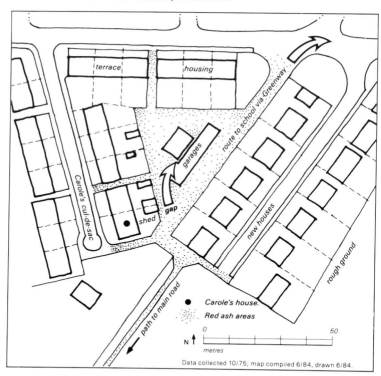

terrace

housing

route to school via Greenway

garages

Carole's cul-de-sac

gap

shed

new houses

rough ground

path to main road

● Carole's house.

Red ash areas

0   50
metres

N

Data collected 10/75; map compiled 6/84, drawn 6/84.

"There's a gap between the garages you can get through..."

Childhood's Domain/*The flowing terrain*

61

18   *Traffic-segregated cycleways and pedestrian paths connecting the study sites to surrounding areas.*
Drawn to the same scale.

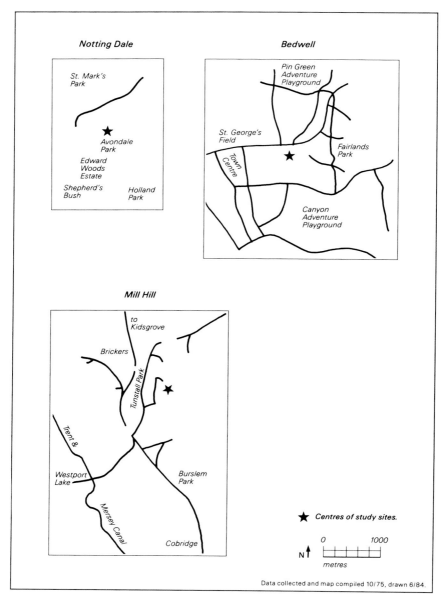

Notting Dale

St. Mark's Park

★
Avondale Park

Edward Woods Estate

Shepherd's Bush   Holland Park

Bedwell

Pin Green Adventure Playground

St. George's Field

Town Centre

★

Fairlands Park

Canyon Adventure Playground

Mill Hill

to Kidsgrove

Brickers

Tunstall Park

★

Trent &

Westport Lake

Mersey Canal

Burslem Park

Cobridge

★ Centres of study sites.

0   1000

N ↑

metres

Data collected and map compiled 10/75, drawn 6/84.

ways in both Stevenage and Tunstall were 'grade-separated,' which meant that they were either sunk in a series of cuttings and underpasses, or lifted up on embankments and overpasses. This had the advantage of making them traffic-free, but it also made them impractical for short trips because the routes were physically cut off from their immediate surroundings. Chris told me he preferred to travel along the street, rather than use the Greenway behind the houses, so that he could "knock up" his friends on the way.

For longer distances, use of the Greenways was limited by the fact that many bridges and viaducts, that once carried the rail lines across the roads, had been demolished. Presumably they had been removed for reasons of liability, or to avoid maintenance expense, or to satisfy some other bureaucratic requirement. At regular intervals, pathway continuity was broken when routes had to drop down to busy intersections, to shake users of all ages out of their solitude and force them to confront the realities of urban traffic. In Stevenage, pedestrians and cyclists remained happily segregated from traffic.

Notting Dale had no major pedestrian routes equivalent to Bedwell or Mill Hill, except for a mile-long strip of space under Westway (the elevated Great West Road extension into central London (Figure 18), that was being developed for community purposes. Unfortunately, no records of use were recorded with Notting Dale children.

BICYCLES

For some children, bikes were an important means of getting around and a primary means of extending territory beyond the limits of foot travel—especially on occasional weekend trips or during the summer when more time was available.

In spite of breaks in continuity, the main Tunstall Greenway allowed bike riders to make territorial extensions to places far beyond the built-up limits of the city. Chris told me that he and his friends sometimes cycled through the countryside as far as Kidsgrove (about three miles away).

The Stevenage cycleways did not have the same potential. They did not follow old railway routes and therefore did not extend beyond the developed fringe of the town. However, the Stevenage system was much better for crosstown travel than the Tunstall Greenways because it had been planned as an evenly spaced network of continuous routes. One day I ran into a group of fourteen-to-fifteen-year-old boys in the Bedwell shopping precinct who told me about a fascinating range of places they went to by bike:

> ...to the Canyon to play commandoes—it's 'smart' down there...down the Dell...on the streets...here at the Bedwell shops... up the lakes...at the bike canyon on the wall of death—it's good on a fine day when you can do wheelies without sliding around. We go out to the duck pond and ride bikes in the bushes...we go to Marks Wood and St. George's Field. We go to places where it's all bumpy...we go down the multistory car park and have lift races. We go to the Little College Dip [in the industrial area] and the Six Hills Burial Ground—there's six Romans buried there—and around the Scout Hut and the garages...we go up the Wild West kind of park and to Knobworth House, where the best adventure playground is. Sometimes we go bike scrambling and play hide-and-seek on the building sites.... We do dares and runouts and....

The places mentioned were located all over town. The boys may have been an especially mobile group; even so, their itinerary clearly implies the importance of two necessary criteria for accessibility: townwide coverage and pathway continuity. It would be interesting to study the bicycle behavior of this age group more thoroughly.

Bicycle ownership was by no means universal. Only about half the children interviewed said they owned bikes and used them on a regular basis (Table 7, Appendix C). Several mentioned that they were "saving up for one" or were getting one for their birthday or for Christmas, or were getting their sister's or brother's old bike. Of those who did have use of a bicycle, one-in-seven said it was broken. Young children cannot normally repair their own machines, and it is a considerable reflection on the lack of parental responsibility that so many bikes were out of commission—for periods of several months in some cases.

On top of this, bike-owning kids who lived in multistory housing faced the additional frustrations of an interior environment not designed for bicycles. Lawrence, who lived in one of the Notting Dale tower blocks, had to keep his bike in the entrance hallway of the flat, which, as his parents explained, not only blocked the way in, but made dirty marks on the floor and wall and looked untidy. But this was nothing compared to the problems Lawrence encountered in going for a ride. We first waited over five minutes for the lift, which eventually arrived crowded with passengers. Lawrence had to shuffle uncomfortably around them and negotiate space for himself and his machine while enduring the disapproving mutterings of two elderly women all the way down. They thought it was shocking that a child should have a bike in the crowded lift (rather than complaining about the inadequate size of the lift or the infrequency of service).[3]

Once outside, all bike-riding kids faced conflict with pedestrians, although it seemed to be more a problem of adult minds than anything else. Certainly there will always be foolhardy bike riders who disregard the possible consequences of their actions, but most children seemed well-aware of potential pedestrian-cycle conflict. In Holland Park, Ricky showed me a long straight path that he called a "bike path." He raced down it with his friends, he said, and added that it was good because it wasn't used by "people" (meaning adult pedestrians). He went on to complain that there were too many people on the other paths that they liked to ride on, and suggested that "they should have people on one path and bikes on another."

In both Stevenage and Tunstall, parallel-but-separate pathways were, in truth, provided for both cyclists and pedestrians. But the segregation rules were often not followed by the users, sometimes for good reasons. In Bedwell, Brian said he always walked on the cycleways with his friends because the group was always too large to fit the narrower footpaths. In Tunstall, where the Greenway cycle and pedestrian pathways were of equal width, users still did not follow the rules. Jill and Lesley said they liked to ride on the "most

"My dad used to go to all kinds of places on his bike.... I like to go to 'big' places like Endon [more than four miles from Tunstall], to the carnival, and to Rudyard Lake [a reservoir almost ten miles away] to go fishing."

interesting parts" of the Greenway regardless of whether they were meant for pedestrians or cyclists. They mentioned a "special circuit" around Pitts Hill (which in fact was a pedestrian path), where they could come "speeding down." Lesley even noted that one path was meant for people and one for bikes and commented, "no one takes any notice of that.... People walk and bike on both paths." So much for rational planning!

Most cycling took place near the children's homes. Those who had roadworthy bikes used them primarily as part of their everyday routine—for moving more quickly around their foot-defined territory. More extensive trips were rare, even though time was available. The most obvious reason was the extreme hazard presented to bike riders of all ages when using major roads. The dangers encountered beyond quiet neighbourhood streets was apparent to most parents, who therefore tended to rigidly control bike riding.

I had a hunch that developmental factors also constrained many of the children. For example, although Mandy was given "free range" over the Stevenage cycleways by her mother, she rarely took advantage of her freedom, but limited herself to riding around in front of the house—with an occasional trip to the park to feed the ducks. She did not feel competent enough for longer trips.

Bike riding was clearly a sensory stimulant. This made topography and differentiation of the terrain significant—to cyclists and pedestrians alike. Andrew showed me how he went "scrambling" on the banks of the Little Park in Mill Hill. Chris told me about doing the same thing on the grassy slopes of Mill Hill's Clanway Stadium. Carole described the circular "race routes" she followed around the red shale paths at the back of her house.

Children on bikes love what adults might perceive as aimless round-and-round riding. The Bedwell shopping plaza presented such an opportunity. One early-closing afternoon I saw a whole gaggle of bike riders gliding in and out among themselves and the fixed features of the space, weaving intricate patterns around concrete planting tubs and a free-standing letterbox. The permutation of circuits added sensory delight to what was an otherwise deserted space.

The most dramatically sensuous bike trip I experienced was with Lawrence in Notting Dale, in the gloomy pedestrian subways under the Shepherd's Bush roundabout. The moment we arrived, Lawrence took-off on the first of several swoops down into the subterranean depths; he on his bike, I tagging behind, trying to look nonchalant, hoping he wasn't going to knock someone down. After one or two near-misses, we reemerged at the point where we had started, having come full circle. These were the subways that some parents would not let their children use, and I understood why. They were dingy and lonely. I was struck by the fact that the road engineers had put the people underground and the cars on the surface. Nonetheless, it was an exciting bike-riding setting—though hazardous to any pedestrians who ventured there.

OTHER WAYS OF TRAVELLING

Tunstall's Greenways had one advantage that major routes in Stevenage lacked. They had been designed for use by horse riders—something that was particularly attractive to children older than the group I was studying. I had the good fortune to run into a group of twelve-

Horseriding on the Tunstall Greenways.

to-fourteen-year-olds who were riding horseback on a Greenway near the centre of Tunstall. It was a wonderful sight. They told me they often rode through the town to Cobridge (a couple of miles away). Before departing, two of the riders made a circuit around the widest part of the Greenway and jumped over one of the park benches, while the others applauded (suggesting the need for more appropriate facilities).

As with the Stevenage cyclists, additional study of the Tunstall horse riders would have been valuable. For instance, how much did horse riding cost? Could horses be hired by the hour? Where could kids learn to ride? Maybe it offered girls an opportunity to even up the score for townwide travel.

Besides walking, horse riding and cycling, two other means of nonmotorised movement were documented: roller-skating and go-carting. Roller-skating was rarely observed, but was several times mentioned. The main problem was the lack of smooth pavements. In Mill Hill, Dawne took me to a sloping asphalt path running across the 'backs' behind her house, where she usually roller-skated. But she complained that the surface was not very good. She wished that someone would fill in the potholes to make it better. It seemed a pity that more opportunities were not available for pursuing such a healthy, energetic activity. Traffic barred it from streets; cracks between paving stones kept it off pavements; park rules banned it in parks.

The traditional childhood craft of go-cart-making was encountered only in Mill Hill (and there quite frequently) because it offered three essential requirements: hilly topography, space at home for construction, and a ready supply of free scrap materials. Mill Hill topography was unsurpassed for its variety of slopes. A large proportion of the housing—even the traditional back-to-backs—had private outdoor areas that could be used for working on small construction projects. Garages were sometimes used, too. Then, of course, widespread industrial sites provided a fertile supply of scrap materials for construction.

Because surface requirements for go-cart racing are less stringent than for roller-skating, go-carts on street pavements were observed several times. The Greenway entrance paths, dropping steeply down the sides of cuttings, seemed to present particularly attractive racing alignments. The crushed red shale provided an excellent riding surface. Chris, an expert, took me to what he had labelled the "roller coaster place" on his drawing. It was an eight-foot-wide path, curving downhill to meet the main Greenway route. He explained that they had races there and that "you try to knock each other on the grass, so you're disqualified." Chris pointed to a low mound rising up on one side of the path and said that it was the best place for "testing-out our trollies." At the bottom of the path he pointed to a curve they had to "swerve around without tipping over" (there were lots of wheel marks there). He mentioned putting bricks on the path to create an obstacle course—"The first one down without touching the bricks is the winner."

Go-cart racing on the Mill Hill topography.

Children often followed unofficial hidden paths, like rabbits or deer making 'runs' through the urban undergrowth, connecting parts of their territories via routes that most adults would not think of using. In Mill Hill, Chris took me on a "quick way," along a path beside a tall brickyard retaining wall to the Clanway Stadium. He showed me how to "get through" a hole in the brickyard fence and cut across Clanway to get home.

"Squeeze through" gaps were made the same size as children's own bodies (most kids can squeeze through nine or ten inches). Simon led me through a gap in the railings in the corner of Tunstall Park, where, as he put it, "the bars have been widened a bit." At the other end of the park, Dawne showed me a similar gap to reach the playground (otherwise inaccessible from the adjacent Greenway).

In places like Tunstall, where large-scale changes were being rapidly made to the landscape, children's pathway privileges were becoming precariously balanced. Carole told me about the "special way we used to go to Westport Lake, to play on the beach." Then she added, "they've built a factory in the way and you can't get through anymore. We went on a wild goose chase last time and found it was blocked." A similar blockage occurred in Bedwell that expressed an unfortunate lack of planning for children's access. Jenny told me she sometimes played in the "field" (park) behind her house, but the way through had been blocked by a high fence at the end of the pedestrian path running past her front gate. "Now I have to walk all the way round in the opposite direction [on the street] to get in," she said.

(Lower left) *Timothy's drawing of his favourite Mill Hill greenway.* (Below) *Heather squeezing under railings to get to the "blackberry place" beside the elevated Metropolitan Line in Notting Dale.*

Childhood's Domain/*The flowing terrain*

One of the clearest expressions of the benefits of continuity in the urban landscape was the way in which children used it as an outdoor gymnasium. As I walked along a Mill Hill street with Paul he continually went darting ahead, leapfrogging over concrete bollards, hopping between paving slabs, balancing along the curbside.

In each study area, certain kids seemed to dance through their surroundings on the look out for microfeatures with which to test their bodies. In Notting Dale, David provided the best sequence. Not only did he, like Paul, jump over gaps between things, go "tightrope walking" along the tops of walls, leapfrog objects on sight, but at one point he went "mountain climbing" up a roughly-built, nine-foot wall that had many serendipitously placed toe and handholds (see photo: p.31). It was as good as any simulated rock-climbing wall in a gymnasium.

David's mother told me her son was "accident prone," meaning that he was not well-coordinated. The reason seemed to be that he had a much more extended motoric relationship with his surroundings than most kids. David was an explorer. He took greater risks, more frequently; this, in turn, led to the increased likelihood of an accident. In fact, the accidents he reported had all occurred in non-routine situations in the course of new explorations and related skill acquisitions.

Mill Hill provided many fine examples of creative interaction with the landscape. Perhaps it was a function of the older, brick-built, small scale domestic architecture. Dawne and best friend Lisa balanced on walls, hopped over cracks between paving slabs, climbed walls and trees, slid down and twirled around railings, leapfrogged dustbins, jumped over streams, did handstands and somersaults on every available patch of grass, and shuffled through leaves. It was an almost continuous gymnastic performance, beautifully meshing the needs of their personalities with the opportunities in their surroundings.

On a small bridge across the Tunstall Greenway, Paul and his friend showed me how they could swing from the supporting rafters, climb up the outside of the bridge, hang on the railings, edge their way along the outside to the centre, and finally drop down to the path below. The bridge served as an effective piece of 'found' play equipment.

David demonstrating the gymnastic, 'motoric' landscape of a Notting Dale street.

Childhood's Domain/*The flowing terrain*

The motoric activities described above can equally well be accommodated by conventional playgrounds—supposing that they are located at regular intervals throughout every neighbourhood inhabited by children.But this was rarely the case. Even when provided, the limited choice of equipment on most designated playgrounds fell far short of satisfying appetites for bodily action. To compensate for this, many residential areas need more built-in play opportunities. Climbable trees are an obvious requirement. Tactile and acoustic dimensions should also be considered—as when children run sticks along railings. On one trip, Lawrence put his ear to a Notting Dale lamppost and said it was like "listening to a timebomb ticking" (the sound of the timing mechanism). The design possibilities are endless.

TOPOGRAPHY

Slopes, changes in level, flights of steps, hills and holes all provided differentiations that had highly expressive effects on children's behaviour. Small grassy slopes offered more opportunities still. Dawne and Lisa took me to what they called the "fields": several sloping lawns rising up around the cul-de-sac at the end of their Mill Hill street. They said they did "dances down the hills," which they demonstrated in a graceful sequence of flowing balletic movement.

Grassy slopes, depending on their size and steepness, stimulated a variety of behaviours. One of the Mill Hill housing estates, built on the side of a hill, was full of possibilities. Andrew, for instance, demonstrated "best man dead" on the grass bank above the pavement. "Someone chooses a weapon," he said, "such as a 'spear' or a 'gun,' and whoever gives the best performance of falling down dead is the next to choose." Andrew told me how an adjacent flight of steps featured as a place to "sit and talk with yer mates," and added that it was also a den in games of tick.

In more extensive landscapes, beyond immediate residential areas, topographic differentiations, and consequential actions, increased in size. Chris showed me some big, twelve-foot piles of clay in the abandoned Mill Hill Brickers (brickworks) where he said kids brought their "scrambler bikes" to ride. He pointed out the remains of an old conveyor belt sticking up in the air, which he said they sometimes climbed to use as a lookout.

Later, we visited an area known to many kids as the Bomb Holes. The 'holes' varied in size and had grassy sides and bottoms. The largest was about fifteen feet across and perhaps eight feet deep. Chris explained that most of them were caved-in mine shafts (subsidence), but that the biggest one was made by "an actual bomb during the war" (a myth). He said they played "jumping games and commandoes" there (remains of Guy Fawkes fireworks were much in evidence). They made camps sometimes by roofing the holes over. He took me to a "special one" that not many people knew about, he said, that had a willow tree growing out of the bottom. He showed

"We slide down the hills on old bits of cardboard."

me how he and his friends climbed down to a little hideaway under the tree, from which they could spy on people walking on the adjacent footpath.

I was also taken to the Bomb Holes by Paul and his friend who said they mostly played "war and hide-and-seek" there. Their favourite hole was a different one from Chris's. It had a line of three small excavations cut out of the side, which they called a "dinosaur print." The excavations were toe marks, Paul said.

HIDE-AND-SEEKNESS

When the degree of differentiation between physical elements reached a certain point it became possible for children to incorporate a repertoire of hide-and-seek games into the flow of their activity. Bedwell's shopping precinct provided a good example. The shops lined two sides of a spacious paved plaza. I was taken there by Brian and met a group of his friends. They said they played "fifty-fifty" around the shops and in between the cars and flower boxes, using the red letterbox as 'base.' The group gave a demonstration, using every differentiated element as a hiding place—the advertisement hoarding at the far end, the supports of the canopy in front of the shops, the planters, the letterbox and the shop buildings (by running around the back of them).

Hideaway games were supported in many ways at different sites. In Mill Hill, Jill said they used to have a camp in "some bushes up on the dump." She took me up the Greenway to an overgrown rubbish tip at a higher elevation ahead of us. She pointed to a group of hawthorn bushes on the side and told me it was where their camp used to be. "We found an old settee on the dump and used to sit up there and chat," she said, "but one day we saw some rats so we don't go anymore.... They were terrible, ugh," she said, grimacing.

In another part of Mill Hill, Tracy showed me the purest example of a naturally-occurring hideaway setting—again in hawthorn bushes. We were walking through the overgrown fields near her house when she pointed to a line of bushes at the top of a bank overlooking the field and said it was where they had their "club and ate picnics.... You've got a lovely view of the golf links from up there," she added. Hawthorns dotted the field. She called them "tree houses," and said they were used for meetings and as hiding places. The

Investigating a "dinosaur print" in the Bomb Holes, Mill Hill.

bushes were surrounded by long grass in such a way that a secluded hideout was formed at each base. Together, the bushes and long grass provided a kind of landscape syntax: a pattern of fixed features complex enough to generate a fluid yet predictable structure of behaviour; as if saying, "come play...here's how."

HARVESTING FOUND OBJECTS

Some terrains offered kids a rich source of play materials and 'found objects' that could be freely picked, plucked, gathered-up and collected for a variety of purposes. Remember Heather's posy in Notting Dale?

In Mill Hill, I walked along the Greenway with Paul and his friend and watched them pick and play with rhododendron buds, snowberries and large orange hips from ornamental roses. They squashed some of the hips to see what was inside and aimed them at the windows of adjacent houses. At one point they started pelting each other in a "rose-hip fight." On other occasions, children collected acorns, small cones from alder trees, seed heads from weeds and grasses and, of course, conkers—usually gathered by throwing sticks up at the tree. Since the fieldwork was conducted during the autumn, the collection of fruit, seeds and nuts occurred frequently. On several occasions, children mentioned "scrumping" in back gardens—a time-honoured childhood activity.

'Loose parts'[4] were the cause of these many fascinating incidents. In the middle of a trip on the Tunstall Greenway, a crowd of kids wandered by with a collection of old car seats balanced on their heads. They set them down on the Greenway bridge, sat and played on them, bouncing up and down and fooling around with great merriment. The purest example of a loose-part/fixed-feature combination took place in the Dip (the Bedwell 'green' described in Chapter 4). On the steepest slope, a deeply-eroded slide had been gouged out. And how did kids travel down it? On plastic milk crates which Philip said they "found" at certain stores in the vicinity.

Special interest was sometimes expressed in "collecting things" —more as a hobby than as a transient play activity. Paul and Simon in Mill Hill provided an outstanding example. They told me they "collected birds [made observations of birds] and rocks," and had "just started collecting toadstools.... One day we were walking along and

A crowd of kids wandered by with a collection of old car seats balanced on their heads...set them down on the Greenway bridge, and produced an instant pantomime...

we found this funny-looking toadstool, so now we collect them."
They also mentioned how they went to a pond near the Bomb Holes
"to catch butterflies, fishes, frogs and water rats."

'Found objects' were often recombined to make something else,
or were used in conjunction with other landscape features. Simon
told me how one day he had carved his name on a lawn in Tunstall
Park with a sharp stick. A subtle, low-key example was shown by
Dawne and Lisa (also in Tunstall Park). Their favourite thing was playing with leaves in Scotia Brook, "helping them along" with little
sticks. Their favourite place to do it was under a large weeping
willow tree. We stood for a while, fascinated by the bright yellow
crescent-moon leaves as they moved slowly on the mirrored black
water in its rock-sided channel.

Another Mill Hill example of interaction with water occurred at
a very different scale on a trip with Chris. We were looking down into a vast marlhole, perhaps a hundred feet deep. In the bottom was a
large pool of water. Chris explained how he and his friends "rolled
all kinds of stuff...car tires, old bike wheels and oil drums down into
the water...we love to watch them bounce off the cliff halfway down
and see how big a splash they make at the bottom," he said. (See Appendix D for a full list of "play objects" recorded during the study.)

A REMINDER

It was impressive to discover how expert some children had been at
finding access to diversity. However, we should bear in mind that
they were chosen as expert users of their surroundings. We must be
careful not to let their creative example obscure the problems that a
majority of children faced. Busy roads and parental anxiety kept
many children away from major neighbourhood resources like Mill
Hill's Tunstall Park and Holland Park in Notting Dale. Mill Hill kids
seemed better-off because their immediate residential environment
was so rich and accessible. Both Notting Dale and Bedwell were less
diverse. Notting Dale children were possibly compensated by the
cultural offerings of the metropolitan setting—though supporting
evidence was hard to come by. Bedwell children may have been
compensated by the added opportunities of the townwide pathway
network and lively town centre. But in fact neither facility seemed
well-used by the under-twelves. Meanwhile, Bedwell had none of

Notting Dale's social diversity or Mill Hill's physical diversity. Did some Bedwell children live in deprived circumstances: equal but different to some of the examples in Notting Dale? It is hard to tell. More study would be needed to answer this kind of question: to assess the negative effects of deprived environments, rather than gauge the positive effects of rich environments—as we are trying to do here.

4   *Habitats around the home*

This chapter investigates in detail home-related, habitual territories: the use of ancillary indoor/outdoor playspaces within the domestic domain (garages, sheds, gardens and yards) and the extension of play into contiguous public spaces (streets, alleyways, mews, 'fronts,' 'backs,' odds and ends of lawn, and other ad hoc left over spaces).

HOME AS HAVEN

What does home mean to a child? The question is worthy of a study in itself. The high rank given to homesites in the drawings indicated home to be the centre of family life and a child's ultimate haven of security and comfort (as we would expect). When children were asked where they went "to be alone," over fifty percent answered "my own room" (Table 5, Appendix C). Privacy is evidently a key function of the domestic indoors.

Nearly all play trips begin and end at home. However, as children grow older, their degree of attachment and dependence becomes more and more varied. Some children continue an indoor orientation because of physical circumstances or because of a natural inclination towards indoor hobbies and bookish study—or because of television. At the other extreme, other children are always off exploring outside, except when sitting at a school desk, eating obligatory meals, or sleeping in bed.[1]

Andrew and his sister chatting on the steps by their house—a Mill Hill niche wedged between the private indoors and the public domain beyond their homesite boundary.

Childhood's Domain/*Habitats around the home*

'Outdoor' children seemed to be either 'pulled' by the intrinsic qualities of the landscape, or 'pushed' by the lack of suitable space at home—where only small amounts of mess and noise were tolerated by parents and other household members. Social constraints at home were reflected in responses to the question: "Where do you go to meet other kids?" Not a single child mentioned his or her own home—although eleven percent of the replies mentioned "a friend's home." Over eighty percent of the replies referred to outdoor locations—implying that only the least disruptive activity occurred in cramped indoor quarters. This meant that ancillary spaces, immediately beyond the purview of tight domestic requirements, provided important transitional zones—wedged between the private domestic indoors and the public domain beyond the homesite boundary.

Zones of this kind varied greatly, both in physical characteristics and the extent to which they were controlled by parents. For children living in Notting Dale tower blocks, such opportunities were virtually nonexistent. Even Bedwell children were severely limited by tightly designed, cost-effective, functional architecture that left little surplus space for ancillary play. It was in Mill Hill that the advantages of more loosely assembled domestic architecture were clearly demonstrated.

SHEDS AND GARAGES

Several Mill Hill girls noted a garden shed or garage on their drawings. "I play quite often in the wooden shed behind my house," Carole told me, "especially when it rains. I play 'house' and 'cafés' with my sister...when we were younger we played 'princesses and queens.' Once, when my dad did the decorating, he put all the furniture out and we stayed all day and played on actual chairs...it was so much fun!"

Jill, who lived in a similar semidetached Mill Hill house, provided the most dramatic example of the value of domestic architecture. She and her best friend Lesley led me down some outdoor steps to a door below their garage. A small bell-shaped notice taped next to the door proclaimed "Hair Bear Mansion." They said the name came from a T.V. program. A length of string hung out of the keyhole with a bent piece of metal rod on the end. "It's Lesley's invention," Jill

Hair Bear Mansion. "You pull on the string and if there's no reply you can go in," Jill said.

said. "You pull on it, and if there's no reply you can go in." Lesley pulled, there was a clanking sound behind the door. She pushed it open and we went in. On the other end of the string was the "bell": an old halfgallon paint can. They said it used to be their rubbish bin but the rubbish kept falling out, so now they had a new rubbish bin: an old galvanized bucket.

In the centre of the room was a table made of a piece of plywood supported on two small trestles. Three or four wooden boxes were used as seats. Opposite the table, a window looked out onto the Greenway—perfect for seeing who was coming and going. They told me they made birthday cards for anyone with a birthday. "We had a birthday party in here last summer on the table *and* with a table cloth," Jill said proudly. Lesley showed me their "food cupboard": a cardboard box—the flaps, with knobs drawn on, were the doors.

Around me was the paraphernalia of a club. Rules were posted on the wall, with details of "competitions" to be held. One competition, they said, was for pieces of material to make costumes. The best piece of cloth would win a prize. Jill said she had written a "play about cavemen" that they were rehearsing. "We're making the costumes—but we haven't got too far yet." She opened a wooden box on the floor and showed me an old dress they had saved.

The girls explained that they were the leaders of the club. Four other girls belonged, plus two boys who were "not really in it, but helped." The club had been founded on August 29th, according to the records stuck on the wall. I was shown the "suggestions box"—an upside-down cardboard box with a slit cut in the top. They checked to make sure no new suggestions had appeared. The list of those made so far was posted on the wall.

The room was a terrific play base, located midway between the house proper and open land. I was struck by the creative social organization of the children. Many topics were embodied: law, economics, drama, art, language, graphic design, cooking, technological invention—in a child-managed community flourishing under the family garage. The two girls had appropriated part of the homesite architecture to create their own social world, with the understanding help and support of parents. Even though a few feet from the house, the psychic distance was sufficient for the children to develop their own world without feeling intimidated. Yet the homesite location meant that play material and recyclable objects were always close at hand. It was a place to play in inclement weather and it showed how an unambiguous line of domestic demarcation could be drawn between child and adult territories.

PLACES FOR PETS

A further advantage of the more open, less controlled, homesite environments of Mill Hill was an increased freedom to keep pets. There were many cats and dogs, of course, but also some less conventional animals. Jill had a fine collection of rabbits in neatly arranged hutches at the side of the house. Glenn kept pigeons. At the beginning of our trip, he took me round the back of his house to a little shed. "Watch out, here they come," he warned as he opened the door. A dozen birds erupted and flapped around us. It was a wonderful beginning to the field trip!

Nothing like this occurred in tidy Bedwell, or high density Notting Dale, where the possibilities for using the homesite as a workspace or resource base were much more limited. Caring for animals provides such an ideal opportunity for children to develop a sense of

"Watch out, here they come!" Glenn said. A dozen birds erupted and flapped around us.

Childhood's Domain/*Habitats around the home*

responsibility and accomplishment. More attention could be paid toward the accommodation of animal facilities, not only on home-sites but in schools, parks and playgrounds—especially in high density areas. Marvellous examples of 'urban farms' and animals on adventure playgrounds do exist, but many more are needed.

YARDS AND GARDENS

Parental control of immediate homesite architecture suggested the need to look at the play opportunities of yards and gardens. Carole said she had a Wendy house, a tent and a paddling pool in her back yard, that she used in the summer with her sister and one or two friends. Tracy used her back yard to "play with the cat, get a chair out...do thumbknit, play cards or dominos...do handstands against the wall—and," she added, "I read there a lot, too."

Examples of such intensive use were rare. More often than not, parents considered their back gardens to be part of their own domain, rather than something to be shared with children. In Notting Dale, Caroline told me how she wished she could grow things in the garden behind their terrace house. I asked if she could show me the spot, but the basement entrance was locked. "Me dad sometimes opens it up in the summer," she said. We went round to the mews and found another locked door in the back yard wall. Caroline said the landlord kept the key. We bunked up the wall, looked over and saw a small, bright green lawn, some planting beds and the remains of annual flowers. On a sunny summer day it must have been very pleasant. Caroline pointed to a young sycamore and said, "Me and my brother have a tree to play on ...we sometimes play Tarzan when we can get in the garden."

Occasionally, back yard space was given over fully to the needs of children. An example was "Stephen's garden," which Dawne took me to in Mill Hill. Behind the house the ground rose steeply and at the upper end of the slope a swing rope hung from a large tree. There was an old carpet under the swing that Dawne said had come from "a man down the street." At that moment Stephen and his friends appeared and we all had a go. The swing was located ideally, at the top of the hill, so that on every swing the ground fell away to boost the sense of height. A bare patch had been worn in the lawn and I noticed a Guy Fawkes bonfire almost ready for ignition. Either

Stephen's parents were extremely tolerant or they simply didn't care. Obviously this kind of activity had a severe impact on fragile garden vegetation so it was understandable that few examples of such boisterous back-garden play were recorded.

Front-garden play was even rarer. The few examples all occurred in Mill Hill. One was with Anne, whose parents did not allow her to stray beyond the length of pavement between the two corners of the street she lived on. So she played "house" in her front garden—a ten-foot square of weeds and patches of earth worn bare by use. She took me to the front garden of her friend, Sharon, a few doors away. In the centre was a small formal rockery supporting a variety of plants. In front were three rocky steps, where they usually sat, Ann said. They played a lot there—"mostly house." She wouldn't go into the garden, but agreed to sit on the front wall to let me take a photograph. At that moment Sharon's mother appeared. "What's all this about?" she asked. I briefly explained. "Wait, I must get my husband," she retorted (this is it, I thought, here's someone who thinks I really am a child-stealer). Sharon's father appeared and looked very suspicious, but thawed out after I re-explained and we parted amicably.

The encounter left me with a sense of the extreme domination that parents can sometimes exert over their children's territory. Sharon herself was one of the few subjects who had refused to come on a trip with me. Her parents needed to keep the front garden neat and tidy in order to communicate respectability to the outside world—an especially difficult task for those who do not like gardening yet feel they have to keep up appearances. Above all, they do not want children messing-up the place.

In point of fact, interest in gardening was seldom encountered among Mill Hill parents. No wonder, the municipal corporation controlled most of the property. Neat and tidy paved areas and closely-mown lawns were standard—with the odd rose bush or piece of goldenrod snuck in by residents. Such spaces offered little intrinsic attraction to children.

The contrasting effect of *unmown* grass was demonstrated very clearly when I was out with Glenn and his friend on the next street over from Anne and Sharon. We crossed to an overgrown front yard which Glenn had shown on his drawing. By the way they approached it and gently parted the strands of tall grass, it was obvious that they knew the place well and that it had a substantial meaning to them. "There isn't much here anymore," Glenn said, dismayed, "but in the summer we found all kinds of things: ladybirds, caterpillars, grasshoppers and beetles." The boys seemed fascinated by the small-scale wildlife. The beauty of the example was that it was available right on their street, rather than in a less accessible, 'rough ground' location.

It is surely time to promote the spread of more wildness in residential areas, as a step towards establishing a more substantial appreciation of the natural world in our cities. But how is this to be achieved in high density housing estates? Children living in lower-density, semidetached, two-story housing in Mill Hill, had many natural resources close at hand. The Bedwell landscape offered some of the same opportunities; although, as discussed in Chapter 9, it could have been managed to better advantage.

In Notting Dale, high density development and tight control of land uses meant that much less space was left for children's play. Ironically, under these conditions of scarcity, the space around buildings seemed protected from human use even more rigidly by the housing authority. Lesley lived in a publicly owned and rehabilitated Notting Dale Georgian terrace, where the former back gardens had been thrown together to make an open lawn. A mound had been formed in the middle which Lesley had shown on her drawing as a favourite place to sit and play with her dolls. Her mother told me it was actually against the rules to play there. She took no notice though, because she thought it was ridiculous to prevent children from using the spot. Lesley took me downstairs to show me how she had to climb over a fence of spiked iron railings to get to the hill—a hazardous undertaking to say the least. Although the hill was nothing more than a mundane patch of elevated lawn, it was the saving grace of Lesley's immediate outdoors. There was literally nowhere else she could go.

It occurred to me that the housing authority, all the way down the line, from elected officials to gardeners, considered themselves both the legal and social 'owners' of residential open spaces under their command. In this sense, landscaping was used solely as a visual commodity by the authority to give a good appearance to housing sites. Tenants had no voice in considering its social function. Lesley's mother told me how difficult it was for children because of the traffic. Even though they lived on a quiet side street, "there's too many

"In summer we find all kinds of things," Glenn said, "ladybirds, caterpillars, grasshoppers, beetles..."

cars for safety," she said. Lesley's need to travel to other play areas could have been considerably reduced by developing the space immediately around her home more appropriately.

'BACKS,' MEWS AND ALLEYS

The terms "fronts" and "backs" are part of the spatial language of every Victorian industrial town with traditional back-to-back housing. I learned much about the opportunities for play in these ubiquitous and culturally significant homesite extensions. In Mill Hill, 'back' referred to almost any shared space behind and beyond the homesite boundary, including even quite large 'fields.' But from the children's point of view, the 'back' alleyways were the greatest boon. They provided traffic-protected play spaces that could accommodate a large variety of traditional games and informal play. And they were still thick on the ground in areas of Mill Hill, where urban redevelopment had not yet swept them away.

Tracy lived in a terrace of five houses with a cul-de-sac 'backs' about thirty yards long and some ten feet wide. The rear walls of the back yards defined one side of the space and the flank wall of the terrace on the next street defined the other. The owners of the end house had made their back yard into a parking space, so there was a single car that occasionally drove through, but it did not seem to inhibit activity.

Tracy wanted her next door best friend to come along on the trip, too, but the family was out for the day. She said they mostly played in the "backs" during the winter—it certainly offered protection from the wind. At the far end she led me to her "favourite spot." It was a ledge formed by a short, low, retaining wall with fireweed sprouting behind. Tracy said she and her friend liked "to sit and talk there...for ages at a time." In front of the ledge was a pair of parallel walls about four-and-a-half feet high and four feet apart. They played a "little game" on them. "It's not much really," she said, and showed me how to slide off the top of one wall, flip round and jump up on the other wall—over and over again. She showed me another game on the I-beam holding up the roof of the neighbour's parking space. She swung back and forth, holding on with her finger tips. Noticing a pile of leaves that had drifted into the corners, from the sycamore trees in the adjacent street, she described the "leaf fights" they had had that autumn.

Tracy provided details of many traditional games played in the 'backs.' First, there were *chasing* games, such as "tick" and "chase" —where the step at the entrance to each back yard was used as a "den," "base," or "docker."[2] In "two-in-a-docker" two people at a time could seek refuge.

Second, there were *gymnastic* games, which included "handstands" and "crabs," both played against the flank wall. Putting her hands on the ground, Tracy demonstrated "crab climbs" by 'climbing' up the wall with her feet behind her, until standing vertically on her hands. She then flipped over, finishing with her stomach facing upwards, head hanging back near the ground, knees and elbows bent crablike. Keeping the same position, she did "walking crabs" on the smooth pavement, walking on all fours, upside-down.[3]

Third, there were *ball* games. These, according to Tracy, included "netball practice...you start with ten points and move along the wall, bouncing the ball as you go...and everytime you miss, you lose a point." There were chanting ball games like "cow-go-over-the-

Tracy demonstrates "crab climbs" in the 'backs' behind her house.

Childhood's Domain/*Habitats around the home*

moon," which was played in pairs, with each person in turn bouncing the ball against the wall and the other person jumping over it on the rebound, while singing "cow—." "Matthew, Mark, Luke and John" was similar, she said, but you had to catch the ball instead of jumping over it. "A-hunting-we-will-go/ catch-a-little-fox-and-put-him-in-a-box" was similar again—but was played by a group of kids rather than a pair.[4]

'Mews' were the London equivalent of Tunstall's 'backs' and likewise offered a refuge from dense traffic conditions. Caroline led me from the busy street where she lived, through an archway in the housing terrace and into narrow, L-shaped, Elgin Mews. On one side was the rear garden wall of her terrace; on the other, a terrace of recently-built housing for the elderly. The first thing she did was play "helicopters" with some seed pods that had fallen from a large maple tree.

The mews felt immediately protective and warm, compared to the busy, windy street we had just come from. The late afternoon sun was shafting down on the stub of the cul-de-sac, where Caroline demonstrated a balancing game on the granite sets. She and her friends often came there to play "rounders," "little racing games" and "tag," she said, and sometimes they sat on the edge of the pavement and played with their dolls. "We dress 'em up and play hospitals and nursing." The street was nice and peaceful for the old folks too, she added, and gave no hint of conflict stemming from their play.

Those Notting Dale children who lived in older terrace buildings, faced highly restricted 'front' situations of narrow pavements and dense traffic. At first glance, the situation looked better in the older lowrise public housing areas where on-site traffic was restricted and open space was provided around the buildings. But in most cases, the hard-surface areas were used for car parking and the manicured, fenced-in lawns had "keep off the grass" signs. Any child playing on lawn or parking area was subject to uncomfortable surveillance by adult tenants passing by or looking out from their windows.

OLD TOWN 'FRONTS'

Traditionally, Mill Hill 'fronts' had provided domestic thresholds right on the pavement, in lines of daily-scrubbed steps. In later housing, garden or yard space appeared between house and street. As far as I could determine, these later spaces were not included in the definition of "front"—which was strictly public, and referred to all space immediately beyond the private domain of the homesite.

The most common 'fronts' in Mill Hill were the small pieces of 'space-left-over-after-planning' so beloved by site planners, to be found in nearly every kind of residential layout. Children called them "lawns," "the grass," "the grass out front," and "the slopes."

Dawne and Lisa showed me a classic example. It included a small triangular patch of grass on the corner of the street, beyond Dawne's front gate. She said it was their favourite place close to home. They played "gymnast" there (and in every other grassy area they could find), doing handstands, cartwheels, front flips and back flips (they originally learned them in school). Hide-and-seek was played using parked cars, front gardens, entryways and flights of steps as hiding places. They said it was especially good at dusk, "when you can't see too well." One of their games provided a particularly good example of play adapted to 'front' elements. It entailed balancing on the narrow edge of a street sign fixed to two posts about two-and-a-half feet above the grass. The idea was to see who could balance the longest. Lisa said she held the record with "140 seconds" (slow counts). Dawne was "up to 135."

Ball play was one of the most frequent 'front' activities observed in all study areas. Andrew was an expert on the subject in the context of Mill Hill corporation housing. He had a "best football place" where he and his friends played. It was a small patch of lawn, not more than twenty-by-thirty feet, facing the corner of the street and flanked by two residential buildings. Even though the space was so small and on a slope, it was heavily used—as indicated by patches of worn grass at each end. Half-a-dozen boys were there, playing football. At one end, a tree, plus a brick on the ground, marked the goal; at the other end, a section of hedge.

Informal ball play is commonplace in housing estates across the country. Even though properly laid out football pitches may be located nearby, short-term kickabouts always seem to occur on the street or in 'front' areas. One clear reason is the time constraint on much of children's play. Between the end of school and suppertime there is simply not enough time to get a proper game organised; whereas, an ad hoc "pick-up" with whoever is around, in whatever space is immediately available, is perfectly feasible.

Even when these time-and-space constraints were absent, many children still preferred to play informal ball games in the more varied

Lisa said the idea was to see who could balance the longest on the street sign. "I hold the record," she added.

spaces available close to home. In such spaces, the ball was used as a loose play-object in conjunction with the fixed features of the surroundings. The prevalence of this type of ball play needs to be better appreciated. Part of its popularity is clearly explained because it is so well adapted to small groups and individual children playing alone. Andrew demonstrated "wally," which consisted of kicking a football back and forth against the retaining wall beside the pavement in front of his home.[5] Opposite the wall, the street trees provided a parallel boundary line. If the ball went over it, the player was "out."

This kind of example shows how difficult it is to be categorical and prescriptive about children's play. It's form and function co-evolve within such very broad, malleable limits. 'Fronts' and 'backs' provided special play opportunities because they were so adaptable and were located close to home. In some cases their potential could have been considerably enhanced by redesign and appropiate management. A few streets away from Andrew's house was an enormous three-acre (1.2 ha) circular lawn-cum-roundabout. Essentially, it was a big 'front' surrounded by houses—a bold geometric feature which gave a strong sense of identity to the immediate area. Kevin said they had bike races round it and played rugby and football on the grass. It was a huge hunk of space, over 400 feet (122 metres) in diameter and large enough to have been planted with a broad band of "hedges and bushes," as Kevin himself suggested, "so we can play hide-and-seek and mess around."

NEW TOWN 'FRONTS'

Bedwell was replete with 'front' spaces. They were the result of the pedestrian-oriented site planning, which excluded all but the most local traffic from residential streets. At every turn there were areas of paving, patches of lawn and modest scatterings of trees and shrubs. Recorded uses of these spaces ranged from incidental activities to substantial standing patterns of behaviour. Amanda took me to a small grassy patch beside her house. It was where they played "rounders," she said, "when the park [one of the 'greens' discussed in the next chapter] is taken over by the boys for football."

Jane introduced me to a rich example resulting from Bedwell's traffic-segregated design: a broad pavement she called the " turning," that ran parallel to her terrace as far as the nearby parking area. She and her friends played "up and down the turning" when they could "only go out for a little while." Their games included "skipping," "hopscotch," "roller-skating," "naughts-and-crosses," "mothers and fathers," "scary house," "two-balls," "catch" and "chalking," she said. "We play there all year round and in the summer we bring out games like bingo."

Brian lived at the end of another Bedwell cul-de-sac. His house faced on to a broad cycle-and-pedestrian path (linked to the citywide system). "In the autumn," he said, "we pile up leaves and jump onto them. We had a pile once that must have been a metre high." In the summer they played cricket on the nearby square of grass, and some-times played football on the patch of concrete in the centre of the walkway. "But people tell us off...and two of the trees are in the wrong place and mess up the game. The other two are good for goalposts, but the others just get in the way." There was a larger patch of grass further down the path and I asked Brian if they ever played there. "The trees are even worse," he said, "they're all in the wrong place." I saw he was right. The trees were scattered at random (for aesthetic effect?), whereas they could have been positioned

Jane's favourite place was the "turning"—a traffic-segregated residential pathway in Bedwell.

Jane's drawing shows the "turning" in detail, including paving joints and 'play marks.' To the right of the pavement is Jane's terrace with her own house indicated; to the left are the back gardens of the opposite terrace, visible from Jane's bedroom window.

people climb over the fence to go to the shops

pond

grass

muddy patch

all mud with patches of grass in other people's garden

little flowers

garden

mud everywhere

steps

my house

bushes

my window

wall

mud

pavement

garden

grass

porch holes

garden

mud

more deliberately around the periphery to create a more usable area. If this had been done, then very likely Brian and his friends would have played football there—without causing so many complaints from the neighbours, as the space was farther away from the houses. Was it possible that the trees had been planted to deliberately inhibit ball games, so that the grass would not be spoiled or residents annoyed? Had the designers assumed that children would take their games to the larger, 'official' play spaces a few minutes walk away? Although close by, they were beyond the habitual range of most children. Brian's ball play took place in the only spaces immediately available: the cycle/pedestrian path between the rows of houses and the nearby garage court.

The variety of Bedwell house groupings, crescents and 'fronts' was impressive. Raymond's house faced directly onto a bulbous cul-de-sac: a road that looped around a pear-shaped 'island' planted with grass, shrubs and trees. Raymond called it "a kind of little park." They had "bike races" round it, played hide-and-seek among the bushes and "we just run around it," he said. "Some people climb the trees," but the younger ones can't get up without help, because the branches are too high to get a 'start.' "

This kind of remark about the trees was made by several children. Most of the Bedwell trees (the majority were sycamore) seemed deliberately pruned to inhibit climbing. It was especially obvious in places where nobody needed to walk under them; yet the lower limbs were still pruned off, regardless. The best climbing tree I came across in Bedwell was an old hawthorn, which (applause for the planners) had been retained from a former farm hedgerow opposite Mandy's house. She said it was her favourite place on the street. In less than a minute she climbed up the gently sloping, twisting, trunk and sat on her "lookout branch."

Philip lived in a squared-off crescent of houses that faced one of the larger 'front' areas in Bedwell. He called it the "green," even though it was not much more than a quarter of an acre (Figure 19). It was situated beyond the cul-de-sac turning-circle serving the houses. A footpath ran around three sides, between the green and the front gardens of the houses. Philip, like Raymond, said they used the footpath for bike races. The likelihood of conflict with pedestrians seemed high, although it was never mentioned by Philip or his parents. He said they played football on the grass. They used a lamppost and a tree as goalposts at one end, and put their jackets on the ground at the other. They played hide-and-seek by using the front garden

19 *Philip's close-to-home territory and rendering of two of his favourite places: the (habitual) 'front' of shared lawn for the crescent of houses where he lived and the (frequented) "Dip," a little way down the street.*

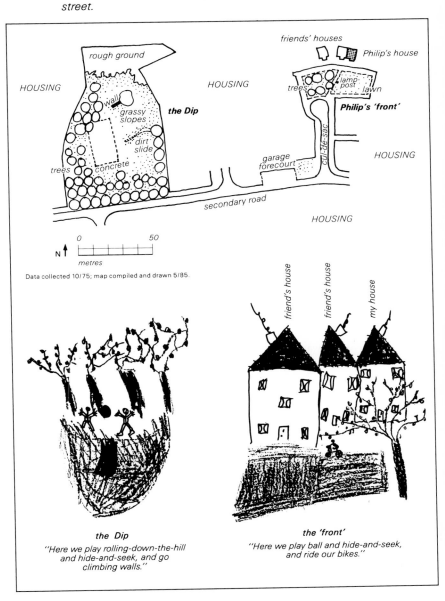

rough ground

HOUSING

HOUSING

friends' houses

Philip's house

trees

lamp post

lawn

wall

grassy slopes

the Dip

Philip's 'front'

dirt slide

trees

concrete

cul-de-sac

garage forecourt

HOUSING

secondary road

HOUSING

0   50

N

metres

Data collected 10/75; map compiled and drawn 5/85.

friend's house

friend's house

my house

the Dip
"Here we play rolling-down-the-hill and hide-and-seek, and go climbing walls."

the 'front'
"Here we play ball and hide-and-seek, and ride our bikes."

hedges (clipped hawthorn), trees and parked cars to hide behind. The lamppost was "base." At this time of year (autumn) he said they liked to sit on the grass or pavement and play with their Dinky Toys. On summer nights some of his friends played "knock down ginger" (ringing people's door bells and running away). "I don't," he added hastily, but in the same breath mentioned playing "dare devils at night. Once we put grass under someone's windshield wipers. We give each other 'dares' like that."[6]

It is plainly unrealistic to think of 'designing out' everyday 'front' activities. Traditional games and ball play can be adapted to almost any set of physical circumstances—hence their cultural survival. Because of their generous size, many Bedwell 'fronts' worked well. They were well-protected from traffic. If they had been designed with more understanding of children's needs, they might have served even better—with less aggravation for some of the neighbours.

CAR SPACES

Some of the most accessible 'front' and 'back' spaces were provided for cars.[7] Many garages in Mill Hill had been built in clusters, on pieces of land left over after the houses were built. In the previous chapter (Figure 17), we were introduced to Carole's habitual territory, including two rows of concrete garages behind her house and the gap between them, about fifteen inches wide, where she liked to play hide-and-seek. She liked to play football around the garages, too.

Bedwell had more orderly garage clusters called "courts"—also a favourite setting for ball games. Brian showed me one a few yards from his house. The garages were back from the street, facing an asphalt area enclosed on two sides by a low brick wall. A group of five-to-eight-year-olds was playing football. One of them showed me the dents in the garage doors caused by fast-moving balls. Brian said the court was the best place to go after school, because it was so near. He said they could also go to the school grounds, but you had to cross a busy road to get there, and they were dangerous because people used them for "golf practice."

Raymond took me to a line of Bedwell garages where he liked to play "chase" and "fighting" with his friends, up on the roofs. He climbed up to show me how easy it was to hide there. "But there's an old lady who always clears us off," he said.

A Bedwell garage "court" — favourite setting for ball games.

Raymond climbing on the garage roofs where he liked to play "chase" and "fighting."

Childhood's Domain/*Habitats around the home*

On both sides of the Atlantic, a number of studies indicate the need to recognise streets as *de facto* playgrounds. It is a centuries-old phenomenon. In a study of Oldham, for instance, fifty-four percent of the children were found playing in the street and on pavements, compared with only three percent in designated playgrounds.[8] Such research results call to question indiscriminate policy objectives like "keep the kids off the streets," which fail to recognize the great variety of playable neighbourhood street spaces. Many streets can provide excellent play opportunities—depending on traffic density, accessibility and physical characteristics. In this regard, the reader is referred to Charles Zerner's marvellous study of children's play in the deadend streets and alleyways of San Francisco.[9] I found, as he did, that cul-de-sacs offered the greatest number of play opportunities, because of the low numbers of slow-moving vehicles. The richest example was recorded in Mill Hill with Carole. She had made such a detailed drawing of the different elements and activities of the cul-de-sac in front of her house that my appetite was whetted. The street itself looked very ordinary, lined with anonymous rows of 1940s semis and small front gardens.

She wanted a "best friend" to come along, so that they could "really play." But one friend was at the hairdresser's and the other had too much homework. So Carole's younger sister acted as a surrogate—which worked fine. They showed me the lamppost that Carole had indicated in her drawing, where they played "shadow tick" in the evenings (using its shadow as "base"). They pointed to the spot behind where a van was usually parked, where they hid in games of hide-and-seek (clearly detailed on Carole's drawing).

We walked to the small turning-circle at the end of the street, where they played ball games. They demonstrated one in which the object was to throw a tennis ball over the telephone wires suspended across the street. Carole said they sometimes tried to do the same thing by bouncing "power balls." The end of the cul-de-sac was particularly good for roller-skating, they said, because it was "extra smooth." The whole street was good for riding bikes because there were "not too many cars."

Five or six kids regularly played in the street, "including my best friends," Carole said. Their games included, "shadow tick," "ball tag," "skipping," and "queenie-eye-o-coco"[10] (a guessing game played along the edge of the curb). They played "sly fox," (the most common of quiet street games recorded by the Opies, known around the

Carole's finely detailed drawing, explaining how she and her friends used the street as a playground.

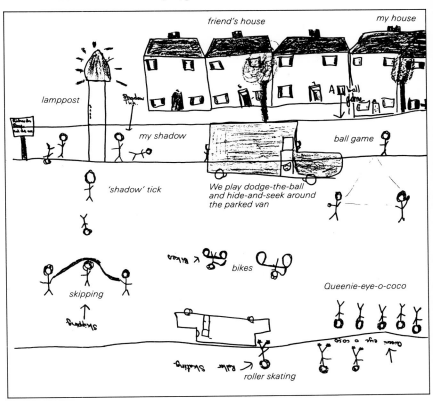

friend's house

my house

lamppost

my shadow

ball game

'shadow' tick

We play dodge-the-ball and hide-and-seek around the parked van

bikes

Queenie-eye-o-coco

skipping

roller skating

country by more than thirty names like "peep behind the curtain," "L-o-n-d-o-n," "White Horse" and "policeman"). And there was "pop stars" (a variation on 'film stars,' which the Opies view as the most popular guessing game in Britain). The way Carole described it: "Someone calls the initial of a pop group. When you've got it, you run to the person who calls out, and the first one there with the right answer is the winner." Other favourites included "stuck-in-the-mud," "chase the bobby" (a variation of "stuck—"), "off-ground tick" and "ball tick."[11] They also played "knock down sticks," a ball game called "polio," and "sometimes we play cops and robbers with the boys," Carole said. "Sometimes we make up our own games, but we always end up arguing about the rules," she commented ruefully.

When traffic density was high, the opportunities of the street depended more on the characteristics of the streetside architecture, than on the carriageway itself. In Notting Dale, Caroline provided a good demonstration of play opportunities in the transition zone between the private space of streetside buildings and the public space of street pavement itself. Her play was limited—by both parents and traffic—to the pavement immediately around her flat (on the first floor of a Georgian terrace). She and her friends had no choice but to fully explore the street's potentials.

We went on a street tour, which Caroline described as "up and down the street, around the corners and everything." She showed me games that she and her friends had invented and adapted to the physical circumstances of the street. We stopped at the entrance to a recently completed underground carpark. Caroline got up on the curved retaining wall and edged her way along, holding onto some metal railings. The garage driveway dropped away below her. When she was standing about five feet above it, she stopped and retraced her steps until she felt comfortable enough to jump. She played around there a lot with her friends, she said, as she sat and played on the small patch of grass on the other side of the driveway.

Up the street a few yards, was another building entrance. It was a tight little space in front of the doors of a nursery school and caretaker's house. A concrete staircase came down into the centre of the space from the upper part of the building. "We play chase, 'had,' and everything here," Caroline said, "and run round-and-round the staircase." She showed me how to swing on the jutting handrail.

Streetside architecture provided serendipitous nooks and perches where children could sit and talk and watch the world go by. Sometimes a game was incorporated. In Mill Hill, Tracy pointed to a low brick wall around the front yard of the hairdresser's, on the corner of the street opposite her house. "I sit there to talk with my friend or we play 'colour car,' she said. "You pick a car colour and the first one to count the number of cars you've decided—with the same colour—is the winner."[12] In another example, also in Mill Hill, two kids had set themselves up with 'guys,' at the entrance to the Tunstall Greenway, to collect firework money. All four of them—the kids and their 'guys'—were perched on the bench beside the pavement, strategically positioned to intercept passersby!

Greater physical depth and complexity of streetside zones stimulated correspondingly richer activities. Paul took me to the local pub "just around the corner" from his house in Mill Hill and showed me a "special hiding place," behind an adjacent fence, that featured in hide-and-chase games. He and his friends used the cars parked beside the pub to hide behind and during "off hours" used the carpark to play football "when there isn't many cars around," Paul said. Farther down the street, he showed me the parking area outside a supermarket where they played football and rode on the shopping trollies.

The most unusual streetside situation was surely Raymond's "danger place," in Bedwell. It was an electricity substation, in reality, enclosed by a seven-and-a-half-foot brick wall. The transformer and switchbox were plainly visible through a narrow barred gate on one side. Raymond showed me how the local kids climbed over the wall by using the remains of an adjacent shrub as a "step." The shrub had been almost totally worn away—giving an idea of how popular the place was. Raymond liked to "get down inside to hear the noise the transformer makes."

5   *Parks and playgrounds*

Playgrounds and parks both appeared high on the list of elements indicated in children's drawings. In the interviews, parks were mentioned most frequently as both places to meet other children and as places to go to be alone (after the children's own rooms). Parks were not only most frequently mentioned as the "farthest place visited," they were the places most frequently prohibited by parents (Table 8, Appendix C). These findings indicate parks and playgrounds to be, or to have the potential for becoming, two of the most strategic outdoor resources available to young people.

I say "potential," because the issue is many sided. There have been polemics written against playgrounds in principle;[1] a number of behaviour-mapping studies have indicated extremely low levels of use;[2] other studies have shown moderate to high levels of use;[3] yet others, as reported here, indicate that regardless of levels of actual use, playgrounds can carry substantial social value to children.

Within this confusing picture, two facts are unassailable. First, there are many city-bound children who *have* to use playgounds, because they have nowhere else to go. Second, public authorities seem determined to continue to build "playgrounds" (actually *play equipment* most of the time), in the name of play provision. On both these counts, the issue of *quality* is paramount, not simply the

An impromptu stage: Dawne and Lisa playing "statues" on the bird table in the Tunstall Park rose garden.

"amount" of provision. What are some of the distinguishing marks of *quality* in playground and park provision?

PLAYGROUNDS IN PARKS

The locational relationship between playgrounds and parks was a clearly identified qualitative factor. Playgrounds (the second most frequent element in children's drawings) were very often shown located within parks (the third most frequent element). In the interviews, parks, rather than playgrounds, were mentioned as the favourite place to go after school. The field trips did much to reinforce the notion that playgrounds were more effectively used when located in or next to a park.

Adults often think of parks as green havens of adult leisure, as places to "get away from it all." Playgrounds, on the other hand, are thought of as places where the kids ought to be—off the streets and out of adults' way. Adult images of playgrounds are often limited to steel-pipe stereotypes or contemporary-looking structures of wood or sculptured concrete. Some experts say that playgrounds are irrelevant to children's "real" needs.

From the perspective of children's actual behaviour, these points of view seem limited. The playgrounds and play equipment identified by children in *Childhood's Domain* were important to them and were well used, especially in park settings. Equally, there were other playgrounds and play equipment areas that were hardly used at all. The point is to recognize the validity of children's own judgements as users of environments especially provided for them, rather than condemning every playground out of hand. One reason why playgrounds are valued by young people is because they provide clearly identifiable pieces of local turf where they can hang out and meet each other. Dawne and Lisa told me that they really liked the Tunstall Park playground when it rained. "We sit in the shelter and talk with each other when no one else is around."

The most popular equipment areas were not found in segregated locations, separate from the park landscape. Children themselves tended not to use the term "playground," but referred to the individual pieces of apparatus that most interested them. In Notting Dale's St. Mark's Park, Heather took me to a large area of asphalt with pieces of standard equipment disbursed across it. The centre of interest was what she called the "big slide" (it must have been fully

Jenny's drawing expresses the prominence of the Fairlands Park playground (centre of the picture), together with the park's additional resources: "lake," "waterfall," paddling (she calls them "swimming") "pools," "horse track" (note her desire for a horse) and "woods" — they feature in Chapter 7.

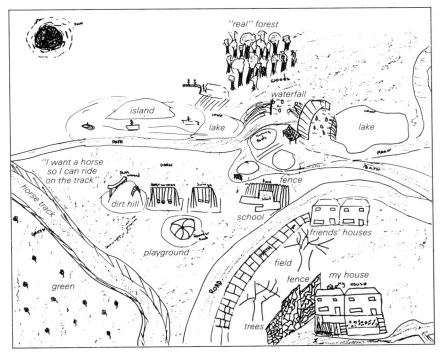

twelve feet high). "I also like the 'spider,' the 'rocket ship,' the swings and sand pit—"we make little villages there," Heather said, "in the sand that looks like brown sugar."

Interview responses indicated that play equipment provided an important social stimulus, regardless of its style of appearance. The play area in Bedwell's Fairlands Park, for instance, was mentioned several times in drawings and interviews. With Raymond I visited what he called the "big dirt hill with a long slide, where we play games an' that" and the nearby "boat": an edifice of concrete and steel pipe railings in the rough form of a boat, surrounded by three paddling pools of different sizes and depths. "Me and my friends sometimes meet and play around here after school," he said.

Raymond's "big dirt hill with a long slide" in Fairlands Park playground. He, too, shows the paddling pools.

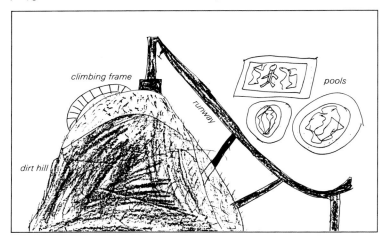

The popularity of Notting Dale's Avondale Park had much to do with its extensive range of traditional play equipment. Lesley said she went nearly every day after school, usually with a friend, or she met a friend there. "Our favourite things are the 'rainbow,' 'witches' hat,' gymnast bars, merry-go-round and swings," she said. David, who lived close to the park said it was his favourite place to meet, too, to play on the 'witches' hat' and the 'jerker.' Several of these heavy swinglike items looked potentially dangerous and have in fact been criticised by consumer groups because of their poor safety record. What made them attractive was the combination of high sensory stimulation and the cooperative social interaction required to make them work. David was enthusiastic about the traditional swings, too, and gave an expert demonstration of "parachuting" (bailing out while riding high) to prove his point.[4]

Children in all three study areas referred to swings as their favourite meeting place. It is tempting to suggest mandatory installation, in sheltered locations, at strategic meeting places in every neighbourhood—in lieu of fully-equipped playgrounds. Swings have been shown to top the bill in several research studies, as the most popular piece of play equipment—whether the traditional type or the wilder, adventure playground Tarzan type. Fine examples of the latter were

Dawn's drawing illustrates the significance of the swings located in an interior Bedwell 'green,' a short walk from her home.

path

bush

grass

seesaw

swings

to be found in the Holland Park Venture (a playpark with some adventure playground characteristics) and the two adventure playgrounds visited in Stevenage. Each Tarzan swing was made out of a length of rope with an old tyre on the end. They were the primary attraction, according to some children. Not only were the Tarzan swings an exciting sensory experience, they also stimulated cooperation. One at a time, kids had to haul the rope up to the jumping-off place, to enable other kids to leap on in succession.

Through observation and conversation it became clear that a brightly painted collection of play equipment often provided the initial pretext for a park visit. It served as a rendezvous and punctuation point for peer interaction, allowing time for friends to gather (after school for instance) and make plans about what to do. The games and joking behaviour stimulated by play equipment sometimes went spinning off into further play sequences extending deeper into the park or neighbourhood territory.

It is unrealistic to imagine that segregated play equipment always works well. The official play areas on the Edward Woods Estate consisted of a few pieces of equipment stuck in the middle of windswept lawns. As a result, kids extended their territory to Avondale and other more inviting local parks as soon as their parents would allow them.

My conclusion is that the location and character of the landscape surrounding each playground or equipment area is just as important as the design of the apparatus itself. The provision of many options for repeatable patterns of behaviour stimulates the interplay between familiarity and creativity. From the children's point of view, the location of playgrounds in parks provides the best of all possible worlds, with the playground functioning as a significant place within a more broadly diversified playscape. Access to diversity is what children really care about, rather than sophisticated play apparatus.

PARKS AS PLAYGROUNDS

The Mill Hill field trips took me to two of Stoke-on-Trent's magnificent Victorian parks, in Tunstall and Burslem (another of the six Pottery Towns). It was from these experiences that many insights emerged concerning the play opportunities of urban parks. Both parks were carefully contrived landscapes of natural forms—concentrated and juxtaposed to heighten sensory experience. Their level of diversity was far above that of the parks in Notting Dale and Bedwell. Their aesthetic appeal was greatly enhanced by the judicious intermingling of elegantly designed artifacts: bandstands, paddling pools, drinking fountains, ornamental features, bridges, retaining walls, toilets and storage facilities. In Burslem Park, Tracy took me to a steep rockery with a little cascade running down it.

"I like to climb around there," she said.

"Why?" I asked.

"I like the way it's 'put'...it just looks nice," she replied.

Trips to Tunstall Park demonstrated how a richly-endowed parkscape can enormously extend and diversify children's behaviour—and by implication, the degree to which behaviour can be limited by bland, monocultural open space. Exploring Tunstall Park with some of its articulate young users convinced me of the value of the arcadian tradition of English park design: the deliberate juxtaposition of natural and cultural forms, the careful taming and shaping of nature to make it a more intimate part of human experience. With

Andrew's drawing of Tunstall Park illustrates his favourite spots: the "Castle," paddling pool, football grounds (where he went to **watch** other children playing, rather than to play himself), the lakes (the smaller one was where he liked to fish) and the "woods"—the rhododendrons with tunnels and "camps and hideouts all the way to the swings" (in the playground at the far end).

diversity as a central theme, the art of park design can be measured by how well such intermingling of forms are handled—in both space and time.

Tunstall Park was a paragon of design in this sense. It provided many lessons showing how an urban park can satisfy the needs of young people and adult users alike. An amazing variety of structures and built forms were interwoven. On a trip with Dawne and Lisa, I was taken to a circular ornamental pool. Dawne said it was "the best place for dragonflies and goldfish, but they're too fast to catch." Next, we arrived at a monument known as the Castle. It seemed to serve no purpose except as an architectural folly. Massive stone retaining walls, topped with heavy balustrades, jutted from the steep grassy slope. We climbed up the slope to where the Castle floor was level with the ground and walked around the balustrade. The girls said they played hide-and-seek there and watched the birds in the

Dawne and Lisa playing at the ornamental pool in Tunstall Park—
"the best place for dragonflies and goldfish," they said.

tree tops alongside. As we were leaving, they had a leaf fight and rolled down the grassy bank overlooking the tennis courts. We arrived at
the rose garden. "It's one of our favourite places," Lisa said. They
climbed up on an old moss-covered stone bird table and tried out
different poses, pretending to be "statues." Tunstall Park had a surfeit
of these 'folly' elements—impromptu stages for spontaneous
theatre—that stimulated equally frivolous behaviour on the part of
the users. Architecturally, they provided a system of landmarks in
contrast to the dominant masses of amorphous vegetation.

On another trip, Simon also took me to the Castle. It had featured prominently in his drawing. He showed me how he and his
friends could climb up the outside at two spots where the buttresses
protruded. We went to the asphalted top surface surrounded by the
balustraded wall. "We can do most things here, like playing war,
chase, and hide-and-seek," he said. Pointing to the flagpole, he remembered that "once, on the Queen's birthday, the ropes were left
hanging off the flagpole and we played Tarzan." He also mentioned
playing on the grass around the Castle "doing somersaults, rolls and
springs."

Simon's drawing of the "Castle" in Tunstall Park, where "we can do most things...like playing war, chase, and hide-and-seek."

We went to the Clock Tower: a solid stone monument, with a door in one side, standing in a little asphalted area on top of a rocky hill covered with flowers and decorative shrubs. Simon said they played "clock-tower tick" there and that the steps on each side of the tower were used as "dens." He noted additional hiding places in the surrounding bushes.

Close by, he showed me the "meteorite": a large rock, about five feet high, partly covered with ivy and steel netting (to protect the ivy!). "It fell out of the sky one night, long ago," he said (recounting a local myth), and added that it was good to climb on, to sit and watch people go by. He demonstrated.

Thickly vegetated parks provide special opportunities for the hide-and-chase games that children play the world over. "We play tick all over Tunstall Park," Simon said, "and dive into piles of leaves and grass—when it's cut." He took me to a group of bushes, pointed to a tough-looking, multistemmed, evergreen shrub and said it was the "best hiding bush...because you can get inside it." He showed me two bushes growing close together that you could "run around and get in between" when playing tick. "The other bushes are no good; they're too spikey," he said.

Simon was very discriminating and articulate in describing the play resources of Tunstall Park and was certainly the expert most qualified to evaluate it's hideaway-spaces. He took me to a long line of rhododendron bushes along the top of a slope adjacent to the

Simon climbing up the "meteorite" in Tunstall Park.

park boundary fence. "There's all kinds of tunnels and hiding places in there," he said. "The main one is called 'great tunnel.' You can run along it, all the way to the playground, without being seen. Then there's 'doom tunnel' which is short and curvy—and some others, but they don't have names." The variety of tunnel-like spaces resulted from the way the shrubs had been planted years earlier, in three staggered rows, about five feet apart. If they had been planted closer together the space would have been too tight to move around in. If planted farther apart, the tunnel effect would have been lost.

On a later trip, Andrew took me to the same rhododendrons and said there were "camps and hideouts all the way to the swings" (in the playground at the far end). Part of the attraction of the bushes was their commanding position at the top of a grassy slope, overlooking one of the main pathways. In the opposite direction, because the bushes were planted along the park boundary railings, one could look out and see what was happening on the adjacent Greenway.

In another part of the park, Simon led me up a steep slope, through some thick bushes, to a large forsythia bush which he said was the "best hiding place around." No wonder. We crouched in a south-facing vantage point, looked out over a flower-decked rockery facing the main entrance to the park and revelled in our invisibility to passersby. In the spring, with the forsythia in full bloom, hiders were immersed in a haze of yellow and surrounded by the many colours of the rockery below. Simon pointed out the "chief parkie's house" near the park entrance and said "it's a good place to spy on him, to see if he's at home or not."

PARKS AS SCARCE RESOURCE AREAS

Parks have traditionally been places to find certain kinds of scarce resources. Animals were a case in point. Tracy told me Hanley Park was "a good place, because there's a horse-and-cart there and you can get rides" (earlier in the trip she had told me she was "mad about horses"). Horses are highly appealing to some children, especially girls.

In Burslem Park, we went straight to the Bird House to see the pigeons and myna birds. Tracy spent a good ten minutes talking to them, making sure they were okay. Simon took me to the small conservatory in Tunstall Park. He pointed to the birds flying around inside and said they stayed there because it was warm. "In the nesting season, I come to watch them up in the baskets and behind the flowers. But some kids poke the nests with stakes," he commented; adding that "kids are not meant to be here without adults" (apparently not defining himself as a "kid").

Dawne and Lisa, too, took me to the Tunstall Park conservatory. Unfortunately it was closed; nonetheless, they pressed their noses against the framed glass doors, peered in at a magnificent display of chrysanthemums banked up on both sides of the central walkway, and said how pretty it was and how much they enjoyed looking at the flowers. They pointed to the notice on the door: "Children must be accompanied by an adult." They thought it was unfair, because (like Simon) they would "never spoil anything." Flowers were also mentioned by Heather, who talked about the flower beds in Avondale Park and how she looked for "interesting plants."

Trees were one of the most commonly-sought natural resources in parks, principally as things to climb. In Avondale Park, David said he climbed one of the two weeping willow trees "because there's a place to sit up there." He climbed into the bowl of the tree, about ten feet above the ground, jumped down and laughed, "I always come down that way" (photo p.49). Trees supplied swirling blizzards of springtime blossom and heaps of autumn leaves. They were the source of play objects such as conkers and supplied things to eat like chestnuts, hazelnuts, cherries and crab apples—an 'edible landscape' that could be further developed in most parks.

Water, in its many forms, was important. Tunstall Park had a large lake, a boat house, and boats for hire. Dawne and Lisa said they cost twenty pence an hour. In the summer they rowed out to a small island to feed the ducks—a favourite activity at the lakes in Tunstall, Burslem and Fairlands Parks. Lakes and ponds also bred fish. Andrew showed me his favourite "fishing spot" on the banks of the smaller pond in Tunstall Park and at the same time admitted that he had never actually caught anything! Other children, mostly boys, said they went fishing or watched others fishing. To a large degree it seemed that this so-called "fishing" was used as a pretext to get away from home and hang out in the park. It provided a plausible answer to parental queries about what their children were "up to."

Besides fishing, there was just plain "playing around" or "mucking about" in water-related places. Jenny showed where she used to

A detail of Hazel's drawing shows her favourite tree in Tunstall Park with a bird's nest, a "hole that you can look through to spy on people," and a spot for sliding her dolls down.

bird's nest

"hole
you can look through
to spy on people"

"sometimes
I slide my dollies
down here"

Details from Raymond's drawing show the "boat" play structure and fishing lake in Fairlands Park.

me fishing

fish

the lake

play in Fairlands Park, on the rocks of a small waterfall connecting two ponds. "But now," she added, "they've put a fence around it" The chestnut-paling fence was temporary-looking, erected to keep children off some recently installed ornamental plants. It looked very ineffective as a protective measure. The rocks, with the water flowing between, were far too attractive as a play resource. Better to plant some hardy, less exotic plants, like willows, rushes and sedges, I

Jenny's close-up of the rocks, bridge, and waterfall in Fairlands Park, where she used to play, "before they put a fence around it."

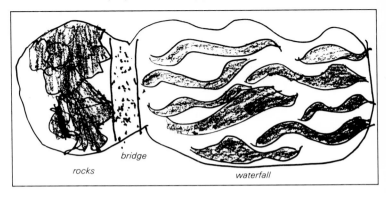

rocks   bridge   waterfall

thought, than try to keep the children off. Here was a classic example of how park managers could create an unresolvable conflict by over-emphasising aesthetic appearance in the wrong place.

Paddling pools were mentioned in each study area and featured on several field trips. Even though the paddling season was over, they attracted attention as places to roller-skate, to do handstands and to kick leaves around. The three shallow concrete pools in Fairlands Park became half-full of water when it rained. On one of the field trips, a group of mothers chatted while their toddlers played at the edge of the water. All the time, two older kids rode bikes back and forth, splashing through the water in the other two pools. It was. a nice example of unintended multipurpose design.

The trees and aquatic elements in both Burslem and Tunstall Parks had a major influence on the range of children's interaction with their environment. Dawne and Andrew both said that "floating leaves down the brook and fishing for them," were favourite things to do in the autumn. The park was situated in the valley of Scotia Brook which fed the two fishing and boating lakes on the way. The brook entered the park in a sheltered corner and cascaded down a natural-looking informal rockery. This was Simon's favourite spot— especially the small pond surrounded by a circle of stone about halfway down. "I often come here with my best friend," he said, "to watch the birds bathing...and sometimes we come with little nets to catch tiddlers." Simon said they never played higher up the rockery, because it was "less interesting and too shady," and they never

Caroline's drawing of Holland Park emphasises her interest in the natural environment. "I go there nearly every day with my brother and a friend," she said.

played in the bottom section either. "It's too near the parkies." He added that it was also too near the big pond where the fishermen shouted at each other too much. "It's quiet and calm up here," he emphasised.

"I'm interested in all the nature around here," Simon volunteered, adding that Tunstall was "more like a 'real park'...it's got two lakes and an island...and lots of places for birds to live.... There's lots of magpies—see those two flying," he interjected, admitting that he knew about fifty kinds of birds, "including pied-wagtails and thrushes.... There's that bluetit again," he whispered.

Parks also housed a miscellany of recreation facilities. Dawne mentioned that she had been to the park to play tennis and "to putt with my dad." Heather said she and her friends sometimes went to the "rec" building to play table tennis. Several children talked about watching sports. In London, Ricky took me to the tennis courts in Holland Park where he liked to "look at the players." The surrounding lawn was elevated above the court on two sides and provided a perfect grandstand view. Several other people were watching, too.

Ricky introduced me to other favourite features of Holland Park, including the "maze": a small geometrically laid out rose garden with beds separated by concrete paths. "You have to find your way through," he said. We passed the Orangery, a rather elegant brick building with arched, full-height windows. "It must be a 'film place,' " Ricky swore, because he had seen "lots of people with cameras there." He thought it was used for weddings. We continued past the park café, "where I get a cup of tea sometimes, when I have enough money," he said.

*Simon in his "best hiding bush...because you can get inside it,"
in Tunstall Park.*

Childhood's Domain/*Parks and playgrounds*

Rickie's drawing of Holland Park, showing the woods, the pathways where he liked to have bike "races" (see p.65) and the adventure playground (Venture), "where I always go."

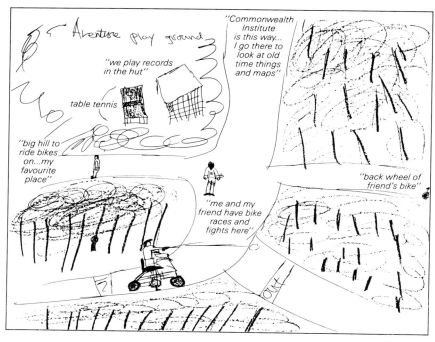

Ricky highlighted the park as a place to find peace and quiet. He ended the trip in a formal garden which he had labelled "the quiet place" in his drawing. "It's peaceful here," he said, as he sat on a wooden bench in contemplation. "I like to come to sit and relax and look at the flowers." Seclusion is a major reason for adults to use parks; why not children also?—especially children from large families living in overcrowded conditions. Also note that parks were the second most frequently mentioned place where children went to be alone. Several trips reinforced the notion of parks as places for children to daydream, to find solitude and to heighten their environmental awareness. In Burslem Park, Tracy pointed to the weeping willow beside the lake, commenting that she liked "how it hangs." She took me down through the fronds, into a completely enveloped space beside the water and pointed to two swans some yards out, gently gliding past. "I just love to sit and watch them," she murmured.

Adults play an unwitting role in park settings—with children who hide in trees or perch high on retaining walls and drop leaves and small twigs on passersby. Strange noises are heard. The idea is to test adult reactions, to see whether playful intrusions are ignored, mis-interpreted, cause annoyance, or are understood and responded to with humour—ah, the sign of an adult friend. Naturally, if an adult gets upset, then further means of annoyance will immediately be in-vented and actively pursued. Much of this 'joking behaviour' is car-ried on in a rather simple manner by children who spy on adults—especially amourous ones—invisibly trailing them by darting around tree trunks and crouching behind shrubs. The unconstrained sur-roundings of parks are ideal for this type of interaction. Most adults seem hardly aware of it.

The most important adults that children encountered were the "parkies" or "keepers." Tracy said she didn't like Tunstall Park as much as Burslem Park, "because there's too many parkies there—and they're mean! They'll take your name just for accidentally stepping on a flower in a game of tick. They really do!" Nonetheless, she still used Tunstall Park "because of all the things there—the swings, the ponds, the rocks, the little stream, the paddling pool and the Castle." Andrew complained that the parkies sent him and his friends off when they played in the plants.

Simon gave a concise rundown on what he called the "men who look after the park: They wear black uniforms and look like police. If you climb the trees, they'll write your name down; the second time, you're banned from the park. The meanest parkies take you to the police. The worst is called Cyril. We call him 'grumpy parkie.' But they don't often catch us—we escape through a hole in the fence." He said there were three kinds of parkies: "nice," "mean," and "in-between." During the trip he pointed out a "nice parkie," who was letting some children help him rake up the leaves.

David said the "keepers" (the London term) in Avondale Park "used to be more friendly.... A man used to push me on the swings. Sometimes I still like going on the baby swings for a change, but the new keeper tells me to get off, so now I can only go on the big swings," he complained. As we left the park, he pointed to the keep-er's house: a large, rather foreboding Victorian building. He said that the "old keeper" first became his friend one night when he went to tell him he had forgotten to lock the park gate—"that way he didn't lose his job," David believed.

If parkies are looked upon as friends, opportunities for mutual education will arise. Park keepers can gain an understanding of children's use of the park landscape and, conversely, children can learn to appreciate the needs of adult users and the play limits of natural resources. If parkies are considered an enemy, mutual mistrust and disrespect will prevail—resulting in nonuse of the site or willful vandalism. A more balanced sex-ratio in park staffing might help. The presence of female keepers would not only affect direct relationships with the children; it could also modify the outlook of male keepers towards children and help some parents feel less apprehensive about their daughters roaming in the parks.

Children like to feel at home in the places that attract them. They don't like to feel adult authority as a daunting challenge—being told to "clear off" when exercising their legitimate right to play. In tightly-structured urban parks like Avondale, play leaders could have accomplished much. A promise unfulfilled.... Avondale's recreation building was not used or mentioned by the kids. Each time I visited, there were two or three adults hanging around the building entrance. It looked as if one was the 'keeper' and the rest were friends dropping round for a chat. They never seemed to move from their hangout, except to tell off a kid occasionally.

Creative play leadership could have animated the Avondale scene, to compensate for the bland physical environment. In such a park, either the physical environment had to change or the social environment had become more creative. Broader age-group interaction could have resulted from encouraging local talent, programming special events, and encouraging everyone in the neighbourhood to get together. In Bedwell, Jenny mentioned the "music shell" in Fairlands Park were she went to concerts with her parents in the summer. She remembered a puppet show that had been great fun.

HALLOWED GROUND?

Parks are one of the longest-term urban investments. "Tunstall Park is years and years old," Simon told me. "It says it was opened in 1903 on the bird table in the rose garden." Adults need to retain vivid memories of favourite childhood environments. Because of their permanence, parks have a better chance of providing a sense of continuity for young people growing up in a rapidly changing urban environment like Tunstall. It is easy to imagine a child such as Simon retaining vivid, fond memories of his childhood in Tunstall Park.

And yet the permanence and social value of urban parks can easily make them into overprotected pieces of the urban status quo. Regardless of quality, perceptions become frozen. Parks then become sentimentally preserved when they should be ripe for reassessment. Rapid changes in society prompt serious questions about current user-needs and their degree of fit with existing environments. Policies are needed to help determine how much change is required, in what direction, and for whom. Difficult judgements are involved because, as with all people-environment assessments, they must be based on what is *not* present in the situation under investigation, as much as what *is*.

An intriguing aspect of the three most popular parks-with-playgrounds (Avondale, Fairlands and Tunstall) was the similarity of their impact, compared to their great variation in size (Figure 20). Each functioned as a *local* park for children living nearby; each was located at a similar distance from the centre of population; each had a similar level of accessibilty. Avondale, however, was much smaller (4.6 a, 1.9 ha) than Fairlands (95.3 a, 38.6 ha) or Tunstall (22.8 a, 9.2 ha), but it was still the most significant spot on the Notting Dale turf map (Figure 10, p.33), appearing on twelve (thirty-five percent) of the drawings. Fairlands was more than twenty times larger than Avondale, yet did not seem to provide many more play opportunities. The Bedwell turf map (Figure 11, p.35) shows the overwhelming majority of mentions (fifty-seven percent) were focused exclusively on the playground—which occupied a minute portion (less than half of one percent) of the site. The "little lake" and the "real forest" received additional small clusters of mentions, but the bulk of the site—the large mown grass areas— were completely ignored. Even in Mill Hill, with its more diversified turf map (Figure 12, p.37), the Tunstall Park playground still made the most frequent appearence on the Mill Hill drawings (twenty-four percent) and was still mentioned more frequently than the rest of Tunstall Park—inspite of its greater diversity of play opportunities.

These wide variations of diversity, play opportunity and physical size, in comparison to the relatively constant level of use, provide a challenging assessment issue. Avondale Park was a prime example. Its play resources included traditional play equipment, a few mature London plane trees and an old, climbable weeping willow. Fenced-in planting beds increased the site's spatial complexity and stimulated games of chase and hide-and-seek. A large area of asphalt (almost sixty percent of the ground surface) supported ball games. On one level

Heather's drawing of Avondale Park shows its basic accoutrements: swings (her favourite spot), "spider," "witch's hat," bench ("for talking with friends") and the weeping willow tree.

spider

"bench I sit on for talking with friends"

me

witch's hat

swings

weeping willow tree

the park seemed to work remarkably well. Its location assured good access. It was well used by children as an everyday meeting ground—particularly after school—to reinforce friendship ties. Large enough to support a sizeable repertoire of conventional play activities; it was a tough, resilient setting that had reached a point of stable adaptation to high-impact urban conditions. What was the problem?

From a more critical point of view, Avondale Park could have been equally well described as a routine, habitual space, where kids could meet, climb a tree, have a swing, play some games, take off.... There were no opportunities for landscape manipulation. Apart from the few trees growing out of the asphalt, vegetation was rendered unavailable by being fenced off in beds of dreary, low-maintenance, slow-growing, evergreen shrubs. The whole place had a gloomy appearance composed of black asphalt, dark tree trunks and dusty dark green bushes. The only flowers were near the park entrance, in a formal "Don't Touch" arrangement. There were no annual plants ('weeds') or natural materials to play with.

20

Avondale, Fairlands and Tunstall Parks, showing their comparative size and shape, and elements mentioned by children.

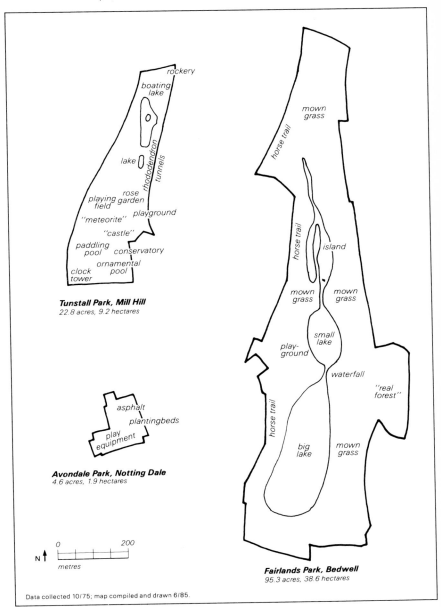

rockery

boating lake

mown grass

horse trail

lake

rhododendron tunnels

rose garden

playing field

playground

"meteorite"

"castle"

paddling pool

conservatory

clock tower

ornamental pool

Tunstall Park, Mill Hill
22.8 acres, 9.2 hectares

horse trail

island

mown grass

mown grass

small lake

play-ground

waterfall

"real forest"

asphalt

plantingbeds

play equipment

Avondale Park, Notting Dale
4.6 acres, 1.9 hectares

horse trail

big lake

mown grass

0   200

N

metres

Fairlands Park, Bedwell
95.3 acres, 38.6 hectares

Data collected 10/75; map compiled and drawn 6/85.

Given this negative assessment, how was Avondale's high level of use to be explained? The answer was easy: no better option was available. Compared to the windswept grounds of the Edward Woods Estate, or the densely-trafficked Notting Dale streets, Avondale was clearly the best, most easily accessible, most satisfactory play environment in the neighbourhood. It was not overshadowed by housing; it had a reasonable microclimate, plenty of space, a variety of play equipment, and was centrally located.

The most obvious missing elements were varied vegetation, dirt and water. The four-acre site was certainly large enough to accommodate additional natural resources. Some of the qualities of Tunstall and Burslem Parks were needed, or even some aspects of Heather's piece of wasteland—provided the local authority was willing to modify the status quo and involve the community in the process.

ADVENTURE PLAYGROUNDS

The qualities proposed for Avondale Park could be found in the adventure playgrounds and playparks mentioned as favourite places by children in Notting Dale and Bedwell. The Venture playpark in Holland Park was one example, but as a major road had to be crossed to reach it, only a small number of children were allowed to go.

There were three adventure playgrounds in Stevenage, within walking distance of the Bedwell children (none were actually within the neighbourhood). Half-a-dozen children mentioned one or another of them as favourite places. I went with Brian to the nearest (Pin Green). We navigated "death bridge"—a raised walkway following a circular route around part of the site. He climbed the "chair of evil"—a crooked branch at the top of a wooden tower structure. He liked to climb the trees and structures, he said, but he never built anything because he didn't go there often enough. After a while he took me beyond the other end of the playground to what he called "the park." It was actually a small copse where he said he liked to play hide-and-seek with his friends (as a group of children was doing at that very moment). Brian's pattern of use was similar to the way children used the parks described earlier. He seemed very familiar with the place, considering how far it was from his house, and I had the impression that he found the adjacent wooded area at least as attractive as the adventure playground proper.

Brian and a friend on the "chair of evil" — the "eye" structure at Pin Green Adventure Playground.

Amanda's drawing of Pin Green Adventure Playground, shows the interior of the hut with it's dartboard (a favourite activity), the rope swing hanging from a tree, and the wooden climbing structures, including the "eye."

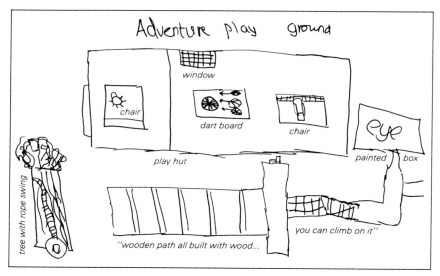

A trip with Amanda and her brother and sister covered all three adventure playgrounds around Bedwell. They loved them and said they went to Pin Green "everyday," to the Canyon "quite frequently" and to Chells Adventure Playground "every now and then." Beginning at the Canyon (a magnificent place developed in an old, overgrown quarry), they showed me how they played on the "giant tyre swing" (a Tarzan rope suspended from a tall tree) and swung back and forth across the central part of the quarry. They showed me the "wiggly tyres," hung on short ropes next to each other so that a group of children could play together. They went sliding down the sides of the quarry on milk crates. The sisters said they occasionally built camps, sometimes played table tennis in the hut and, apart from that, just "played around." We moved on to Chells where the atmosphere was very lively, with lots of camp-building going on. Amanda said they didn't come frequently enough to build anything and mostly played on the "rope swings" and the "bridge" (an elevated structure). At Pin Green, the trio went climbing and swinging around again. Amanda said they never built anything there but "once helped some boys build a hut."

Amanda on the "giant tire swing" at the Canyon Adventure
Playground.

Dean's drawing expresses the three dimensional complexity of the summer adventure playground in Notting Dale, "about ten minutes walk from home...I went there about every day to swing and climb...to meet my friends...to play 'had'...and do building. Hello down there!" he is shouting from the top of the structure.

It is difficult to draw conclusions from these few snippets of field data. However, note that thirteen additional children (mostly from Bedwell) told me they were *not* allowed to go to the adventure playgrounds because their parents considered them to be too dirty and/or too dangerous. A few parents expressed these concerns directly. One mother said the Canyon bothered her because, even though she'd been over there with her daughter, she couldn't believe it wasn't dangerous. Another said she wouldn't let her daughter go, "because it's not supervised enough and all kinds of things go on there." A Notting Dale mother said Holland Park Venture was "okay, because it's well supervised."

Some children told me they wanted an adventure playground in their neighbourhood. After a trip across rough ground in Mill Hill, Chris suddenly said, "They should do an adventure playground here. I've been to the one at Chell Heath but it's too far away and they steal your bikes there." He had seen a TV program about adventure playgrounds and said he would use one if it were nearer. I was puzzled by his request because it seemed to contradict the substantial freedom he already had to roam an extensive and adventuresome territory. I asked him why he liked adventure playgrounds.

"Because you can do what you like there and not get told off," he replied without hesitation. "In most of the places where we play, we're always getting chased out." For Chris, an adventure playground would provide a secure space for the legitimate pursuit of manipulative activities.

Adventure playgrounds encourage environmental participation by concentrating the interactive qualities of the environment in one place: combining natural resources, scrap materials and play leadership. Holland Park Venture was a successful example, but such combinations were rare. In the adventure playgounds visited, no attention was paid to natural resources. Trees were sometimes burnt and mutilated. No instances were seen of tree-planting or other forms of revegetation. No gardens were in evidence. The lack of attention by play leaders and children to growing and protecting natural resources surely helped foster appearances that adults found unacceptable.

These observations suggest that natural resources should be more energetically integrated into all types of playgrounds, not only to improve their utility as places for children, but to improve their public image and attractiveness to parents and adults generally. One way to achieve this is by locating playgrounds and play equipment within park settings, whenever possible.

6 *Greens*

Each of the study areas contained enormous open areas of mown grass. Because of their large size and monotonous appearance they were not used by neighbourhood children—except for team sports. They certainly did not feature in the children's drawings or interviews. However, several examples were encountered of smaller mown-grass areas which were well-used. They were larger than 'fronts,' with visual characteristics that fell somewhere between parks and rough ground. None of the examples went by the official title of "green," although in appearance and type of use they were reminiscent of traditional town greens.

SCHOOL GROUNDS

Notting Dale had one of the best examples: the landscaped grounds of a new primary school—a piece of official space used in an unofficial manner. Heather and her young sister, Sheryl, took me to the site at the end of their street. The single-story school building was centrally sited nearly 100 feet from the boundary fence and about ten feet below the surrounding ground level. An asphalt path sloped down to the building from the locked entrance gate.

Heather led the climb over the fence. "They always keep that gate locked," she muttered. I didn't need to ask whether other kids came there, too. The completely worn-off paint where we climbed over was the answer. "We're always coming here in the summer to sunbathe on the grassy bank," Heather said. "We wear backless dresses to get a good tan." The bank was less than a tenth of an acre (less than a twentieth of a hectare). Near the school building was a covered, padlocked sandbox, about twelve feet square. Unconcerned that they could not play with the sand, Heather said they liked to lay on the galvanized metal cover when the sun was out, "to warm our stomachs." In the next breath she revealed that "boys come and smash the windows at night and light fires in the planters." Evidence of the latter was plainly visible in the charred remains of several shrubs against the wall of the school building. (I wondered if such things would have happened if the grounds had been left open for public use, after hours. Then other users would have informally policed the site.)

Next to the sandbox was a set of bars. The girls did a couple of quick "twist overs." Heather reeled off some of the games she and her friends played on the surrounding asphalt: "'Queen Anne,'[1] 'chainy' [or 'chain-he'[2] where players link hands when caught and chase together], 'rounders' and football with the boys...sometimes."

Heather (right) and her sister at the spot where they climbed over the fence into the locked grounds of Thomas Jones Primary School.

Heather and her sister (facing camera) laying on the sandpit cover to, "get our stomachs warm," in the grounds of Thomas Jones Primary School.

As we started up the path to leave, a chilly wind reappeared. I suddenly realized how pleasant the microclimate had been down by the sheltered, south-facing side of the school building. It was a private, protected dell. After school hours it offered an alternative hangout to the busy streets around Heather's home. As we left, she commented, "there's a school-keeper lady who lives there, who always chases us out—especially off the grass."

The school grounds were well used because of their central location in the neighbourhood. The newness of the site pointed to a need for education and recreation authorities to coordinate their plans *before* schools were constructed so that after-school use could be integrated into the site. Maximum use has to be made of such scarce community resources. It is unfair to expect children to stay away from something they reasonably assume they have a right to use (school sites, above all). Verbal abuse for doing so only makes matters worse and paves the way for retaliatory vandalism—as I had observed.

BEDWELL'S FIELDS

Most greens were not so rigidly controlled and in fact one of the main advantages was their openness and accessibility. They were commonplace throughout Stevenage, where much of the public landscape consisted of large tidily-mown lawns. Bedwell children called them "fields." Jenny said she and her friends walked across the "field" behind their houses because it was a quick way to get to the shops. "We don't play in the middle, there's nothing there," she said. "We just cross it to go on errands...or we sometimes play in the 'pretend' forest" (two lines of sycamores along one edge). She couldn't remember anything that they played specifically in the "pretend" forest. I asked if there were any "real forests" around. She recalled the one she had drawn that was "down by the [Fairlands Park] lakes" (see drawing, p.111, and description, p.170). Jenny's friend, Jane, told me the main thing they did in the "field" was to "jump in piles of leaves [from the sycamores], kick them around, roll in them, and bury ourselves in the autumn."

The smaller Bedwell greens were integrated into the housing layout, which gave them a much stronger sense of enclosure. Raymond took me to one that was developed, in part, as a conventional play area with swings. He called it a "park" and also "a 'dump,' because it's so messy." It certainly looked untidy, principally because the remains of a bonfire were scattered around.

"It was our Guy Fawkes fire," Raymond said. "Some of the big kids lit it early." Then, "I like the swings and seesaw," he went on. "We play 'relays' [a racing game with sticks] and 'fifty-fifty'.... Someone counts to fifty in 'fives,' everyone hides, he shouts 'I see so-and-so, then everyone tries to get back to base and say 'fifty-fifty.'[3] We also hide in the hedges around the park and sometimes we sit on the grass and talk or play football. There's not much out here," he added, "but I still come a lot because it's near my house. One thing we need is more swings."

Mandy showed me the same bonfire remains and said she had helped build it, adding in dismay, "It gets burnt down early every year." She liked to swing and play hide-and-seek, too, and had shown a special bush on her drawing that she liked to hide in. "They need to put more bushes in here," she commented.

THE DIP

The Dip was Bedwell's most interesting green: a large, neatly mown, grassy bowl, fifteen-to-eighteen feet deep, 200 feet across, and encircled by rows of standard Stevenage sycamores. Down in the bottom, looking strangely out of place, was a rectangle of asphalt and a free-standing brick wall with the word CHELSEA painted on it. What Philip called the "milk crate slide" ran down the steepest slope. According to him, you had to "bring your own crate...you get 'em round the back of the shops," he admitted, openly. He liked the Dip because "you can do anything you like here...climb the wall, climb the trees [including a dead tree laying on its side], play hide-and-seek and kick a football around," (on a rectangle of concrete near the wall.

Carlo's drawing of the Dip shows the CHELSEA wall, milk crate slide, old tree and rectangle of concrete

The "milk crate slide" at the Dip.

The Dip had a pleasant microclimate, provided a good sense of enclosure and was well-separated from the surrounding housing. Martin said it had been made by a bomb, during the war. According to Brian's mother, the Dip had been "reclaimed" from an overgrown, natural depression. It had once been "the best place for blackberries in the neighbourhood," she said, but "the Corporation tidied it up." I suspected that the significance of the place could have been further heightened by reintroducing some of its former character—by planting shrubs and leaving part of the grass unmown.

THE BANKS

The same could have been said for many of Mill Hill's steep, grassy slopes, where the varied topography of the residential estates made the greens intrinsically more interesting than the equivalent flat spaces in Bedwell. Andrew took me to a spot known as the Banks: an acre of undulating, closely-cropped lawn at the top of the hill above his house. His seven-year-old sister came along too. Together, they showed me a sharp fold in the lawn that they called the "best ditch" where they played "war" and "tick" with their friends. Sometimes they rolled around on the grass and played "combat" in a small clump of trees and bushes. Andrew said he went "walking up the Banks" with his dog. The views across the city were magnificent on a clear day

SCHOOL GROUNDS AGAIN

Lesley and Jill took me to a flat green that was part of the grounds of the Catholic school at the end of Lesley's street (Figure 21). We turned up the driveway towards the school; to the right were large expanses of windy playing field, Lesley said they never played there. To the left, between the driveway and hard-surfaced tennis courts, was a small (less than a quarter acre, tenth of a hectare) triangle of turf supporting several large lime trees. The driveway marked the first side. The back fence of the last house on the street defined the second side, and the tennis court fence marked the third side. Lesley said they sometimes played tennis, but mostly they played football there. They also played hide-and-seek in the twelve-foot-wide passage between the next side of the tennis courts and the back garden fences.

21

The corner of the Tunstall Catholic School grounds where Lesley and Jill liked to play, and (below) a detail from Lesley's drawing of the same spot where she liked to play football, "just up the road."

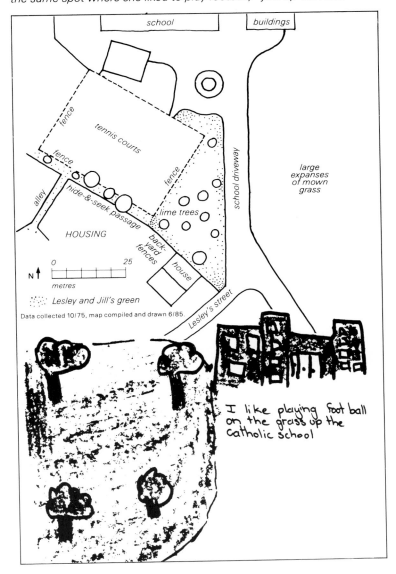

school

buildings

fence

tennis courts

fence

fence

hide-&-seek passage

alley

lime trees

school driveway

large expanses of mown grass

HOUSING

back-yard fences

house

N

0   25

metres

Lesley and Jill's green

Data collected 10/75, map compiled and drawn 6/85

Lesley's street

I like playing football on the grass up the catholic school

The episode demonstrated how a strong sense of enclosure and physical differentiation could stimulate the use of a small portion of an otherwise large, underused, open space.

GREENWAY EDGES

In Mill Hill, particularly, children were attracted to the unreclaimed edges of the greens. In these 'behavioural ecotones' play flourished because of the high density of resources to be found. The great advantage of many Mill Hill banks was that they were too steep to be mown. Tracy took me along one of the Greenways to a "blackberry patch" beside the back fence of one of the houses. "Me and my friends pick blackberries to make blackberry pie or 'lollies' in the fridge," she said.

Simon showed me how they played hide-and-seek along the steep, overgrown bank of another Greenway. I asked if he had a favourite spot. He took me to a hawthorn bush growing about four

Simon showing where they played hide-and-seek along the edge of the Tunstall Greenway.

feet below the top of the bank, thus making its underside level with the edge of the path. "It's the best hiding place I know, because it's so well camouflaged. "There's plenty of space in there," he said, as he crawled in under the foliage. "The others are not so good...but we hide in all of them on the way home from school and spy on people."

Later, Philip and Paul took me to the very same area. They climbed some of the same trees and bounced up and down on the branches of a mature shrub and said the bank was "a favourite place for hide-and-seek and chase." One of their hiding places was the same "best" one Simon had shown me. The vegetated bank was essentially a small rough-ground territory (as discussed in the next chapter). Despite its small size, it was able to absorb large amounts of interactive play and represented a type of landscape quality that could be designed into parkland edges (like the rhododendrons in Tunstall Park), to attract play away from more sensitive vegetation.

Annette's drawing shows a section of the Greenway between her house and the shops, where she liked to play and to watch others play (boy with kite).

Paul's drawing illustrates the significance of the open, grassy areas of the Greenways as a year-round playground

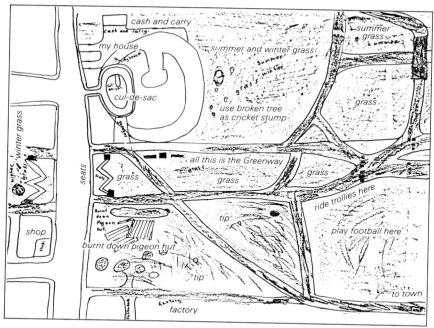

SPORTS FIELDS

Some greens revealed extra-special surprises. With Paul and Philip I squeezed through a gap in the fence surrounding the large bowl-shaped Clanway Sports Stadium. As we came down the grassy slope towards the flat playing area, Paul gestured to a steaming crack in the ground. He called it a "volcano." It was actually the spontaneously combusting buried remains of a refuse refuse tip that had formerly occupied the site (which, before becoming a tip, had been a large marlhole). The boys were fascinated by the smelly vapours issuing forth, blackening the grass. It didn't look very healthy to me, but to them it was a magic spot. They mostly came to play football and to watch people flying radio-controlled aeroplanes, but it was a good place, too, for playing hide-and-seek. They described how one could travel around among the bushes at the top of the stadium banks without being seen.

Tom's drawing shows where he played football in St. Mark's Park.

Large amounts of space in Tunstall, it seemed, were provided for sport. Much of it appeared underused much of the time. Glenn and Kevin took me to the local football team's "training ground" and said they sometimes went to watch the training sessions there. But other things happened on the way, as we toured the attractions of an adjacent playing field.

Our first stop was a small lake by the Burslem Greenway. Glenn said he often brought his dog Shandy there for a swim and regretted that he hadn't brought her on this trip. He said they once took their shoes and socks off and "walked in up to our middles—that's how deep the lake is....we come with nets sometimes to catch tiddlers."

We followed what the boys called "the sewer"—an open gully with periodic wooden erosion control devices—that drained the field into the lake. "I fell in once, when it was flooded, and went home smelling vile," Kevin said. The boys stopped to play around on a bridge over the gully, where a smaller ditch entered. We followed it along the edge of the field and found ourselves in an intimate, little space, instead of the huge, windy playing field. Several four-to-six-year-olds were playing with a trickle of water in the ditch bottom. To one side, a group of twelve-to-fourteen-year-olds had strung a "tight-rope" across, between two large trees, to see who could go the farthest, hand-over-hand.

THE LITTLE PARK

Most greens attracted children because they contained unusual features or special possibilities for play—like "the sewer," "the volcano," model aeroplanes, banks and bushes. In this regard, the Little Park in Mill Hill was an outstanding example (Figure 22). It was located across the street from one end of Tunstall Park, covered just under two acres (less than one hectare) and was bounded on two sides by

22   *The Little Park—a classic "green" offering a wide range of play opportunities (plan orientated the same as Jill's drawing opposite).*

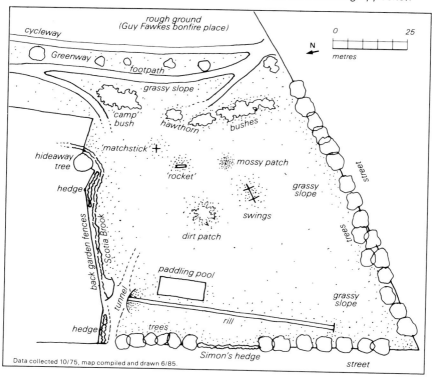

roads. The third side rose steeply to the Pitts Hill Greenway. Along the fourth side was a line of bungalows and back-garden fences. A gentle slope ran across the main area which was several feet below the level of the surrounding terrain.

From a distance, the Little Park looked like nothing more than an open field with a few items of play equipment plonked down in the middle. But the place was at least as popular as Tunstall Park—for reasons that emerged in the course of several field trips. The first at-

Jill's drawing of the Little Park shows its many attractive features: 'matchstick' centrepiece, 'rocket,' swings, brook adjacent to the bungalows' back fence, dirt patch ("sand pit"), sliding bank, hawthorn bushes and trees. A Guy Fawkes bonfire is plainly shown in the making (top right corner). Notice how the Greenway access system, linking Jill's house and the Little Park, is clearly described. Notice, too, that the Greenway "cyclist path" and "footpath" are clearly labelled as separate routes, even though Jill admitted (pp.65-66) that she and her friends rode their bikes on the "most interesting parts," regardless of official designations!

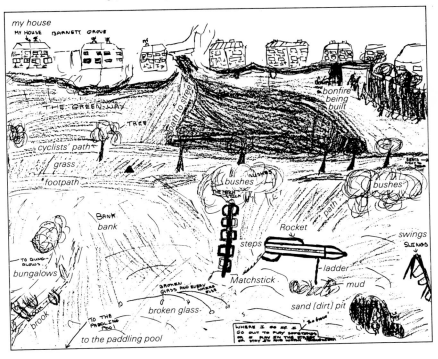

traction was the play equipment. Simon introduced the "rocket ship," where he and friends played "man on Mars" and pretended that "monsters were coming out of the bushes." He described further games they played on the "matchstick" which, like the "rocket ship," was made of welded pipe and used as a climbing frame. The grassy slope on one side of the central space was topped by a privet hedge, two-and-a-half feet high. "We dive over the hedge and roll down the banks," he said, and demonstrated—pushing his way between the plants then, repeating the sequence, he described doing "backrolls" down one particular slope, commenting that "the others are too steep." (The one he was on had a gradient of about forty degrees.)

Jill and Lesley introduced me to more of the Little Park's advantages. In another privet hedge, dividing the park from the back gardens of adjacent houses, they showed me some old birds nests they had discovered. A hawthorn bush in one corner of the park was used as a "club house...for telling secrets and things." They took me to "the brook" (Scotia Brook) that flowed from under the back fence of one of the adjacent houses, followed the fence line for about 150 feet (46 metres), turned sharply into the park, flowed through a fat

Simon diving over the hedge around the Little Park....

ten-foot-long pipe under the main path, and continued along a stone and concrete rill (narrow channel). Eventually, the water disappeared through a grating at the far end of the main lawn, went under the street, entered Tunstall Park and cascaded down the rockery (where Simon liked to play). The girls bent double and went through the pipe. "We look for frogs in the brook and play hide-and-seek in the bushes," they recalled, as they played follow-my-leader along an eighteen-inch strip of land between brook and bungalow fences.

"Oh, they've cut down all the nice long grass," Jill exclaimed (a large pile of grass and wild plants lay beside the stream, evidently trimmed by the City Parks Department). "It's no fun anymore. You can't hide and there's nothing to hold on to," she complained.

The girls pointed to a section of hedge growing between the brook and the flank wall of one of the bungalows and said it was "like a tunnel behind...a good place to hide." Farther along, the branches of a large hawthorn tree drooped over the fence to create a second, shady hiding place beside the stream. This part of the brook was "best for catching 'tiddlers' that sometimes escape upstream from ponds in people's gardens," they said.

Downstream, the brook broadened and went through the big

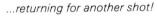

...returning for another shot!

pipe. Jill and Lesley said they played a lot around there, built dams in the summer and looked for "scrawly things...ones with hundreds of legs and babies attached. The best place is over there," Jill shouted, pointing to the stone-edged rill on the other side of the pipe. They called it the "muddy place." The water was several inches deep, much slower flowing, with a bottom-layer of mud. The girls concentrated on looking for "wiggly things" (freshwater shrimp). As they didn't like to pick them up with their fingers they tried a series of makeshift implements: an old stick, a potato crisp bag and part of a plastic bottle. I asked if they knew the name of what they were searching for. "Maybe 'water lice,'" Jill said, "like we found in the 'pond study' we did at school." They described worms they had caught that lived in the mud. They enjoyed the microcosmic fishing activity immensely.

Jill and Lesley looking for "wiggly things" in the stone-edged rill in the Little Park.

Near the channel was an empty concrete paddling pool, strewn with broken glass. Both girls said the glass was a problem in the summer and mentioned that they wore "pumps" (light shoes) when they went paddling. An added complaint was that the water was never turned on at the right time, "when it's a nice hot day."

Our next stop was the "sandpit": a section of sandy soil about fifteen feet across, in the centre of the main grassy area. The middle six feet or so of soil was completely exposed and bore evidence of constant use. There was no real edge to the pit. The dirt gradually gave way to grass. On the uphill side, children had burrowed into the ground, to create a miniature, undulating cliff.

"We make streams in the sand when it rains and water comes down the hill," the girls said. They got down on their hands and knees and embarked on a sequence of sand play. Within a few minutes, they had laid out a network of "roads" running around the humpy surface of the fine, hard-packed, sandy soil—qualities that allowed one to both mould the top inch or so and/or dig deeper. Lesley was making a "town with a motorway" with scattered groups of "houses" (small mounds of dirt). Jill was working on a larger mound which she called a "manor house." I asked how she knew about manor houses. "From my class at school...and I visited a stately home with my parents," she said. Lesley was putting "'odd' houses in the countryside...and a mansion," she said. It was a fine display of (iconic) dirt play with connections to both home and school.

Attention shifted to the unevenly-surfaced grassy slope beyond the sandpit. Jill said they used to ride their bikes down the slope—but not anymore, because once she had fallen off. I questioned them closely about where, specifically, they played on the grass. They took me to a small, "soft and mossy," level spot where they mentioned doing handstands and "just sitting around." Down on our hands and knees, we felt the velvety spongy texture of a subtly differentiated patch of dark green compact moss; conditioned, presumably, by the character of the soil or some combination of micro-ecological factors.

At the top end of the sloping lawn, large hawthorn bushes grew on a steep bank between the Greenway and the Park. When the grass was long, the girls slid down the bank on bits of cardboard, they said, but the grass was too short at the moment. The summer before last they had made a clubhouse under one of the bushes, and they showed me a cavelike space where someone (not they) had dug out a flat area on either side of the trunk. Kids hid there to watch people

Jill and Lesley constructing an imaginary landscape in the exposed patch of dirt in the Little Park.

in the park, they said. Later, during another trip, I saw a boy using the hawthorn hideaway, just so. The girls said they had tried to build a tree house there but it was too difficult—the hawthorn was "too spikey."

It was a fascinating trip. Because Lesley came along too, both children achieved a deeper level of play. I was astonished by the diversity of opportunities and depth of involvement within such a small territory. The children related to just about every physical differentiation—even discriminating between grass and moss textures. Their behaviour emphasised the importance of using tough bushes like privet and hawthorn, sited against fences and buildings and planted on grassy slopes.

ESSENTIAL INGREDIENTS

The Little Park reminded me of the 'recs' (recreation grounds) to be found in many British towns and villages, that consist typically of an expanse of mown grass, some items of play equipment and nothing much else. There were several in the town where I grew up, that I recall being used principally as places for ball play and as hangouts for older children and adolescents.

The Little Park offered something more to help explain its attractiveness:

- Centrally positioned play equipment, that signalled the entire space as a legitimate child-territory.
- Easy access from surrounding residential areas.
- Clear geographical identity, for parents wanting to know where their children were.
- Strong sense of enclosure, produced by the sunken site.
- Varied topography of surrounding slopes and undulating lawn.
- Better-than-average microclimate—again a function of the sunken grade of the site.
- Diversity of play opportunities: equipment, stream, pipe, paddling pool, hedges, bushes against fences and buildings, sandy/earthy/muddy areas, long grass, wild vegetation and climbable trees.
- Absence of "parkies."

At one level, the Little Park was just another mundane green space, the character of which was summed-up derisively by Simon, who said: "Oh...it's just got swings." Yet he was one of several children who valued the place highly and spent plenty of time there. It seemed attractive simply because it was neither park nor playground but had the character of both—as well as some of the rough ground character discussed in the next chapter.

Jill and Lesley used the natural resources of the Little Park in ways which would surely have attracted the parkies' attention if done in Tunstall Park. In the Little Park, Scotia Brook was partly contained in a soft-sided natural channel, and partly in a hard-edged rill. This allowed for a variety of play with water, mud and aquatic life— with the added bonus of the big pipe to crawl through. In Tunstall Park, Scotia Brook had a more elegant appearance that curtailed interaction. It was good for jumping over, for splashing with sticks and for floating leaves, but not much else. It also fed a series of ponds and lakes which offered play opportunities, but they were dominated by fishermen and boating couples; besides, their size was out of scale with most children's play needs. There was the rockery where Scotia Brook entered Tunstall Park, with its miniature pools and waterfalls, which Simon and others found attractive. But the children who played there still felt the menacing presence of the parkies. The Little Park was free of such intimidations. The steep banks and undulating ground surface provided an unusual setting for special activities like roly-poly, cardboard-sliding and bicycle tricks. Play equipment was another important factor, especially in combination with natural resources. The Little Park's brightly-painted "matchstick" stood out like a beckoning exclamation mark, ringed by grassy slopes and bushes.

Most of the greens I documented were overmaintained and underused 'resource voids' that left much to be desired, compared to the Little Park. Yet most of its prime characteristics could be introduced into many open spaces, through a program of selective physical modification and alternative resource management. Local authorities might give some thought to this.

7   *Rough ground and abandoned places*

Beyond the adult-determined surroundings of home, traffic-loaded streets, greens, and official parks and playgrounds, children took me to places where they could assert a greater sense of possession. Children are born curious. They have an innate motivation to explore and learn through cause-effect interactions with their surroundings. To fully experience the thrill of discovery, they need places to play and learn in their own way, shielded from adult interference.[1] They need places off the beaten track; places that can stimulate creative interaction—and places that can also absorb the sometimes untidy results.

'Rough ground' and 'abandoned places' were distinctly different entities, although they lay along a similar dimension of experience and were often found in association with each other. 'Rough' denotes a more physical quality, indicative of an unkempt, unordered, unmanicured appearance. Unmown grass and weedy waysides have it. So do unpruned trees, holes in the ground, varied topography and water features. Rough ground can accommodate a range of activites not usually found in parks and greens—like fire-making, excavating, manipulating water courses, throwing things, collecting things, playing with vegetation, climbing trees, sliding down banks, observing and collecting small animals, making "camps," "dens," "hideouts" and "clubhouses;" and that beautiful catchall of children's play, "messing around."[1]

Looking for "good pieces" of china in the shraff and rubbish of a
Tunstall marlhole.

Rough areas were referred to sometimes as "fields" (as greens were). Some were publicly owned, some were private (in which case children exercised a tenuous privilege of use). Sometimes the land was still in marginal use—like the Tunstall marlholes and Marat Farm in Bedwell.

Abandoned places were haunted by a residual human presence that stimulated the imagination and made it easy for children to anthropomorphise their surroundings; to muse, to make up stories about what might have gone on there, to create a kind of local mythology from found fragments of the past. They were places without purpose, open to individual interpretation, unconditioned by institutional directives: not yet cleaned up, cleared away, or otherwise conventionalised by the existing social order; available for children to colonise and create their own world—a "no-man's-land" or *niemansländ* (the German equivalent[2]) of abandoned, transitional, economically fallow spaces throughout the city.

Abandonment gave a visually readable 'archeological' dimension to a place, indicating previous human activity and former ownership. For kids, it was a beckoning invitation to explore. Abandoned places were not yet redefined by adults as 'historical heritage'—either because insufficient time had elapsed, or because insufficient material remained to meet adult criteria for preservation; or simply, the historical significance was, in fact, minor.

Such places did not attract all children, or even a majority. They were widely scattered and invariably located on the territorial fringe. As a result, parental concerns about physical and social safety were far more likely to be raised. Abandoned places included both land and buildings—frequently in a state of economic transition—suburbanising farmland, exhausted mineral workings and urban renewal sites. They were the most indeterminate of settings, and attracted those children who had both a strong exploratory urge and the trust of their parents.

THE GROGS

The Grogs was one of the most interesting of Tunstall's diverse range of rough-ground places. Located next to the Tunstall Greenway, to the uninformed eye the Grogs looked like just another piece of nondescript wasteland. For several Mill Hill kids, however, it was a favourite place: a piece of flat, overgrown land, no more than two

Chris leading a tour around the Grogs—an exemplary piece of rough ground.

acres (0.8 hectares) in extent, covered with weeds, patchy long grass and a few bushes. I asked Chris where the name came from.

"When kids came back from playing there, their mums used to say they were all 'black and grubby'...that's how it's called the Grogs—from 'grubby.' "[3] He said it used to be a crockery tip until "*they* flattened it out to make a football pitch. The pitch hasn't been finished yet," he added, "so we still call it the Grogs even though it's all been changed." The ground surface was made up of a mixture of broken crocks and red shale: a beach comber's paradise. Chris explained how they sometimes excavated the surface, looking for "whole mugs." When he found one he took it home, cleaned it up, and decorated it with "transfers."

On another trip, Paul showed me how they looked for "glass." Within five minutes he had half-a-dozen pieces of decorated pottery in his hand, assuring me that kids called it "glass," not pottery. What irony! Imagine these kids, mimicing their dads down the pits, mining for treasures thrown out by their mothers as waste from pottery factories, to be taken home as prized discoveries and lovingly pre-

Paul and his friend looking for pieces of "glass" (broken pottery) on the surface of the Grogs.

sented to parents as something of special value: a powerful metaphor of contrasting childhood and adult values, linked by fragments of Tunstall's economic base—the reason for the town's existence.

"One summer when the grass was really high," said Paul (uncovering more of the Grog's opportunities), "me and a group of friends built a camp out of sticks, oil drums, two old doors and lots of grass...then *they* came along, cut the grass down and bashed our camp... For fun we rolled the drums down the hill at the back." He and a friend led me through a hole in a high privet hedge, into a patch of tall grass and fireweed, behind some back-to-backs waiting to be demolished. "It's a good place for hide-and-seek, because of the long grass," Paul said. They "did things" there, he commented. The two of them set up a pyramid of old tin cans for a game of cockshy and had a great time whooping around as one or the other scored a bull's eye. Here, it was harmless sport. In a public park or recreation ground it would have been impossible, without disturbing other users.

GUY FAWKES

Chris said the Grogs was a good place for Guy Fawkes[4] bonfires and showed me where last year's fire had been. He mentioned that their "enemy's fire" (shown on his drawing) had already been burnt down. Apparently it was a local tradition for rival gangs to burn each others fires, before Guy Fawkes Night. In Tunstall, these rival burnings were taken for granted, and were carried out with a certain amount of humour and zeal.

In Stevenage, on the other hand, where accessible rough ground and bonfire materials were scarce, local kids treated rival burnings with great dismay—literally as an act of vandalism. The lack of resources in Stevenage made Guy Fawkes into a precarious, 'precious' event, organised and controlled by adults, consequently lacking the participation of children; done *for* them, rather than *with* them, or *by* them.

In Tunstall, Guy Fawkes still lived on as an authentic part of childhood culture. Walking back one evening at the end of a field trip, I saw, off in the distance, across the weedy 'fields' of mining subsidence, a great blaze of yet another rival burning, ringed by the silhouettes of twilight victory dancers. It rekindled my own Guy Fawkes memories of great heaps of anything burnable, scavanged by a gang of us, without benefit of adult advice or assistance—except at the conflagration itself, to keep sparks out of the box of fireworks and to make sure no one got injured. The fire building was truely a child-planned, child-executed tradition. I wondered if it was still that way where I grew up, now that suburban housing covered the land. In Tunstall, Guy Fawkes was certainly threatened by the City's plans to convert every piece of rough ground to a 'higher and better use' without consulting the existing users.

The ubiquitous evidence of fires—the burnt patches and charred remains—blended naturally with the unkempt appearance of the

Paul setting up a cockshy of old tin cans, surrounded by fireweed in a redevelopment area at the far end of the Grogs.

Grogs. It even helped maintain textural interest and ecological diversity of the ground surface each spring, when the burnt patches were reinvaded by a new crop of weeds and grasses. In Stevenage, the same Guy Fawkes activity had a disasterous impact on the monocultural greens. The half-burnt remains and blackened areas looked horrible. It took months for the lawns to regain their pristine appearance. This raises a question for those who plan new family housing: Ask yourselves where young residents will be able to find sites and materials for Guy Fawkes bonfires? The answers should indicate which outdoor areas, if any, will be suitable for 'adventure play.'

Rough-ground areas in Notting Dale were much smaller than in Tunstall, but were surprisingly common—more so than in Bedwell where, although densities were lower, every piece of land had a planned purpose. Notting Dale seemed better off because it was older. Most of the rough ground areas were redevelopment sites, temporarily on the market for childhood use (five years represented use by a complete generation of eight-to-twelve-year-olds). Presumably, some decades hence, when urban redevelopment starts in Stevenage, similar rough-ground, 'meanwhile' opportunities could arise there, too.

To return to Notting Dale.... Heather's piece of wasteland was a fine example of an abandoned place: a redevelopment site, down the end of her cul-de-sac in the heart of the neighbourhood. It was a partly filled basement, measuring 80 by 250 feet (24 by 76 metres), with a humpy, dirt-dumped surface, overgrown with wildflowers, weeds and grasses. Rubbish, building debris, broken glass and miscellaneous objects were strewn around. The site looked as if it had been vacant for three or four years.

The ground surface was about three feet below the level of the adjacent streets. A corrugated-iron screen surrounded the site and rose eight feet from street level, enclosing the site to a height of some twelve feet. This gave a strong sense of containment and also provided protection against the wind. The microclimatic effect was reinforced considerably by a length of freshly-installed galvanized sheets which reflected the sun's rays into the place, to give it an immediate feeling of peaceful warmth and security—in contrast to the hectic, noisy streets outside.

To an outsider, it looked like just another piece of waste ground. Luckily for me, Heather and her seven-year-old sister, Cheryl, were expert interpreters of the possibilities of bare earth, varied topography and vegetation. The way they moved around the place and talked about it, indicated a strong sense of territorial proprietorship. They obviously spent lots of time there, in their private sanctuary.

They picked some rosebay willowherb (fireweed *Ebilobium augustifolium*). "There used to be some lovely white flowers over there, too," Heather said. "My mother calls them 'London pride' (*Saxifraga urbium*), but the boys are always bashing them down."

"Here's a treasure chest," Cheryl said.

"Don't be silly, it's just an old box," Heather retorted, illustrating the transition from fantasy to practicality that comes with age. The level-headed older sister didn't keep a level head for long, however, but continued with a bubbling stream of recollections.

"A man got blew-up once, fiddling with electric wires. I think it used to be a garage. Watch out for the stinging nettles....We used to come here picking blackberries. We play with the stuff that looks like wheat (tall grass). See it over there. We suck it and pretended we're cavemen. There's lots of ladybirds here, and bees' nests—but the boys are always burning them." She pointed to a hollow in the ground, where she said a bees' nest used to be before the boys dug it up.

During the whole of the conversation, Heather had been carefully assembling the posy of wildflowers and grasses for her mum, described in the opening of Chapter 1. "Look how it's been nibbled," she said, pointing to the leaf of one of the small plants.

MARAT FARM

Bedwell had no incidental rough-ground areas resembling the Grogs or Heather's building site. But situated just beyond the housing area, on the far side of the school, there was Marat Farm: one of the last remaining segments of landholding, yet to be appropriated for the extension of Fairlands Park. Brian, who had talked about Marat at length in his interview, took me there one foggy morning, a few minutes walk from his home. We ducked under a strand of barbed wire beside the road and entered an overgrown, abandoned orchard. Large old fruit trees, unpruned for years, grew in disarray. Thick undergrowth surrounded the site. The center was fairly open with two or three narrow paths winding through a ground cover of wild plants. The old farm house was just visible in the background.

Brian took me to a gnarled crab apple tree he and his friends liked to climb. Judging from the shine on the limbs, it happened frequently. We looked at the crown of an elm tree laying on the ground, which Brian said had blown down the previous summer. He showed me the remains of a "camp" they had built between the grounded branches. Another "camp" was located on the other side of the orchard, in a cozy 'found' space under the low-hanging branches of a yew tree: a special place, by definition, since it was the only yew in the whole area. Alongside, was an ancient apple tree with an upwardly-curving trunk that Brian called his "lookout tree," as he climbed to a horizontal fork, about seven feet off the ground.

"We often come down to Marat's to play in the woods," he said . "It's a good place for playing games and climbing trees." A magnificent horse chestnut tree in one corner of the orchard was his "favourite conker place." He pointed to a great mound of blackberry briars that formed part of the overgrown hedge surrounding the site, and mentioned how he liked to eat the fruit. It was a fine example of a small 'play wood,' barely three acres (1.2 hectares) in extent. Yet there were climbable, unusual trees; a rough, overgrown terrain, crisscrossed by narrow, twisting paths; things to harvest like apples, blackberries and conkers; and a sense of privacy and possession. The only problem Brian mentioned was the stinging nettles!

"The government's bought the land," he said, "and is trying to get the owners out, but they've refused to move. One day they'll knock the house down and take it over," he predicted. "They should make it into a place like the Canyon, because the trees are good enough to put planks on and make slides." Brian obviously wanted more loose parts to play with. I wondered if it could be done without altering the character of the old orchard too much.

As we were leaving, Brian showed me a garden enclosed behind a sturdy brick wall. "See all the good vegetables growing there," he observed. As we walked along a gravelled driveway, beside the red brick farm buildings, Brian counted eight of a rumoured twenty-two cats. He gestured towards "the barn where onions and things get cut up."

"How do you know that," I asked?

"We can see it through a gap in the window."

Farther up the driveway we walked past what Brian called "the most important blackberry patch'—a large section of hedge entirely interwoven by briars. We walked through the long grass next to two elm trees ("good for climbing"), squeezed through a wire fence and arrived back in the lane that we had first entered by. We had navigated, full-circle, the last piece of rough landscape close to Bedwell—a slice of social history remaining from the time Stevenage was just a stretch of farmland—now appreciated by children, while awaiting the knell of development.

The rest of the farm was already part of Fairlands Park: a regional recreation facility with a well-used boating lake, paddling pools, bandstand, playground and horse trails, interspersed with acres of closely-mown grass—little-used except for ball games. It looked as if the New Town planners had decided to redo the whole landscape, instead of conserving sections of the original farmland as an integral part of the local scene. I wondered if the 'landscape assessors' had really dismissed the farm as insignificant. Brian, for one, saw it as an important wild place. One thing was certain: It would be impossible to re-create such a landscape, once it was removed.

We continued up the valley beyond the farm and came to a pond filled with mud. Brian called it "Marat's toffee." There was a small concrete drainage structure at the end of the pond where he said they played a game by "sliding little stones down the slope to see how far they go." Our trip ended there, but Brian said they went farther up the valley in the summer, once or twice a month, to play hide-and-seek, "where there's good hills and trees to climb...near the 'sewage pipes.' " I made a mental note to take a look at this intriguing boundary-marker of Brian's occasional territory.

WOODS

Patches of woodland like the Marat orchard are an excellent example of rough ground. Bedwell children had access to several other similar copses and wooded areas, although, Marat Farm excepted, they were beyond the frequented territory of most children. (Notting Dale and Tunstall had fewer wooded areas and fewer individual trees, except those growing in the streets and parks.) After visiting her "pretend forest" (p.141), Jenny took me to her "real forest," on the far side of Fairlands Park. We followed an asphalt path across the mown swards, past the lakes and waterfall, to a point where the path turned into an informal gravelly trail and entered a piece of indigenous woodland: the "real forest."

"We come here to look for squirrels," Jenny said. "In the spring we pick bluebells—not *too* many though. We chase around, but not hide-and-seek, in case one of us gets lost" (the wood was five acres— two ha.). Other kids were playing there, whooping among the trees.

We followed a sunken path and wandered among the trees. A few large oaks rose above multitudes of multistemmed elderberry bushes spaced eight-to-ten feet apart. Bright sunlight shafted through the amber autumn leaves and reflected off the golden carpet of those already fallen. The effect was magical. Few words passed; they didn't need to, the reality of the "real forest" enveloped us so strongly.

Jenny leads a trip through the "real forest"—on the way encountering other children playing.

Next day I paid a visit to the intriguing "sewage pipes" that marked the edge of Brian's occasional territory. They were real enough, standing vertically out of the ground, topped by manhole covers at what seemed to be the street level of a future housing development. For now, the area was yet another 'meanwhile,' fieldlike terrain covered by weeds and long grasses. Steep, rough-hewn banks rose up on each side of an asphalted path. On one side, narrow 'runs' cut through the long grass, connecting places where children had beaten down the grass to create hideaways and lookouts. On the other side of the asphalt path, a steep earthen slide descended. Beyond the top of the bank lay a two-acre (0.8 ha) copse, also laced with pathway traces.

Although the term "fields" was used by both Bedwell and Mill Hill kids, the characteristics on the ground were very different in the two neighbourhoods. Since all present-day Bedwell 'fields' were mown greens, the term had surely originated with the early settlers, whose new houses had once been surrounded by farm fields. Presumably the Mill Hill term had had a similar origin, although most present-day 'fields' were fallow mine workings or areas of subsidence. Because of Tunstall's piecemeal development, many 'fields' were still in a rough-ground state, although reclamation was converting them to greens.

"Shall I take you to the 'fields,' " Tracy asked, "where I go with my friends pretty often?" We crossed busy High Lane, went up a short side street, round the corner to a cul-de-sac, and down a narrow path between two houses. Suddenly, we emerged into a wide expanse of shoulder-high grass, with Chell Heath Valley stretched before us. "Sometimes we go on hikes across there in the summer," Tracy reported, tracing in the air the route taken, pointing to a green band running through the housing estate on the distant hill (about one-and-a-half miles away). "It wasn't 'arf a long way....We phoned our mum from up there—once after lunch and once after tea—from the phone box by the church" (visible from where we stood).

We walked farther down the path to a pigeon loft standing in the middle of the field and were greeted by Blackie the dog. Tracy also talked about a dog called Jenny, belonging to neighbours. "We can take her out anytime we like...sometimes for hours." She spoke to Blackie, who guarded the birds, and said "hello" to the pigeons. "I see them every time I come down to the fields," she said, and added that she and her friends did handstands on the path there.

Fields on the fringe of Bedwell, adjacent to the spot Brian called the "sewage pipes." Note the extreme contrast between the rough-ground character of these fields and the broad expanses of smoothly-graded, mown 'fields' of Fairlands Park, visible in the background. The residential part of the neighbourhood can be seen on the horizon.

Farther down the hill we came to a flat shelf where a thick slab of black tar had been dumped long ago. "We sometimes play on it in the summer," she said, and described how it got soft in the sun so you could see your footprints.

TRACY'S MARLHOLE

"I'll take you to the marlhole,[5] if you don't mind grasshoppers... there's millions of them around there." Tracy headed off through the long grass to the marlhole a hundred yards away. It was ancient look-ing, obviously abandoned long ago, sheathed in a covering of down-like grasses and wild plants. We half-climbed, half-slid down a steep path that she said were used for "races." There were two small ponds in the bottom that Tracy frequented twice a week for "frogging and newting...and to look for minnows, tadpoles, water spiders, and water beetles."

She climbed onto the remains of a half-submerged tractor cabin and peered into the water. There were several "stories" about how the tractor got there, she said. "One I heard was about a man driving along in the dark. He came crashing down and is buried underneath, in the water. It's one of the least likely—I don't believe it."

"We throw things in the water to scare the frogs," she went on, "so they come to the surface. Usually we wear our Wellingtons and spend maybe five hours, maybe the whole day, down there." The well-worn pathways around the ponds spelt heavy use. The main pond looked attractive with lots of reeds growing around and halfway in it, camouflaging any rubbish. The second pond (right under the cliff) was not so well protected and was more visibly full of junk. Tracy said they sometimes had fun "throwing things in the water off the top of the cliff." Getting to the top was like "climbing the South Face of Everest." She pointed to an old box they had put in the second pond so they could stand in the middle. I asked if she liked all the junk. "Not at all," she emphasised, neatly illustrating the contrast of values between the joy of throwing things into the water and the unsightly consequences!

Tracy sliding into her marlhole "where the sun gets you."

Tracy relating the story about how the half-submerged tractor cabin came to be in the bottom of the marlhole.

I asked why she liked being down in the marlhole so much. "Because of all the sun that gets you," she replied. I couldn't imagine a better phrase to describe the marlhole's sheltering microclimate. "You're allowed to do anything you want," she went on. "If you tread on the flowers, or something, even the police can't do anything...it's just waste ground. All your friends can come down and have lots of fun. We always have a laugh down here...funny things are always happening. And you've got good views at the top, too." Her environmental awareness was remarkably well developed; her political sense, too.... "You know what," she concluded, "we could get together and buy it so it will always be here."

We returned topside and were surrounded by waves of long grass. I asked Tracy what she did there. "We play hide-and-seek, tick, and bully-beef-and-chips," she said, and explained that in the latter game, "one of the kids is 'on' ('it') and the rest are 'chips'.... It's like hide-and-seek, but the 'chips' have to be on the move all the time—you're not allowed to stay in one place." It seemed to me that this game was well-adapted to such a sizeable area of really long grass. It wouldn't have worked otherwise, because the players would have been too visible.

We started talking about wildlife. Tracy said they looked for or had seen in the area: rabbits, mice, birds, pigeons, cats and dogs, lizards, ladybirds, grasshoppers and spiders—plus the things in the pond. Long grass obviously added immensely to Tracy's wildlife experience by providing a habitat for many more species than mown grass ever could.

GLENN'S MARLHOLE

A second unforgettable, though very different, marlhole trip happened with two boys: Glenn and his best friend Kevin. Glenn's marlhole was vast by comparison to Tracy's and was in the process of being filled with municipal refuse and *shraff*.[6] We stood on the rim and tried to guess how much longer the filling operation would take. "Me mum don't really mind me coming here," Glenn said, "as long as I bring something good up. You can find all kinds of things down there—ornaments, plates, everything. Me mate found forty-pounds-worth of plates once."

We scrambled down the banks to an intermediate level. Glenn said they used to "roll old settees down the cliff onto chairs at the

Glenn and Kevin on the rim of their marlhole, surveying the latest changes, before our descent. Note the screes of white shraff *(middle ground, left) and active tipping area (middle ground, right).*

bottom and watch them get squashed.... We try to find 'things' there.... What's there now ain't nothing to what it used to be," he reminisced. "It was all grassy once, before they started filling it in. We used to go down the banks on trollies and have stone fights between two sides of friends. There used to be a big lake at the bottom. It was 'dead deep.' We once buried a dead pigeon where the bottom used to be. It's private, you know, but they let us go in." He remarked that "tramps used to live in caves in the sides of the hole."

Hundreds of little red plastic hemispheres, mixed with a few yellow ones, were scattered around. The boys started looking for "yellows" (the rare ones, naturally) to fit together, to make little plastic balls. They looked like part of a child's game. The boys explored a huge rock outcropping on the one side of the hole and picked away at the shale/coal strata.

"It used to be all hills here until they started filling it," Kevin remarked.

"I suppose it will be all flat by the time they're finished," Glenn accurately perceived.

We reached a small pond at the bottom. A fifteen-foot-high bank of pottery waste rose to our right. Glenn and Kevin started looking

Kevin explores the remains of a coal outcropping in the bottom of the marlhole.

for "good pieces." All manner of plates, cups, teapots and ornamental animals were systematically inspected, and rapidly discarded or thrown in the water. The main idea was to find a piece that was glazed. Nearly all the shraff was unglazed and therefore not usable as "real china."

"Here's the kind of plate you serve turkeys on," Kevin shouted, holding up a large platter printed with the traditional willow pattern (but not glazed).

"You can find some good things an' all," Glenn said, holding up the bottom half of a porcelain figurine.

"Hey, anyone want a toilet?"

Kevin laughed and pointed to half-a-dozen damaged porcelain toilet bowls laying on the tip.

"We play 'flying saucers' with the plates and skim them on the water sometimes," Glenn chimed in.

"You have to get used to the smell," Kevin joked, commenting on the aroma of municipal rubbish.

I asked about *shotties*. Several Mill Hill kids had mentioned them before. Within seconds Kevin was back with one. It was roughly spherical; a smooth, white ball of china or porcelain. He told me kids in the Potteries used them to play "shottie"—a game similar to marbles. They were used in the china works. He didn't know how, exactly.

We returned to the top of the tip and about a hundred yards away could see where active tipping was still underway. A constant flow of lorries was coming and going, while a bulldozer levelled the rubbish. At the foot of the tip, about ten kids could be seen hovering around, pulling stuff out of the advancing piles, like wasps around a jam pot. "Shall we go over?" asked Glenn. They don't mind kids being there." The boys went ahead while I took some pictures, before anyone noticed me. It wasn't long

"Why do you want to photograph this lot?" the bulldozer driver asked, when I arrived. "We already gave up with them. It's impossible to keep them away. We've even had the school inspector down here. But it's no good, they just keep coming back." The tip was an amazing collection of stuff: polythene sheet, plastic pipe, rope, bits of machinery, building rubble, plastic stampings.... Each boy had collected his own small pile of booty from the larger heap. Thirteen-year-old Michael said he was collecting copper. He had a big sack of old wire to "take home to burn to get the metal and sell

to a scrap dealer for twenty-pounds-a-hundredweight.... I spend the whole day at the tip," he said, usually from seven-thirty in the morning." I asked if he went to school.

"When I feel like it," he replied.

He was a likeable, friendly boy, apparently addicted to collecting scrap. He showed me his pickings for the morning. In addition to the wire, his scrap-heap treasure trove included aluminum ducting, a steel window frame and bits of a car engine. He climbed out of the marlhole with us. Before saying goodbye, he reverted to childhood behaviour for a few moments to play hide-and-seek with Glenn and Kevin among the hummocks and long grass around the marlhole edge (marked on Glenn's drawing).

Thinking about the experience afterwards brought childhood memories of my own favourite rubbish tips. In Tunstall they were so attractive that children cut school to hang out there from the early hours of the morning? Yet why not? It was real work. Useful too: salvaging nonrenewable resources back into the economy. Part of the attraction was the sheer diversity of stuff thrown together in one spot. There was the delight of not knowing what would turn up next. And there was the financial stake...the excitement of a treasure hunt, of finding something valuable in the dirt, the satisfaction of getting something for nothing, something to take home to parents— who might have even made the object!

The tip was an incredible mixture of quintessential *stuff*—like pebbles on the beach, only a thousand times more varied. It is interesting to note that in recent years "scrap projects" have been set up in cities on both sides of the Atlantic to salvage industrial waste and surplus items and make them available to community groups working with children. A more radical parallel enterprise would be to make selected scrap resources directly accessible to children at special 'tips,' in rough ground areas.

HEATHER'S OLD GARAGE

Round the back of Heather's Notting Dale terrace was the roofless shell of a small industrial building. "It belonged to an old man," she said. "We used to bring him tea and biscuits, because he never had time to go to the café; then he got sick and the garage had to close."

Heather and her sister at their "camp" in the abandoned garage behind their Notting Dale house.

She went on about how "the boys used to let off fireworks in the garage after it closed.... One day they made a big fire and the fire brigade had to come to put it out. After that they blocked up the entrance, but the boys bashed it down again."

The principal significance of the old garage, for Heather, was a "camp" built at the back against one of the walls. It was made of four sheets of corrugated iron (two for the walls and two spanning across for the roof) and other miscellaneous odds and ends. In front was a small climb-through entrance. The camp measured about six feet square and was little more than two feet high. Inside, Heather proudly pointed to three old car seats they had set up. Her best friend had had the idea of the camp, she said, and her "boy friend" had helped build it the previous summer. The corrugated iron had been "nicked" from her 'meanwhile' play area, described earlier. The remaining building materials had been gleaned from a pile of junk stacked against the garage wall.

The garage space was enclosed by high walls. A couple of trees gave additional camouflage. The access route was very indirect. You wouldn't know the space was there, unless someone showed you. On a warm summer's day it must have been a cool secluded haven, just a few yards from Notting Dale's main shopping street.

LAWRENCE'S CAMPS

Lawrence took me around a whole system of camps and camplike spaces in the redevelopment zone of Notting Dale. We headed down a narrow side street (which he called a "shortcut," although actually it was a longer way around), through an intimately-scaled area of two-story terraces and mews. Most of the houses stood empty, their windows blocked up, their residents flown. The area was deserted, awaiting demolition.

We stopped under the balcony of an upper flat. Lawrence said a rope used to hang there and described how he and his best friend used to swing on it, "before it disappeared." Only they knew about the spot, he confided. A great patch of Boston ivy stretched across the roofs of the adjacent garages. "It's been there for years," said Lawrence, and added that they had used an old taxi that once parked there, "to hide from the Jamaican kids" (Lawrence's parents were from India).

Lawrence stands guard in front of his "camp" in the old garage behind him.

Lawrence's drawing of his third camp—and his "enemy's" camp.

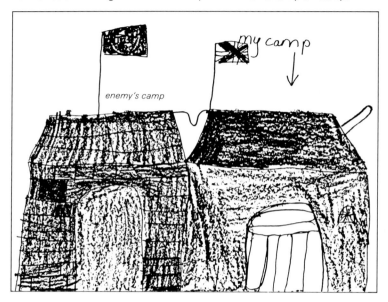

The next hiding place was a small patch of overgrown land, overlooked by a multistory commercial building, in the centre of Shepherds Bush, on the extremity of Notting Dale. It looked as if it had once been someone's back garden. Lawrence scooted under the fence and ran to his "camp" under a large weeping willow tree (in the midst of brand-new urban development). He went there sometimes, "to hide from my enemies."

Lawrence's next camp was more elaborate. It was situated inside an abandoned building that, ironically, had been last used as a youth club. We climbed up a jagged corner of the brick building and peered in. Lawrence had lots of tales to tell—about fires, fights and boxing matches (there had been a boxing ring inside, he said). It was hard to tell whether the tales were imaginary or factual. Some may have been based on real events, witnessed by Lawrence; others seemed based on hearsay, coloured by Lawrence's fertile imagination. Either way, they featured central characters that Lawrence insisted hung around in that part of the neighbourhood: street people, squatters, and members of teenage gangs.

The third "camp" was the one shown in Lawrence's drawing: an old garage in an industrial mews backing onto the main highway. At first, Lawrence was vague about where it was, saying he couldn't show it to me as it was "secret" and because there were "guard dogs everywhere." Gradually however, without any prodding on my part, we advanced down the mews. Lawrence said he couldn't remember which garage it was; but after opening a couple of wrong doors, he found it. Inside were some large rolls of cardboard, which he said were used for building additional rooms. We were both a little scared about being there. Lawrence was obviously using me as a 'front' to re-explore his occasional territory. Dogs could be heard clearly in the factory yard across the way. I suggested that we leave. "We're trespassing, you know," Lawrence said. "Don't tell me mum we came here.... I don't want anyone to know our secret ways."

THE "STUDIO"

The largest abandoned building I visited in Notting Dale, was part of David's territory. He had mentioned it several times in his interview. Formally a school, the Victorian building had at some time been converted into a multipurpose community studio. Most recently it had caught fire, which explained the desolate and hazardous-looking burnt-out shell we were looking at.

David showed me how to enter through a hole in the fence and we started on a tour of the place. He pointed to a barricaded window and said that he and his friend had a hideout behind it. "They've blocked it up, but I can still show you how we get in," he said. We went into the main building, being careful not to fall through the holes in the floor. His hideout was a small room at the back. He and his friend had "swept the floor and fixed-up some furniture," he said, as he gestured proudly towards an old stove and a board to sit on, propped-up on a couple of bricks. "There's been seven or eight fires here.... Big kids do it," he explained, adding that a second hideout had been upstairs, before the fires started. We gingerly climbed what had been the main stone staircase and looked across a roofless, floorless, void to where the other hideout used to be.

David said they sometimes looked across to the flats (where he lived), to see how many holes in the roof there were. He pointed to a patch of new tiles, said that it had once been a hole, and described

how he had once climbed into the space under the roof to look
through the hole, before it had been mended. David had drawn the
most accurate, most elaborate, most extensive map of all the Notting
Dale kids and had demonstrated a natural aptitude for understanding
the spatial form of his territory. To search out the hole in the roof,
with the realisation that he could look back at the Studio, was
powerful evidence.

"Do you know how these plants got here?" he asked, breaking
in on my thoughts. In front of us, hundreds of little seedlings were
sprouting among the charred remains in the upper section of the
building. "The big plants give seeds. They get blown up here and
when it rains you get all these sprouts. Plants come from other
plants, you know" (his latest discovery about the workings of the
world).

Downstairs once more, David told me he and his friends once
worked for some builders in the Studio, after the fire, stacking up
bricks for fifteen pence a day. "They gave us a pound on the last
day," he said proudly.

He didn't go to the Studio anymore he said because "if the
police find you they'll take your name and address...and also tramps

sleep in there at night sometimes." David's mother told me, "They used to play over there a lot, but not anymore—it's too dangerous." She seemed relaxed about the situation. It didn't seem as if her son was absolutely forbidden to go there, or anywhere else for that matter (including the nearby Union Grand Canal). The building was obviously hazardous and looked as if it would collapse at a moment's notice. Considering the safety objections sometimes raised against adventure playgrounds, it was amazing to find such a shakey structure still standing (presumably with the knowledge of the local authority).

HAUNTED HOUSE

Mill Hill had its share of abandoned buildings because, as in Notting Dale, redevelopment was underway. One of Tracy's favourite places was a vacant house standing in its own grounds. We could get there, she explained, by climbing over the fence from the street, "but the nasty old lady opposite will tell us off. Let's walk round by the front." On the way she told me, "It's been passed around that the house is haunted. I'm scared to go there on my own. I don't believe in ghosts, but there could be nasty men there. It used to belong to a doctor, but he went away and never came back."

The two-story, boarded-up house was surrounded by overgrown gardens. Tracy showed me a small tree they sometimes climbed. She led the way round the back, through an open door. I began to feel uncomfortable, thinking that one of the neighbours would see us' and suspect me of abducting her or something.

In the front room sheets of sunlight squeezed through gaps between the boards. "This is where we decide who's going to do the murder," Tracy said. "We have a long stick and whoever gets touched is dead. Sometimes we play 'murder in the dark,' except it's in the daytime and there's a whole crowd of children, so we don't get too frightened. We spend ages arguing about who's going to go upstairs, it makes you so scared."

Outside once more, Tracy explained that sometimes they picked blackberries and hunted ladybirds in the back garden, "but mostly the boys play there. The girls play on the concrete (the floor of a former garage) with their roller skates—I should have brought mine to show you." The large limb of a tree was laying on the ground in front of the house. Tracy climbed on it and started rocking back and forth. She broke off a few side branches, saying, "I'm always breaking things to make other things out of the pieces. I made a seesaw once...it was a laugh...it was really funny."

CHRIS'S CAMP

Chris took me to a redevelopment site, close to the centre of Tunstall, in the 'backs' of a section of vacant terrace housing. Most of the houses were bricked-up, awaiting demolition. He showed me two that "used to have camps inside, but *they* kept bricking-up the windows so you couldn't get in. Also, the lady with the red door kept complaining—I don't know why; maybe it's because she's the last person living there." He showed me an outhouse that he and his friends had used to store their Guy Fawkes wood. More recently, they had moved it a couple of houses down, he said, "so our enemies can't find it."

Chris in front of his "camp" behind the Greengates potbank (he called it "Wedgewood") in Tunstall.

Chris' drawing of his camp, woodhouse (Guy Fawkes wood store) and entrance gate. Note his enemy's bonfire and the bricked-up windows.

We came to a wooden gate set in a low brick wall. Chris climbed over the gate, opened it from the other side and led me into a small brick-paved yard hidden behind the Greengates Pottery. Clumps of willowherb spattered the ground, growing between the bricks. He opened the door of a small shed with a slate roof. Inside, the space was subdivided by a shoulder-height wall. Chris explained that they were planning to store their Guy Fawkes wood in the first space and to clean up the second space, to meet in. It was going to be their "new camp." They were going to use an old car seat for furniture, with a cupboard that was already there and an old settee which they had stashed somewhere else. Chris said there were seven kids in the gang—all boys between nine and fifteen years old.

THE BRICKERS

This was another of Chris's favourite places: an abandoned brick-works on top of a hill overlooking the neighbourhood, ten minutes walk away.

He introduced the "toilet and office block": a small, broken-down, single-story building overlooking a huge marlhole. We peered in the window at a steel safe where, Chris said, "they used to keep the

Paul and his friend on top of a clay mound at the Brickers, throwing stones onto the corrugated asbestos roof of the old kiln building.

money." He described how he and his friends could get in through a hole in the roof. The building was going to be converted into a clubhouse for the golf course that was being constructed in the vicinity, he thought.

Chris called another building the "power house" and described how the electricity used to hum inside. He showed me the remains of a weighbridge "where they used to weigh the lorries" and some old flood lights, shakily suspended high on a pole, that once illuminated dark winter afternoons.

Paul and his friend took me later to a different section of the Brickers where wild games were possible. The collosal, open-kiln roof of corrugated asbestos cement, supported by a steel frame, had once protected great stacks of 'green' bricks from the weather during firing. The boys scrambled to the top of a twenty-foot mound of clay and began throwing small stones at the sloping roof—aiming for a line of square openings of former skylights. They rarely succeeded; so the stones made a wonderfully resonant clanking sound, as they rolled back down the asbestos.

Building sites could take on the character of an abandoned place, during nonworking hours; especially if security was low. Chris told me about some garages that were being built in the British Rail goods yard, where he and his friends liked to jump off the roofs into a sand pile. They had used "pieces of wood laying around to build camps inside the transport containers parked there.... But now the containers are never left there long enough to make it worthwhile," he added.

Another time, Chris described all the games they had played around a recently completed bungalow—"when the builders were on strike.... We still do a lot of stuff like that," he emphasised. The scattered, small-scale rebuilding underway throughout Tunstall, provided many opportunities to play in half-finished buildings on summer evenings and weekends.

Stevenage still offered a few remaining opportunities—like the "sewer pipes"—but construction was almost complete (until some distant era of "New Town renewal"). There was an initial impression in Stevenage of undeveloped land being conserved between neighbourhoods. However, the large size of both built-up sectors and open land, meant that rough-ground opportunities were located far from the bulk of users. Also, the abrupt demarcation, between built-up sectors and open land, made it easy for parents to limit occasional travel with rules like, "you mustn't go beyond the neighbourhood."

The differences in temporal and spatial character, between the Tunstall and Stevenage landscapes, clearly accounted for great differences in the number of adventure play opportunities they each offered. The many incisions, open wounds and partly healed scars in Tunstall, provided relationships with the landscape rarely available to Bedwell children. Tunstall had a long way to go before it would match Bedwell's tidiness.

Notting Dale still provided adventure play opportunities in a variety of abandoned and decaying quarters, but once new building took over, they would become drastically curtailed by dense multi-story construction and tight autocratic management.

Conserving and creating childhood domains

The child shall have full opportunity for play and recreation which should be directed to the same purposes as education: society and the public authorities shall endeavour to promote the enjoyment of this right.
— United Nations Declaration of the Rights of the Child

8 *Hidden dimensions*

Why did children living a few streets, or even a few doors, from each other have such widely differing patterns of use of their surroundings? As I talked with them, went out with them and interviewed their parents, I realised that each pattern was influenced by a complex set of interlocking factors: relationships with parents, family and friends; television; cultural attitudes in the community (towards private property and appearance, for example); the perception of social and physical hazards in the surrounding environment; the influences of school, youth organizations and other institutions; and, of course, the aptitudes and genetic inheritance of each individual child. Some factors seemed to apply to most children, some to a few. My purpose is to expose aspects of these hidden dimensions that seem relevant to childhood environment policy, ie., the effect of some of the social-ecological factors contained in Figure 1 (p.5).

PERSONALITY

Children exhibited a striking variety of personal styles. Lawrence, for example, took me on an action-packed sequence of visits to abandoned buildings and secluded corners in Notting Dale, simultaneously entertaining me with a string of tales about events, real and imagined, associated with the places we were passing through.

"See that Jamaican man looking at us?," Lawrence suddenly said, while we were looking at the back of a terrace house. "He thinks me and Perry set fire to the curtains of his house, but it wasn't us. I swear it. It was some other boys. He called the police and now he don't like us at all. It's a shame 'cause we've known him for years."

Fact and fiction became intertwined on Lawrence's territorial stage. He and his friends climbed, swung, hid, camped, spied, ambushed, fought battles, escaped—invariably in response to some physical object or attribute of the physical setting: an abandoned building, a garage roof, a weeping willow tree on vacant land, subways under the street. These were the sources of inspiration for Lawrence's storybook of outrageous tales, stimulated by his self-teaching territory—both reinforcing and being reinforced by his aptitude for language.

MILIEU

What if Lawrence had not had access to such a rough-and-ready domain, uncolonized or rather *de*colonized in the process of Notting Dale's redevelopment. What difference did it make to *his* development? What added advantage did he gain by being able to recount his tales to attentive parents? What if his parents had not allowed him freedom to explore, or had mocked his stories? What will kids like Lawrence do when Notting Dale's urban renewal is complete, when the last remaining pieces of Tom Tiddler's Ground[1] are replaced with conventional parks and playgrounds? Will television become the eventual replacement for personal adventure?

David, another Notting Dale explorer, was always on the lookout for something beyond the routine use of his surroundings. He had demonstrated an unusual level of cognitive skill in the accuracy and detail of his drawing. His field trip was much slower and quieter than Lawrence's, but equally rewarding. David was more contemplative, more of a loner. He seemed more involved in his surroundings for their own sake, more appreciative of their sensory impact, expressing in his style of movement unvoiced feelings like, "This is my tree, with its broad dark brown and deeply textured trunk that helps me climb.... This is my pavement with its uneven curb stones that I can balance on and hop along." His self-learning was expressed in sensory awareness and body language rather than verbal dexterity.

David's mother had a kind of laissez-faire philosophy about her son's outdoor escapades (although she was clearly a loving parent). "I leave him to it," she said. "I'm not really afraid, but sometimes I must say I wonder how he survives." As both parents worked, the children were often left to their own devices. David took full advantage of his spatial freedom, but it was evident that he had nothing like the verbal reinforcement at home that Lawrence had. David's mother had a 3R's classroom view of education, so that although she helped David read school texts, she had little knowledge of her son's wealth of experience outdoors and did not see it as a source of verbal exercise. She also showed little recognition of her son's unusual graphic skills, even when I expressed my own enthusiasm.

Heather was another confounder of working-class stereotypes. Her reading level was way above average. On the way to Avondale Park she read aloud, without hesitation, the plaque on the Old Bottle Kiln (a historic monument) opposite the park. She articulated stimulating descriptions about everything around her and expressed great interest in natural phenomena. Her parents had bought her a biology book for Christmas because "that's what she had asked for." Heather called biology her "hobby." Her mother called it her "unusual interest" and seemed to have a clear grasp of her daughter's need for assistance.

Heather made full use of her freedom to explore. On the other hand, she exhibited an unusual degree of social precociousness compared to most other children I worked with. She was just twelve years old, yet wore stockings, high heels and make-up, and made constant references to "boy friends." It seemed as if she was becoming enveloped by the dominant working-class atmosphere of the neighbourhood, leaving less and less time for serious pursuits—unless one of her school teachers could take her future in hand. Her's was a classic case of the bright working-class kid facing inevitable value-conflicts—a situation greatly worsened by the terrible housing conditions: an overcrowded, dark, damp, basement with no room for quiet study.

Tracy, in Mill Hill, did not have those problems. She was an only child and lived in a comfortable renovated back-to-back. Her mother seemed truly in accord with her daughter's experiential needs. "I had a wonderful childhood in the country just outside Stoke," she told me. "I was very happpy and I'm doing my best to bring up Tracy as my mother brought up me." Tracy was the outstanding 'child-environment expert' of the whole study. Not only did she play in the broadest range of places, she demonstrated great verbal skill in describing them. Her mother was unusually reticent about Tracy's gift for language; although, in contrast to Heather's situation, she transmitted a definite sense of upbringing, as related to appearance, manners, doing homework on time and "getting on in the world." The decent house they lived in surely helped.

To emphasise the tremendous range of influence that family background can have on children's use of the outdoors, take the example of Anne who lived just a few streets from Tracy. Anne's parents told me she was allowed to go "just around the block to the shops." The family never went out, except to the Working Men's Club where the parents worked. The family went on holiday each year to the Mediterranean—to Spain or Majorca. Her father proudly told me his daughter had been to Venice, "and had had experiences most children never get." Yet Anne's experience of her immediate neighbourhood was extremely curtailed. My hunch was that she spent most of her time watching T.V., or playing in her front yard, or in Sharon's front yard down the street. Her parents' big fear was "strangers." They really believed their daughter would be abducted if she went far from home.

Anne (and Jane, in Bedwell) represented extreme cases of unreasonable parental restriction, which mercifully did not occur often. But insufficient evidence left key questions unanswered. How much did it matter that some children grew up with such limited territories? Would Anne and Jane transmit the same fears and restrictions to their own children? Was the pattern passed from generation to generation?

Would a child like Jill, who lived in the same neighbourhood as Anne, who had a very different relationship with her parents, who used her surroundings far more extensively, become a different type of parent? Her mother offered me coffee and explained that Jill was "very sensible" and could "obviously take care of herself." She and her husband had grown up in rural surroundings and she recalled walks taken as a child "all over the fields and woods, mushrooming and picking primroses." She wanted Jill to have the same kind of experiences, although it was more difficult now, she said, because they lived "in the city."

Many children had parents who both worked to provide the essentials of life: rent, gas and electricity, food and clothing. Some, like Dawne's parents (who kept a shop in Tunstall), worked long hours, seven-days-a-week. Little time or energy was left over for their children. The situation bothered them a great deal, but it was difficult to pinpoint any ill-effects; maybe this was because Dawne had several close friends to play with in the relatively safe, easily accessible and varied surroundings of her neighbourhood, while her own parents were away.

In examples like this, where both parents worked, or where there was only one parent, children acquired greater freedom for self-directed activity. As long as parents provided a framework of social and spatial limits, and as long as the child lived in a stable, relatively homogeneous community, with access to playmates and diverse surroundings, the trade-off seemed acceptable. If one or more of these conditions were lacking, the negative effects were apparent. For example, the Woods Estate 'tower children' in Notting Dale suffered severe limitations because they lacked direct access to the outdoors—which in turn reinforced apprehension and over-protection among parents.

TELEVISION

Two-thirds of the children said they watched television "more than two hours a day" (Table 9, Appendix C). Over one-third watched it more than three hours a day. Some watched it even longer and said things like "most all the time," "as long as I can," "all day," or "until it goes off."

Additional demands were also made on children's time, too. Most had to help with household chores, a few had paying jobs such as paper rounds, and there was homework to be done. However, according to the interviews, television was the most constant and largest competitor for their time, especially on weekends. During the week, television-watching could happen in the evening and still allow time for after-school outdoor play.

To draw reliable conclusions about relationships between television-watching and children's use of the outdoors would require more study. There is more to the issue than meets the eye. For instance, some of the most expert children, who used the outdoors extensively and were articulate in their descriptions, were also avid television fans. Some even cropped up in the 'more than three hours a day' category.

NEIGHBOURS NICE AND NASTY

Most field trips gave the impression that children were treated with passive toleration by the large majority of unrelated adults they encountered. There were isolated examples of where adults and children had developed a strong rapport—for instance the "nice parkies" in Tunstall Park and the Notting Dale garage proprietor whom Heather had served with cups of tea. There were equally negative examples, too, like the Bedwell lady who shouted at Jenny for trying to reach through the garden fence to get some chalk to play with. There was Brian's example, too: the flat roof of a shed at the end of a neighbour's garden where he used to play before "the new people living there told us to clear off."

Sometimes, adult objections to children's play seemed justifiable, especially in relation to private property. But this was not always the case. Chris had had a rope swing on a large poplar tree on one side of the Tunstall Greenway where he and friends played. "This old man kept cutting the ropes down," he explained. "He has a whole shed full of them...so now we use slipknots and take them away with us" (not a completely negative example, since the old man's behaviour had taught Chris a lesson in ingenuity).

Finding climbable trees was a perennial problem. Dawne and Lisa took me to a couple of Mill Hill poplar trees that Dawne had shown on her drawing. Both girls quickly scrambled up into the spreading branches. In a moment, a lady living in an adjacent house rapped on her window (the trees were actually on her property boundary). The girls descended rapidly and we left in a hurry. They said they usually went there when the lady was not at home and remarked that they could be seen more easily at that time of year because the trees were losing their leaves.

The worst example of unwarranted adult intervention happened at the Bedwell shops while I was talking with Brian and his friends after lunch, on early closing day. Partway through our conversation, a local shopkeeper (who was painting the outside of his shop behind us) turned and said, "What do you want with these bloody kids, they're just a damn nuisance, always coming round here making trouble."

"Hey, have you got any kids, mister?" one of the group responded, in defense.

"You know this man is from the police, taking pictures for the files, don't you," the shopkeeper interjected. Shocked surprise appeared on the kids' faces, portraying a broken trust.

"Don't take any notice of him," I said. "Do you believe him? Do I look like a policeman?"

It was a nasty moment, which I wouldn't have succeeded in rectifying had Brian not been there to vouch for me. Within a couple of minutes their trusting looks returned and our conversation continued. But the unpleasantries of the afternoon did not end there. A few moments later, a middle-aged man pushing his bike past us, reprimanded Brian in a nasty tone. "Hey, you, get your foot off the planter. You'll break the shrubs." In fact, Brian was standing beside the planter barely resting his heel on the corner—quite innocently—not touching any of the plants.

It was no coincidence that these events occurred in the deserted precinct of the shopping centre, where a group of highly visible young people were hanging out. Adults assumed they were up to no good. Although such extremely negative attitudes seemed rare (less than one in ten of the children's dislikes about the outdoors, or their suggestions for change, had to do with negative adults), few such incidents would be needed to build up resentment in young people to the point of retaliatory vandalism.

BOUNDARIES

When children were asked: "Is there anywhere you are not allowed to go?" thirteen percent of the mentions indicated relatively loose geographical control by their parents, with answers such as, "Not really" or, "I go most places." Seven percent of the mentions indicated tight limits such as, "Not too far." or, "I have to stay near the house." A further nine percent indicated neighbourhood-based restrictions, with limits such as "not beyond the street," "not off the estate" or "not out of the neighbourhood" (Table 8, Appendix C).

The largest majority of answers referred to specific places outside the immediate neighbourhood ("the lakes," "the marlhole," "downtown," "the old houses"); less frequently, they referred to general boundaries ("out of the neighbourhood," "across the main road," "off the estate").

Parks and open space, plus several mentions of adventure playgrounds, represented just under a quarter of prohibited places. Other specific places and boundaries, and the crossing of major roads, represented just under another quarter of the mentions. Commercial areas ("shopping centre," "town centre," "next town") accounted for just over a tenth of the mentions. These results give a good sense of the kind of places used as landmarks by children and parents in negotiating territorial limits. They also reflect parental apprehensions about traffic, physical hazards, social threats, and fears about their children getting lost or being abducted.

In reply to the question, "What is the farthest place you've been to alone or just with your friends?" by far the largest number of mentions (nearly half, Table 8, Appendix C) referred to town centres or commercial areas like the West End of London (Figure 23). This indicated the significant 'pull' of commercial places—especially town centres—not only for buying everyday things like sweets, small toys and hobby paraphernalia; but also for window-shopping and making cost-comparisons of more substantial items such as bikes, roller skates, pets, clothes, sports gear, and the latest electronic wizardry. The main attraction of commercial districts like Notting Dale's neighbouring Shepherds Bush market and the crowded town centre of Stevenage (which was especially attractive perhaps because there was no competition), was the intense blend of people and things to be found there. For Notting Dale and Bedwell kids, these centers of social, cultural and economic activity were clear-cut geographic goals—places to hang out, to enjoy the scene and feel part of the community—while at the same time trying to resolve impossible equations between material desire and ability to pay.

Nearly half the commercial centres mentioned related to the "next town" or "another town." These were even more exotic destinations and represented the ultimate *occasional* goals of children travelling alone or with peers, either by bus or occasionally by bike. This was especially true for the Mill Hill kids. They did not find Tunstall centre particularly attractive, but went there mainly to use the swimming baths or to catch buses to other Pottery Towns: Burslem, Hanley, Stoke, Fenton and Longton, as well as to Newcastle-under-Lyme and outlying townships like Kidsgrove. Children said they biked to the small settlements of Knypersley and Mow Cop

23   *Furthest places travelled to alone or with friends.*

Drawn to the same scale.

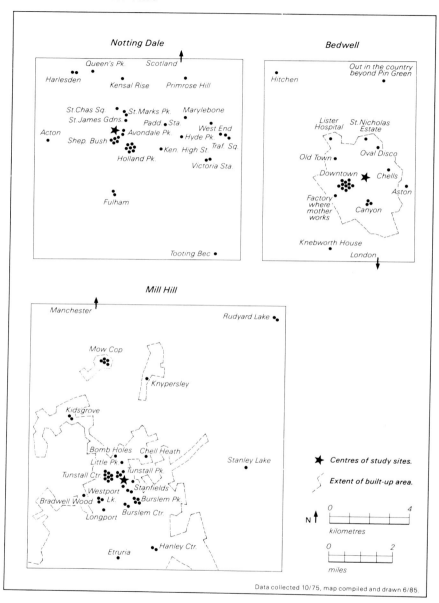

Data collected 10/75, map compiled and drawn 6/85.

202

(Figure 23) both almost four miles (6 kms) north of Tunstall. The latter, an ancient hilltop development, was particularly attractive because of a "castle" that children went to explore and "look at old things," Helen said. A London equivalent of this kind of exploration were trips to famous landmarks like Piccadilly and Trafalgar Square—"we float things in the fountains," David said—and the mainline stations like Paddington, and Victoria with its continental comings and goings. Many of the farthest Notting Dale trips were made to friends and relations by bus and occasionally by tube.

Parks, open spaces and adventure playgrounds, were not only sometimes prohibited places, they were also mentioned about one-in-seven times as the "farthest place travelled to." Holland Park was the most popular Notting Dale destination. In Tunstall, Andrew reported that he sometimes walked to Westport Lakes. He showed me how he sat on the jetty to watch the sailboats on the "big lake" and from the wooden bench by the "small lake," watched the radio-controlled boats.

The remaining scatter of 'farthest places' included extra-special resources like Rudyard Lake, that Paul and Andrew both biked almost ten miles (16 kms) to from Tunstall, to fish (q.v., p.65); and Stanley Lake, a little nearer, where Andrew went, "not to fish" but, as he put it, "just to have a bit of fun." An equivalent Bedwell example was given by Richard, who described biking to Aston (Figure 23) "to catch frogs in the pool under the bridge." These were special expeditions, each with a specific geographic goal usually in mind. Alan had biked to Knebworth House, two and a half miles (4 kms) south of Bedwell; Tracy talked about walking with her friends several times to Etruria, about the same distance south of Tunstall. Some journeys were less goal-orientated and more expressive simply of a desire to get out into the country, "two or three miles beyond Pin Green," Bedwell Brian said, "where we like to climb trees, chew wheat, muck about, and play games."

The most frequently mentioned territorial limits (commercial centres, open space and main roads) and particular special places were also available to parents to use as a framework for territorial negotiations with their children or to mark (temporarily) 'non-negotiable' limits to territorial expansion. Because Gill lived halfway up a Woods Estate tower block, informal access to the outdoors was impossible. With good reason, her parents were so apprehensive and protective they did not allow their daughter to go beyond the estate boundary—clearly defined by its junction with adjacent Victorian terraces and older, low-rise public housing. In other words, no 'margin of negotiation' was available for the gradual expansion of Gill's territory. Instead, she faced the single big hurdle of the estate boundary sometime in the future. At some point Gill would be allowed to go to school on her own and to the park and to the Ladbrook Grove shops, but these watershed events (which had already occurred for most Notting Dale kids) were yet to happen. She seemed already resigned to the situation—which was surely affecting her development—of being trapped on the Woods Estate with its mediocre play environment, terrible microclimate and repressive management.[2]

I came face-to-face with the management myself, at the beginning of the trip with Lawrence. I was accosted by a council employee who demanded that I have a permit to take photographs on council property. Lawrence's parents told me that the man in question bullied kids on the estate. On one occasion they had seen him "destroy a harmless game children had set up with a few pieces of scrap wood and some string."

Two other Notting Dale girls were constrained by parental anxiety. Both lived in Victorian terraces. At least they had access to small 'back' areas they could call their own. Lesley had her grassy "little hill" (p.90). Caroline had her sheltered mews (p.94). Gill's territory offered no such relief.

The Woods Estate had no saving graces as far as I could see. The introduction of creative play leaders and a play centre of some kind would have helped greatly. But the negative physical environment and overt managerial resistance made it easy to imagine the enormous effort that would be required to make anything but a marginal impact on the lives of the children.[3]

The more expansive yet well-defined neighbourhood boundaries of Bedwell provided a more flexible basis for territorial negotiation between children and parents. The main feeder-roads that defined the free-range boundary of Bedwell (Figure 24) enveloped an area of greater diversity than the Woods Estate and, for most children, provided a dividing line between their habitual and frequented territories. Furthermore, the way Stevenage neigbourhoods were laid out seemed to provide a clear system for journey-taking within and between neighbourhoods (although most kids taking advantage of the system were older than those I was working with).

The Woods Estate boundaries were not so provident, primarily because the territory they enclosed did not contain sufficient diversity to satisfy the play needs of large numbers of children.

Clear geographic boundaries were always used by parents and children to define general limits of behaviour. In London, major roads such as the elevated A41 and Holland Park Avenue were used. In Mill Hill, major roads were used, together with Greenways and large areas of open space or derelict land (Figure 24). Carole's mother illustrated the use of Mill Hill boundaries by referring to her own free childhood ("playing in the woods and fields all day") in contrast to the limitations she felt obliged to place on her daughter because of apprehension about strangers. In one direction a main arterial road was used as a permanent boundary. In the other direction no clear-cut permanent limits were set. Mother and daughter worked out a changing set of agreements over the course of time.

Many parents suffered anxiety about their children's outdoor play. The Woods Estate 'tower children' were trapped indoors by the configuration of their surroundings. Bedwell was much better, but still provided a set of dull choices. Tunstall's intimate residential paths and varied spaces gave parents the greatest number of options for negotiating spatial range with their children. In all three sites, the majority of parents succeeded in controlling their fears sufficiently that they did not limit their children's behaviour unreasonably. Whatever the degree of control, children were less likely to suffer harmful consequences if the immediate environment was reasonably diverse and accessible.

Physical barriers such as rail lines, major roads, canals and industrial zones are an inevitable part of the urban scene and serve positive functions such as helping to define neighbourhood indentity. Nonetheless, since such clearly defined boundaries do limit behaviour (reasonably or unreasonably), their *location* should be carefully considered in neighbourhood planning and design.

PARENTAL FEARS

Fear of traffic, fear of strangers and fear of physical hazards were the principal reasons given by children when asked about places their parents did not allow them to visit (Table 10, Appendix C).

A third of the replies mentioned "fast traffic," "too many cars" and "busy streets" as limiting factors on their behaviour. With good

24   *Territorial barriers around study sites.*

Drawn to the same scale as Fig. 23.

Notting Dale

Bedwell

Mill Hill

★   Centres of study sites.

—   Solid barriers: embankments, etc.

– – –   Passable barriers: major roads.

N ↑

0   4
kilometres

0   2
miles

Data collected 10/75, map compiled and drawn 6/85.

reason. According to figures from the Royal Society for the Prevention of Accidents, over forty percent of pedestrians and cyclists killed or injured each year are children, even though they constitute only twenty-three percent of the total population.[4] In other words, children are twice as likely as any other age group to get hit by traffic.

Social threats, particularly 'fear of strangers' (a less tangible and therefore more frightening phenomenon than traffic), accounted for almost one-in-five mentions. Some social threats emanated from "bullies" or "teenagers" who could "beat you up," "steal your money" or "get you in a corner." The significance of this was further emphasised by the fact that "rough kids," "ruffians" and "big boys" were mentioned over one-in-four times as children's greatest dislike about the outdoors (Table 12, Appendix C).

The most common fear for parents was child molesters, who were sometimes imagined lurking practically everywhere. The Bedwell parents of eleven-year-old Jane were so frightened that their daughter would be assaulted that her outdoor territory was restricted to a short length of pavement beside the house. Jane's drawing consisted of a highly detailed rendering of the pavement (p.99), complete with hopscotch chalkings and other markings related to play activities. Details of next door's garden were also included because, as she said,"that's what I can see from my bedroom window" (indicating considerable amounts of time spent gazing out).

Anxiety about 'strangers' was most often expressed with euphemistic phrases, such as, "You never know these days." or "There's some pretty weird characters around here." Occasional remarks were made about "discos" and "pubs" as places where undesirables hung out. Sometimes references were made to newspaper reports of crimes against children. Most commonly, a kind of general apprehension was expressed that a child could be lost or carried-off and never seen again—sentiments that one might feel for a highly-prized possession. Children themselves mostly did not seem fearful but simply referred to the fear of their parents as a reason for not playing somewhere; or it was the reason why they had to say where they were going; or it was why they had to be home by a certain time.

The most serious consequences of the 'fear of strangers' were the unreasonable territorial constraints imposed by some parents. A larger-scale study would be required to find out the true extent of this kind of situation, but the fact that several cases turned up in such a small sample is indicative of an issue that should be investigated further. A particularly pertinent aspect was that girls were more heavily controlled than boys—in both the general growth of their territory as well as the severity of prohibition in the use of certain kinds of places. The effect of this double standard was clearly indicated by the difficulty I encountered in finding as many 'expert' girls as boys in all three study sites.

Besides traffic and 'strangers,' parents fear of physical hazards such as water, abandoned buildings and high elevations, were mentioned almost one-in-five times as reasons why certain places or activities were prohibited. Again, children themselves did not seem irrationally fearful and were generally realistic in their assessments of hazards.

This observation would not be so true of younger children, whose knowledge of their surroundings is not so well developed. It is also important to note that all children have accidents, especially accidents that result from the unforeseen consequences of poorly designed or badly maintained play equipment—an issue that has been well-publicized in recent years. The collection and publication of injury statistics relating to the full range of environments used by children—including traffic accidents, drownings and accidents in the home—would be very helpful in reducing the gap between parental imagination and statistical fact. Take the frequency of drownings for example. Surely the level of actual occurrence (excluding seaside accidents) would never justify the level of apprehension some parents feel about water play. Philip, for example, was allowed to roam to most places in Bedwell, except to the lakes in Fairlands Park, because of his mother's fear of drowning. She admitted it was due partly to the fact that she could not swim.

NEGOTIATING TERRITORIAL LIMITS

In order to reconcile their own apprehensions with their children's developing desire and ability to travel farther afield, parents engaged in a continuous process of renegotiating permitted boundaries—similar to the descriptions given by Roger Hart for New England families.[5] He found that permissions varied according to whether trips were taken alone, with other children or with another adult. The sex of the child, the characteristics of the territory under negotiation and the extent of the parents' firsthand knowledge of it, were further significant factors in both Hart's study and the one reported here. The studies by both Björklid and Holme and Massie shed further useful light on the complex nature of these and other social factors that influence children's territorial behaviour.[6]

In the most successful examples of negotiation, both parties engaged in a frequent reconsideration of permitted limits in both space and time—somewhere between what was already accepted by the parent (usually the mother) and the new extension hoped for by the child. Take the example of Woods Estate Lawrence. His parents allowed him considerable spatial freedom and had recently given him a bicycle—making it easier for him to escape the boring surroundings of the estate. His parents noted a couple of major arterial streets in their interview as the new boundaries of Lawrence's 'bike range.' However, he took me far beyond these presumed boundaries and it was done in such a matter-of-fact way, I felt he sensed that his parents knew that the boundaries were being transgressed.

This difference between stated rule and actual behaviour provided an added margin of security for the parents, as well as an added sense of autonomy for the child. In other words, there was an implicit understanding that the rules were not quite as tight as the negotiated agreement indicated. In any case, beyond a certain age (that varies greatly) there comes a point where the child doesn't really care about territorial rules; at which point, parents cannot do much about enforcement.

Less successful cases of negotiation resulted in polarized, child-adult tension: between the child trying to push the boundaries as much as possible and the parents trying to hold back as much as possible. Take the case of Lesley in Notting Dale. At one level there seemed to be a close understanding between mother and daughter. Lesley's drawing was an accurate expression of her play world. It showed a happy association with Avondale Park. It was an important place to her, and she had recently been given permission to go there on her own. However, I discovered by accident that she had secretly expanded her territorial limits well-beyond the formal agreements with her mother. As I was leaving the flat with Lesley to photograph her "hill," her mother asked if she could read the transcript of her daughter's interview which was laying on the table. Without reflection I said yes.

Thus her mother discovered that Lesley went to Holland Park with a thirteen-year-old friend, something which she was clearly not allowed to do. It was an embarrassing moment because it was obvious to Lesley that I had betrayed her. I tried to explain myself to her mother. I think she understood and accepted my point of view (hopefully avoiding unpleasant repercussions after I left). In this example it seemed to me that there was too much of a lag between the child's knowledge of her own capabilities and her mother's assumptions about them. Lesley and her mother lived alone. Earlier in the interview her mother had spoken movingly about allowing her daughter more spatial independence. Although she felt it necessary for her daughter to learn to cope with the world, she found it difficult to release the reins. This overly-tight margin of negotiation then forced Lesley into a deceitful territorial expansion well beyond her mother's limit of psychological comfort.

In the majority of cases, an open and reasonable compromise—between the child's urge to explore and intolerable levels of parental anxiety—seemed to prevail. Simon, for example, was given plenty of freedom by his parents. Their major fear was that he would get picked up by strangers. He could go to the Bomb Holes, but not the "big marlhole"—it was considered "too dangerous." He could go to Tunstall town centre and to Westport Lakes—"about once a month to look at the swans with an older cousin." He was allowed to spend hours at a time in Tunstall Park. His parents said he was "not allowed to go *too* far away" (i.e., compared to existing permissions) and always had to give his destination and time of return before leaving the house.

MOTHERS AND FATHERS

Simon was one of a minority of cases where the setting of territorial limits was decided jointly with both parents. In most cases limits were more likely set by mothers, although this impression may have been exaggerated because I was able to conduct so few interviews with fathers—they simply were not around the house (in itself expressing a difference in parental role). Mothers nearly always seemed more knowledgeable about their child's territory. While fathers were at work, mothers had taught their children how to deal with an expanding environment in shopping trips, on journeys back and forth from school, and on visits to parks and playgrounds. Tracy told me how her mother had taught her the highway code before she was allowed to cross the busy street outside their house in Tunstall. "Then, when I was eight-and-a-half," she said, "Mum let me go on my own; but for quite a while, she watched from the front windows, to make sure I was doing it right."

Because they were more knowledgeable about their child's outdoor play, mothers tended to be less apprehensive and more discriminating about the strengths and weaknesses of their offspring's ability to deal with their surroundings. An exception to this general rule was a case where the mother herself had suffered a traumatic experience as a child.

Fathers seldom acquired knowledge of their child's whole territory. More likely it was limited to a few places of special male interest, such as football pitches and fishing spots shared with sons. There were no equivalent place-connections between fathers and daughters (who remained even more exclusively in the company of their mothers). Whereas mothers might express anxiety about a specific street-crossing, or an unused corner of the park, fathers expressed more general and pervasive fears, reflecting their lack of knowledge about their child's territory and her/his ability to cope with it. Thus fathers, who as boys more than likely experienced a more diverse and extensive play environment, helped, ironically, to perpetuate the more severe territorial limitations of daughters.

The difference between mothers' and fathers' perceptions had special significance in cases where fathers dominated family decision making and thus overruled more knowledgeable and discriminating mothers on territorial questions. Paul's father reflected on the great amount of freedom he had had as a child growing up in a small village outside Tunstall; yet he expressed greater concern than Paul's mother about their son's security outdoors.

Some fathers made a sharp distinction between "playing" and "learning," especially with regard to their son's education and future career. Philip's father for instance expressed little interest in his son's play (his daughter's was never mentioned), compared to his firm attitude about "getting on well in school." At the same time, he spoke playfully about his own "archaeological interest" in things he unearthed at work as a cable layer.

An obvious issue is raised here. It is men rather than women who have largely decided the form of cities, the layout of neighbourhoods and the design of housing—with little regard for the needs of mothers and children. Yet historically, it is women rather than men who have carried the burden of caring for young children and who, as a result have developed a fuller understanding of children's play and its environmental requirements. The general movement of women back into the workforce and their more rapid employment after childbirth, is helping to shift childcare responsibility in other directions—towards fathers certainly, but also towards other childcare settings that are still largely run by women. An equitable distribution of responsibility between the sexes is still far from being achieved.

Gaps and discontinuities still persist in these shifting systems of responsibility that leave children without adequate care. Consequently, they depend more on their nonhuman surroundings for developmental support. Yet environmental design decisions are still more likely to be made by male professionals, still more than likely with less understanding of children's needs than their female colleagues.

SPECIAL TRIPS

Children who did not yet have permission to go alone to the local park, or to downtown, or to cross the main roads around their neighbourhood, could feel confident that permission would eventually be granted. Maybe they had already made trips there with their parents, or with older siblings, or with other family members; or perhaps they had friends who already had.

Caroline's Notting Dale territory was bounded by two busy streets which parents and daughter had agreed were the current boundaries (south and west). To the east was the mews behind her house, used as a day-to-day, habitual play space. North led away from Notting Dale towards Bayswater, the next closest commercial centre. The route was explored by Caroline and a group of friends each week on their Saturday morning walk to the "pictures" at the Bayswater Odeon. The fact that Caroline was allowed to make such a lopsided extension to her territory indicated her parents' willingness, as time went on, to negotiate other appropriate extensions.

Other children mentioned "going to the cinema" or "to the pictures." Others, still, organised picnic trips to the local park or further afield. These were repeated special events, tied to known locations during specific time periods. Parents thus felt comfortable with them as extensions of everyday turf. Church-related trips served a similar role. Tracy reported her Sunday school trip in detail, saying that she "played around the church, swinging on a big pipe." She also men-

"My mum takes me and a friend to St. Mark's Park sometimes,"
Sandra said, "and we have a picnic on the grass." The illustration is
from Sandra's drawing

Picknick

tioned that the church was next to Burslem Park, where she went to
play before and after Sunday school. As a result, she was the only
Mill Hill child who knew about the special attractions of Burslem
Park: myna birds, swans, the waterfall, and pony rides.

Swimming pools (including summer paddling pools) were the
most frequently mentioned community facility. Swimming was
especially popular in Notting Dale, where a new pool had been built
near the centre of the neighbourhood. It was highly prized—an important sign of positive change in a community torn apart by a
decade of urban renewal.

Watching football games at the local field or at more distant
stadia was mentioned with regularity—but only by boys, who usually went with their fathers, older brothers, or other male relations.

Other types of community facilities were introduced on several
field trips. Philip took me to the Stevenage Museum, where he said

he had been a couple of times with his mum. The museum was on the periphery of Stevenage Town Centre and could be reached via the walkway network from Bedwell. Philip looked around and pointed out things of interest about the history of the area. He also went to the nearby County Library and remarked that he would have used the museum and library more often if they had been nearer his home or if he had been allowed there on his own.

Caroline took me to a place near her house where she came after school with her Notting Dale friends "to dance and play games." It was called the Lancaster Club and was housed in a single-story building set back from the street. Unfortunately it was closed the afternoon we went there. Caroline was obviously disappointed. Just down the street was the public library. As we walked past Caroline said she only went to the library on Friday afternoons—with her class—and never on her own or with friends. Maybe, unlike Philip, her parents didn't encourage her; or perhaps the sedate, bookish atmosphere of the library wasn't appealing, or was too strongly associated with 'school.'

Cultural facilities available to Notting Dale children included the Commonwealth Institute. It was sometimes mentioned as a favourite place, even though situated across the other side of Holland Park, far from the neighbourhood (Figure 6, p.26). The building itself was striking: a bulging parabolic roof and flags of the Commonwealth Countries lined-up in front. As we entered the forecourt, Ricky showed me the "wishing well"—an elongated shallow pool with coins scattered on the cement bottom. He said he liked the Institute because it was warm inside and there were all kinds of things to look at. We walked slowly around the open-plan, multilevel interior, looked at models of native dwellings from Canada and handicrafts from India, and went to the theatre to see a film about African wildlife.

Ricky's favourite spot was the West Indian section where, by pressing a button, he could see a filmclip about the Jamaican Carnival projected on a small screen set in the wall. For a few moments his fascination was captured by the steel band and brightly-coloured costumes of the parade. Ricky told me his family was from St. Vincent and that he had arrived in England when he was a year old. The attraction of the Carnival was not difficult to understand. I reflected on Ricky's situation, thinking, on the one hand, how nice to be able to walk in off the street for a few moments exposure to his cultural heritage; and on the other hand, how sad that it was reduced to a push-button secondary experience. I wondered if the Institute staff were aware of kids like Ricky and whether they encouraged participation by children in the Institute's programmes. Ricky said he had been there a couple of times with his teacher who also was West Indian.

Heather was another of the few children who mentioned school trips to special places. She talked about a trip to a nature centre outside London with great excitement. It was the only example anyone described in detail.

Apart from parks and swimming pools, community facilities were mentioned so rarely it is difficult to imagine them having a substantial influence. The low rate of mention could have been for three possible reasons: lack of provision, difficulty of access, or lack of personal interest. The study sample was too small to draw firm conclusions. Even so, access difficulties rather than lack of interest seemed more likely. Organizations such as the Brownies, Cub Scouts, youth clubs and schools—which could provide access and encourage interest—were rarely mentioned. Nonetheless, an impression was reaffirmed that community facilities and community organizations had little memorable impact on children's lives. Considering the extent to which adult concern for children's leisure and learning is almost entirely channeled through specialised facilities and programmes—rather than opportunities for self-directed play—an important issue is raised.

WEEKEND VISITS

Weekend trips and visits to special places were made with parents and other family members, thereby extending territorial limits. The most common were shopping expeditions to local downtown areas, that many children would not have made alone.

"Visiting our relatives" was regularly mentioned as a special weekend activity. Notting Dale children visited relatives who had "moved out farther west," into less congested areas of London. Bedwell families said they made regular visits to relatives who still lived in central London. In some ways, children may have benefited from this scattering of traditionally homogeneous communities. Now, instead of visiting grandparents, uncles and aunts everyday, down the street, trips were made on special weekends, to new places full of surprises.

In Mill Hill, extended-family trips were less common because the community still maintained a closeknit working-class social network. It had not yet been disrupted by rapid regional economic development, or by high levels of car ownership or by rising affluence. Some Mill Hill children mentioned weekend visits to see friends, "where we used to live" (reflecting the impact of a rehousing programme that had been underway for years, to replace back-to-backs with Corporation estates). But the overall impact of urban renewal on traditional Tunstall lifestyles did not seem substantial.

In all study areas, besides occasional visits to see relatives (by car, bus or train), family recreational trips were rarely taken. It was hard to see these families as part of the much heralded 'new age of leisure.' Most parents had to work hard, for long hours, to meet basic everyday needs. Little time or money was left for relaxation. Notting Dale families mentioned occasional trips to Hyde Park, to the Serpentine, to other London parks, and to exhibitions and museums. In Stevenage, stately homes, country parks and particular lakes were mentioned. Even when families said they made an effort to get out on weekends, it seemed to happen only two or three times each summer. Sometimes, annual family holidays or youth organization camps provided an important extension to the child's everyday turf. Caroline's family went to Ireland every year. Jill's mother said they liked to moor their canal boat and "go for long walks...and explore churches, museums and stately homes." For most children such holidays were a rare event, if they happened at all.

PUBLIC TRANSPORT

Buses, trains and the London Underground were important for one-in-seven children as a means to extend their territory—especially on weekends (Table 6, Appendix C). The significance of public transport was reinforced by the number of children who answered "next town" or "another town," when asked for the "farthest place travelled to alone or with a friend." Buses were most popular. They provided a frequent service, close to home. The routes had closely-spaced stops and passengers could maintain visual contact with their surroundings. Trains and the Underground lacked this immediacy. Only two or three Notting Dale children actually were allowed to use the Underground. Parents saw it as a far more risky venture than bus travel. From the child's point of view, the greater distances between stations meant that the Underground (and all fixed-rail systems for that matter) did not fit their normal territorial needs so well. It was good for occasional trips, however.

TRAVELLING COMPANIONS

Few children were allowed to ride the buses alone. Many went with a companion—usually an older brother, sister, cousin, or close friend trusted by parents. David's mother told me her son had been on 'Red Rover' trips (using a special weekend unlimited-travel ticket) with his older brother because, "they get on well together." Trips to unusual places, whether by public transport or not, most often required an older companion, especially for events such as football games where crowds were gathered. To be trusted, companions usually had to be family members. This seemed equally true in Notting Dale's strong ethnic enclaves, in Tunstall's traditional working-class community and to a surprising degree in emigré Bedwell. In matters of child care and supervision, family relationships were extremely signifi-cant. The role of older sisters and brothers as protectors, guides and teachers was a critical factor in helping younger children extend their territorial boundaries and encounter new experiences.[7]

9   *Environmental change*

People and environments are interdependent. Each reflects the other. The social history of cities, accumulated in their buildings and spaces, can be highlighted and conserved, or torn down and squandered, during each cycle of development and redevelopment. Old values may be supported and/or new ones introduced, depending on how trade-offs between economics and social needs are managed and the degree to which inhabitants are involved in the process.

This book has been concerned with identifying opportunities for supporting children's development in the physical environment, so that children's needs can be given more emphasis in the process of managing urban change. Yet many aspects of people-environment relations are essentially cultural phenomena— impossible to codify as truths for all time and all situations. Hence the comparative approach used here, of looking at children's use of their surroundings in three contrasting neighbourhoods. In this chapter the cultural and political aspects of environmental change are discussed, including the views of the children themselves.

EXISTING CONDITIONS

At one extreme was Stevenage, a new settlement deliberately planned to meet human needs; a rationally ordered, pleasantly modulated environment; a model solution for keeping the automobile in its place.

On the negative side, little was left to chance—open to the influences of neighbourhood residents or the vagaries of nature. Each neighbourhood had been built as a self-contained unit during a relatively short period of time, leaving no raggedness, no raw edges, no wildness. This impression was partly due to the pristine appearance of the immature landscape; which, with the passage of time, would undoubtedly acquire more richness and variation—but still, only within ecological limits predetermined by design. If only something had been allowed to go to seed occasionally, to counteract the uniformly tidy appearance. A little ecological anarchy needed to be set in motion to stimulate children's exploration.

While Stevenage was congratulating itself for having created a spacious, culturally progressive, clean twentieth-century image, Tunstall was partway through a massive tidying-up of the antithesis: a messy, decaying nineteenth-century legacy. The unintentional landscape of Tunstall, with its haphazard intermingling of built and unbuilt land, had been historically determined by the location of mineral deposits and the need to house workers and factories close together. But since the late sixties a cycle of deliberate change had been imposed, to transform the chaos, dirt and decay into what the local newspaper had dubbed a "garden city." As a consequence, many physical reminders of the city's formative era had been removed.

Notting Dale had some of Tunstall's character, though more subdued, since industry and housing had not been so intimately associated. Both were old, physically complex environments that had undergone many cycles of growth, decay, conservation and renewal. As a result, both provided a greater diversity of play opportunities than Bedwell's carefully planned surroundings. The richness of traditional children's games was particularly noticeable in Mill Hill, where the number of times they were observed and mentioned by children contrasted strongly with their sparseness in Bedwell.[1]

In Notting Dale, the recently redeveloped sections stood in sharp contrast to the old areas of intimate Victorian terraces and early estates. Advanced building technology, in the hands of centralized government, had transformed the scene with massive blocks of flats. It was a simple, orderly solution, conceived by planners and political leaders unconcerned about human consequences: the disintegration of a culture that had evolved during centuries of street life and close-knit neighbourly relations.

Against this historical backdrop of new and old environments, children's desires for change were modest—if they existed at all. When asked the question: "What would you like to see added or changed in the outdoors," a third of the children answered: "I don't know." This sizeable group either did not understand the point of the question (even when prompted) or could not conceive of changing the conditions that they were so used to. They had learnt to accept reality—with a working-class 'know thy place' outlook—not to question it.

It is provocative to note that when the identical question was asked of a similar sample of Northern California children, very few had nothing to say—possibly reflecting a more pronounced self-expressive cultural style. Or perhaps it reflected the American habit of constantly evaluating material existence, versus a British habit of resignedly accepting things the way they are: an intriguing cultural difference. Only two British children said *everything* in their outdoor environment was okay. One said indoors was preferable.[2]

For the British children, the largest number of proposed changes and additions were for new resources like "football stadium" and "hut to camp in." The majority related to play equipment and facilities (Table 13, Appendix C). This suggests that children attached most importance to official play-places, even though (in the interviews) playgrounds and play structures were mentioned explicitly only one-in-sixteen times as favourite places. This difference—between suggestions for the future and response to existing conditions—indicates a need for improved quality in both new and old facilities.

Natural resources such as "bushes," "flowers," "trees," "animals" and "water" were mentioned in more than half the replies. Specific suggestions were made, to "plant better conker trees" and " put a little zoo in the park." Requests for animals or animal-related facilities were small compared to the level of interest that children showed for pets and small animals during the field trips. Perhaps it reflected a lack of understanding that urban wildlife can be increased by improving shelter conditions and food supplies.

Few references were made to climatic factors. This again should not be interpreted as a lack of interest. Most children realized the impossibility of asking for year-round summer weather, yet they did not consider microclimate as something changeable. Field trip comments about phenomena such as "warm spots" indicated an awareness of microclimatic factors. But children didn't understand that microclimate could be deliberately modified by design. Climate modification, vegetation establishment and urban wildlife conservation are gaps in knowledge that could be remedied through environmental education: a worthwhile step that would help children turn a more critical eye towards the quality of their local surroundings.

Some children were well-aware that other aspects of their surroundings could be changed, and made suggestions such as "get rid of the cars on my street," "bring the library nearer," "put more stuff in the park," "make streets smoother for roller-skating" and "make a place for horse riding." The bulk of suggestions were for small, inexpensive changes. Unfortunately, there was insufficient time to probe the reasons why some children could readily imagine changes and additions, while others could not.

If the study had had a stronger environmental education emphasis, a more extensive list of desired changes would have most likely resulted. But to what degree should children be educated to propose change or, on the other hand, to appreciate the status quo? Too much emphasis on change could discount present values and lead to cynicism from unfulfilled expectations. Yet many changes made to the environment are not in the best interest of children. They must therefore be educated to appreciate the gamut of political, economic and social dimensions of change and taught to discriminate between positive and negative costs and benefits.

IN WHOSE INTERESTS?

Brian's mother summed up her perception of Bedwell. "There used to be some lovely bits of waste ground around here...they're nearly all gone now...even Marat Farm will be part of the park soon." She went on to explain how she grew up in rural Essex, had spent her holidays on a family farm, and as a result valued indigenous, unmanicured landscapes. She pointed to her own back garden and said, as if apologising, "it's so untidy, but it's good for wildlife and ecology...what else can I do?" Parental sentiments such as this were not usually expressed in Bedwell (or anywhere else for that matter). However, similar questions were raised by children at every turn in Tunstall, since most of them had grown up amid the many changes wrought to their surroundings by the City's landscape reclamation programme. The more articulate conveyed a sense of the contrast, in terms of their own values, between current and bygone conditions. Jill told me how the Greenway near her home had been "better the way it used to be...after the trains stopped running...before it got changed.... It was longer grass before. We built camps all over and rode our bikes up and down the hills."

Jill's mother agreed that it had been more interesting for the children, but "also more dirty." Then she commented, "On the other hand, all this work has improved the city no end. It's unrecognizable. Look at the nice view we have now." She gestured towards the green sweep of reclaimed land behind their house, extending up to Clanway Hill. "It'll be perfect, once they clear the 'brickworks' off," she observed. The gaunt remains of the Brickers' old kiln building (Paul's special place) were clearly outlined. Admittedly it was a blemish on the skyline, even if one appreciated industrial architecture.

Although Jill's mother was well aware of her daughter's play environment and recognized the negative impact of reclamation, she also expressed a keen desire for the more attractive surroundings that were beginning to replace dereliction and decay. Their house had overlooked the blackened remains of old railway sidings for so many years that, understandably, she valued the improved view more highly than her daughter's lost play opportunities.

There can be no argument against reclamation in principle. Reservations stem from the insensitive way it had been carried out in some cases. A large proportion of Tunstall's derelict land was a dull and useless mess which everyone wanted cleaned up. But mixed-in were specific places that were (or had been) highly attractive to both children and other age-groups in the community.

"We used to play 'scramble' where the railway lines met," Simon said. "There used to be a bridge, but they took it down because it was collapsing. There used to be hills and banks. We made lots of camps. We had a special one on a hill that looked like an upturned cup. We used to have a lookout and played cops and robbers before it was changed." I asked what improvements could be made. "They should get lots of lorries full of soil and dump it and make more hills with tall banks and grass to hide in, again."

We turned down an unpaved road into a small area being cleared for redevelopment. Beyond was a group of old garages overlooking the Greenway. "We play hide-and-seek around them," Simon said. "There's lots of places to hide in-between. You can get up on the roofs if you're good enough.... They're taking them down now, because they keep falling on to the Greenway." I asked what he thought would happen after the buildings were removed. "They'll probably just level it off with more grass."

Back home, Simon's dad sketched his own picture of change. "When I grew up, it was all fields around here.... Trains used to stop at Tunstall Station. Then houses were built in the fields and the railway was turned into a Greenway." His feeling was that the reclamation work had been the "greatest thing since they discovered coal. I saw a big discussion about it on telly," he said. "They reckoned the reclamation programme had been a godsend...and the city was going to be one of the most modern in Britain before long."

He thought the old rail line had been dangerous, but Simon's mother interjected, "I used to play up at Pitts Hill Station. It was an exciting place. No one ever got hurt—except a deaf man who was killed by a train one day." We debated the issue for a while, but it wasn't an easy conversation. Eventually the father admitted that "maybe places like the Bomb Holes are special and should be retained."

"My son still plays football in the street," he went on, "even though they have all that grass down on the Greenway. In the end the kids'll have no choice. As more people get cars they won't be able to play in the street anymore. It's already very busy around here. In the summer, kids have nowhere to go. They should keep the schools open. They chase kids out of the park for collecting conkers, but they're not doing any harm."

Here was a parent with mixed perceptions about what was going on. His ideas for using the schools for recreation during the summer, and for changing the park rules, expressed concern for his son's welfare, yet he did not see the possibility of making reclaimed areas more relevant to his son's needs. He spoke so freely about playing in the fields when he was young, yet at the same time projected a narrow football-playing image on his 'play expert' son. He numbered among several parents who had difficulty transposing the qualities of their own childhood landscapes to present day conditions.

Simon's father communicated such a pervasive sense of inevitability, that nothing could be done, that an anonymous "they" was in command. The idea that design policy could be influenced, or at least questioned, never entered consideration. So to the final question: Will Simon grow up any different, any less forgetful of all he once knew about his surroundings? How is it that people forget or revalue this childhood wisdom, as they grow up? Is it an inevitable function of the human psyche?[3] Does it happen in all societies? Or does it stem from a working-class sense of powerlessness—whereby people feel they cannot take responsibility and control over their own lives and those of their children—believing that such matters are in the hands of experts who know best, who speak in ways hard to understand?

Technically speaking, there was no reason why reclamation had to be such an all-or-nothing affair. The 'greening' of the city could still have been dramatic, while at the same time retaining and/or enhancing the landscape qualities relevant to young people and other groups. One difficulty that does arise, in meeting children's environmental needs, is the different scale of experience and perception of children, compared to adults. It is an issue that applies particularly to policy-makers and planners, who inevitably must focus on the broader perspective of city and regional development. Since human perception and landscape values are interdependent, ways must be found to appreciate urban landscapes beyond their surface appearances, to see their deeper connections to human development

Tracy's marlhole provided an ideal muse on this question. After the trip, I remember thinking to myself, supposing such a place had been created naturally instead of as a by-product of industry. Supposing there was only one such hole in the whole of Tunstall, or in the whole of Stoke-on-Trent? If so, it would surely have been preserved and protected as a unique natural feature—with kids excluded from the "site of special significance." But because it was "just another marlhole," among dozens scattered throughout the city, it was not highly regarded. Yet for Tracy it was the kind of feature that every neighbourhood should have—a special habitat, where life could flourish, where special things could happen.

A constant threat is directed at these anonymous childhood places, that they will be filled-in or levelled-off. Ironically, preservation would probably be far more likely if they contained a threatened species of rare plant or animal, instead of our own human progeny.

On the other side of Mill Hill, Chris demonstrated (like Tracy), a high quality relationship with his surroundings. By inventing his own naming system for special places, he provided a perfect example of true territorial possession. We climbed down into a vast, partly-overgrown, abandoned marlhole below the Brickers, and came to a small rush-covered pond. It was the "number-one newting pond," Chris said. A few yards farther on we came to "number-two." He said it had once been "very good, with lots of pond weed. Newts and water insects used to live in it"; but now, it was "half dried-up." Chris explained that there were eight ponds altogether and that six of them had "numbers in order of goodness." Next in line was "number-three." It was good for chucking stones and broken bricks into. Then there were three more, in decreasing order.

The two top ponds had extra-special names, Chris explained. He showed me one called "Ex-Queenie": a body of clear bluish water, with a clump of rushes growing at one end. It was called "Ex-Queenie" because it was "the next best after 'Queenie'—the best pond." I asked where "Queenie" was. "Way over there," Chris said, pointing to a couple of giant earth-scrapers moving back and forth against the skyline, off in the distance. "Queenie had had everything," he said, "frogs, toads, newts and tadpoles, but it's probably filled-in by now.... They're going to turn the whole place into a golf course," he explained. "They're flattening it all out. They're going to fill the marlhole.... See them getting nearer? Soon they'll be up to here and we won't be able to play no more. We won't have nowhere to go. They've already 'seeded' half of it. Sometimes we go over to the hill where you can look down on the scrapers zooming around underneath you." (The advancing scrapers were shown on his drawing.)

When children invent their own toponyms (place names), it indicates a degree of proprietorship that can only happen when adult culture does not dominate the scene too heavily. Children need landscapes that are open to creative verbal interpretation, not ones limited by simplistic environmental change that overlooks the history, language and culture embodied in our physical surroundings. Such embodiments can be remarkably resilient. When I came to write up Chris's "roller-coaster place" (described on p.69), I suddenly recalled that I had photographed a short, steep, go-cart ramp near the same spot, while surveying the site six years earlier (before reclamation had begun). Bulldozers had, in the meantime, reconstructed the whole area. Its appearance has been dramatically altered, and yet the play tradition in this spot had survived, to be passed from one childhood generation to the next. Who will ensure the conservation of nameable places in Tunstall and other 'old town' landscapes? Will Chris, or Tracy, or Simon, or the others, raise objections to the elimination of the toponymy of their youth, when they reach adulthood? Will they attempt to conserve it for their own children? Or will they merely 'give permission' for its use (if any of it remains by then) as their own parents did? Arguably, I suppose, one could let such a toponymically-rich landscape disappear, on the grounds that it is used only by a minority of children and that future generations will inevitably adapt their play to a different-yet-equal environment. Maybe concern should be centered instead on the quality of the close-to-home environment of the majority of children, where needed improvements are more obvious, here the impact on behaviour would be more visible. Better still, why not attend to both these policy extremes—and everything in between.

BACKLASH

Chris remarked that "all the places I like to play are disappearing...the camps in the old houses...the ponds up the Brickers." He seemed acutely aware of what was happening, literally before his eyes. His attitude conveyed resigned acceptance of the all-powerful "they," who were taking his territory piece-by-piece. I shared his sense of powerlessness existentially, feeling the relentless inevitability of it all; and yet, I thought, there must be an alternative way to proceed. At the very least, children's participation must be encouraged so that their values can be incorporated on behalf of future generations.

Many smaller, close-to-home, rough-ground areas in Tunstall had already been converted to mown grass. With continuance, one might have expected damaging activities to shift to other open spaces, or to shift back to the reclaimed areas themselves—where former freedoms were no longer accommodated. For instance, down on the banks of the Tunstall Greenway, where the soil was particularly thin, groups of kids had started to burrow into the side of the hill to rediscover the archaeological remains of what had once been there:

bits of pottery, machinery parts, and miscellaneous junk. Many brickbats and piles of uninteresting rubbish were also uncovered and spewed down the bank on to the footpath and bikeway. It was a mess. And yet if it had happened in an unreclaimed area, say up on the Grogs, in the long grass and weeds, it would have not bothered anyone.

This type of damage could be regarded as attempts to re-establish older patterns of creative behaviour. In other cases, the attacks were more willful. In some of the newly reclaimed areas of dull topography and mown lawn, the top of every 'standard' tree had been broken off. These nursery products, with their long spindly trunks and small crowns of foliage, were planted in scattered groups, surrounded by acres of lawn. Their chance of survival was slender because they provided the only source of differentiation and interest in an otherwise bland landscape. Sticking conspicuously out of the ground, they inevitably attracted attention. There was no intervening vegetation to provide a transition between mown grass and tree tops. Such a landscape looked pretentious, trying to be a park too soon, rather than looking like an immature landscape, evolving in its own time.

Chris described with exhilaration the time he rolled an old tyre down the hundred-foot Brickers' cliff and watched it pummel with a great splash into one of his ponds—the kind of thrill that children seek the world over. Like many Tunstall children, he had strong relationships with what many adults would consider "degraded" surroundings. For children like Chris they provided special opportunities for adventure play, seldom found in more conventional park settings and tidy residential sectors.

Chris was at the apex of childhood. His understanding parents allowed him considerable territorial autonomy and he did not feel he abused the privilege. Some of the things he did, like messing around in old houses, could have been construed as being near or beyond the margin of the law. But he did not like to feel they were illegitimate. They were not done to challenge adult authority, but rather for the intrinsic quality of the experience itself, to fulfill the need to explore, to interact with and learn from his surroundings.

Children and other members of the community will lose important recreational opportunities unless their landscape values are represented in the decision-making process. The issue seems equally pertinent to 'old town' renewal, New Town development and suburban growth. In each situation there is a need to deliberately conserve parts of the landscape and/or increase the possibilities for manipulative interaction. If not, children will do it for themselves as "vandals."[4] If opportunities to exercise natural aggression toward the environment cannot be found, children will be forced into situations where the results of their actions will not be tolerated by the adult community.

EVOKING A SENSE OF HISTORY

Tunstall seemed to be gaining a new image at children's expense. In their eyes, the derelict landscape contained a rich language of meaning in the pervasive Victorian buildings and industrial bric-a-brac. If just a few of these artifacts were left in place—protected and softened by long grass—kids could absorb a feeling for their historical roots and grow up with an intuitive feeling for their birthplace. Why did their dads have injured backs? Why did grandfathers die from 'black lung'? What did mothers do in the pot banks everyday? In his impassioned and eloquent *What Went Wrong*, Jeremy Seabrook reminds us how lethal the pottery industry was. People died like flies from the coal-fired kilns and lead glazing—children included. Yet there also developed out of the misery a stoic working-class culture built on pride of work, independence, discipline, and the elevation of human relations above material possessions.[5]

If children can pick up a sense of their social history in their everyday surroundings, their curiosity will be motivated to find out more by reading, by visits to local museums, by trips to the library, by talking with teachers and family (embracing all modes of playing and learning).

How can 'playable history' be conserved when the landscape is being renewed on such a massive scale? Is it technically feasible to create Piranesian[6] landscapes in a state of arrested decay, or to allow for their gradual transformation by the forces of nature? Perhaps the notion is completely unrealistic in the context of bureaucratic systems that have to transform relationships into official products to justify their own existence. Public works cannot be undertaken for their own sake, how could they be accounted?

Official action was expressed by a particularly curious monument sited at the street entrance to one of the Tunstall Greenways: a pair of old railway engine wheels mounted on a concrete podium. Paul and his friend climbed on the wheels and said they ran races round the podium. The wheels commemorated the opening of the Greenway. Mounted as in a museum, they evoked a strangeness that guaranteed attention as an object divorced from historical context. If simply left 'laying around' (especially if still attached to the railway engine!), they could have evoked a much stronger historical feeling. Child users had sensed the bogus transformation, judging by the way in which the plaque had been scratched and mutilated; or perhaps they did not understand the commemorative words describing the grand afternoon when such and such a politician had officially open-ed the Greenway.

It cannot be denied that such events symbolise important moments of local history. In Tunstall, they highlighted the rebirth of the town and the replacement of many bitter memories with hopes for the future.[7] But still, not all industrial artifacts have to be trans-formed into token gestures. Labelling things and putting them on pedestals might be reasonable as long as it is not the only treatment. 'Living history' needs to be conserved and re-created, lest all artifacts are turned into freeze-dried abstractions, set apart from children's sense of their cultural heritage. In *What Time Is This Place?* Kevin Lynch has raised the issue of conservation from the point of view of future inhabitants of cities like Stoke-on-Trent.[8] His philosophy sug-gests the incorporation of artifacts informally into the landscape, as if designing an archaeological site. While never offering the powerful mystery of prehistoric remains, informal treatment would increase the impact on children and maybe on some adults, too. Artifacts such as industrial objects, old structures and engineering works, could be left *in situ*, undefined and unframed, to be discovered and rediscovered, filling the imagination with stories and myths that are the true substance of history. Yet they would remain a living aspect of the present.[9] Artifacts sited in rough ground, surrounded by vegetation, would convey a necessary feeling of transformation. The viewer would then see the object both growing out of the land and being simultaneously reclaimed by the land.

The qualitative distinction I am trying to make was well illus-trated by what kids called the "Sausage Tunnel," located at the ex-tremity of the Tunstall Greenway. The Sausage Tunnel was a narrow, brick-arched, pedestrian passageway under the elevated railbed. It had been mentioned several times as a favourite place by kids and parents. Paul and his friend took me there and demonstrated the "sausage game," a form of 'tick' played on the embankments and brick retaining walls at each end of the tunnel. Paul said he came blackberrying on the embankments and recognized it as a good place to catch butterflies. Why the name "Sausage Tunnel" I could never determine. Its significance was expressed in the way the children spoke about the place as well as by what they did there. It seemed to focus their feelings for the whole surrounding area, including the adjacent Bomb Holes.

In a stable, parochial community like Tunstall (if you lived there, it was almost certain you were born there), it is difficult for inhabitants to get an adequate perspective on their own cultural situation. As Jean-Paul Sartre once reflected, people can become so immersed in their own history they cannot see their true selves. Yet people must learn otherwise—enough to recognize the consequences of technological change on traditional lifestyles—before, as Seabrook fears, the old industrial base becomes only a folk memory.[10]

PURITY AND DISORDER

Childhood environments must provide both security and serendipity to stimulate both predictable and unpredictable consequences. Nature itself is genetically controlled, demanding certain absolute conditions for survival and healthy growth, yet also able to tolerate and adapt to a range of circumstances that promote varied character development.

In *The Uses of Disorder*[11] Richard Sennett comments on the "purified thinking" of contemporary urban planning that he sees as reinforcement of the trend towards urban monoculture. Purified thinking leads inevitably to an ordered, alienating mode of living; formed, according to Sennett, by two coacting factors: first, the "unresolved identity crisis of adolescence, carried into adulthood as a fear of freedom"; and second, by a "mechanical mode of conceiving and acting" which is a direct result of technological innovation. In this latter process, mechanistic modes are applied inappropriately to the realm of human relations—in particular by the bureaucratic methods of 'top-down' city planning and management. Such modes of decision making, divorced from a detailed knowledge and understanding of how people actually live, result in grossly oversimplified assumptions and proposals.

Is it inevitable that childhood experience must be replaced by sentimental clichés, that oblige children to perceive situations and objects as culturally determined certainties? For a few brief years children have the gift of intuitive perception. As they explore and play with their surroundings, is there a way to involve them in processes of deliberately creating and validating their future, rather than accepting it without question? Children need to build their own reality, to reconcile (assimilate/accommodate) the dialectic between themselves and culture extant. Each generation must start anew. In her aptly titled, *Between Past and Future*, Hannah Arendt describes perfectly the issue:

> Basically we are always educating for a world that is or is becoming out of joint, for this is the basic human situation, in which the world is created by mortal hands to serve mortals for a limited time as home. Because the world is made by mortals it wears out; and because it continuously changes its inhabitants it runs the risk of becoming as mortal as they. To preserve the world against the mortality of its creators and inhabitants it must be constantly set right anew. The problem is simply to educate in such a way that a setting-right remains actually possible.... Our hope always hangs on the new which every generation brings; but precisely because we can base our hope only on this, we destroy everything if we so try to control the new that we, the old, can dictate how it will look. Exactly for the sake of what is new and revolutionary in every child, education must be conservative; it must preserve this newness and introduce it as a new thing into an old world, which, however revolutionary its actions may be, is always, from the standpoint of the next generation, superannuated and close to destruction.[12]

A gulf exists between formal education and informal experience. It is a gulf which is surely greatest and most poignant during middle-childhood, when people are as free as they will ever be to seek out environments they can respond to and learn from by experience-for-its-own-sake. Consider the liberating possibilities for children and adults learning together in relationships based on mutual exploration. Now compare the quality of this situaiton to the parallel course of events in school, where children must digest verbal, abstract knowledge, divorced from its experiential roots.

Environmental professionals think of landscapes as 'objective' resources to be classified and manipulated on their own terms. There is nothing wrong in this. Landscapes do have their own intrinsic qualities and integrity. They are also social artifacts, used and experienced by a dependent human species. We need them to survive. The antithesis of "purification" need not be a total "muddling through."[13] Recognition must be given to *polysemy*[14] as an essential characteristic of social change—just as it is a characteristic of adventure play, where options are juggled to ensure a positive outcome, where neither ends nor means are known ahead of time. The antithesis of this process is competitive sport—or war—where all ends and all means are predetermined.

At the heart of the so-called environmental crisis is a three-way conflict between the values of 'conservationists'—who would protect intrinsic and historical values; 'exploiters'—who use the environment in the name of economic progress; and 'everyday users'—whose needs are many, yet rarely articulated with clarity. It is not the moment to examine these conflicts in detail except to note a gaping void of understanding about the role of childhood experience in the development of environmental values. Since major users of the local environment are children, and since values are acquired through experience, then the values underlying adult environmental behaviour must be partly rooted in childhood environmental experience. The quality of such experience merits a level of attention which is curiously absent from most child development literature.

In *Small is Beautiful*, E.F. Schumacher[15] expressed dismay about the transition from childhood to adulthood which seems to lead inevitably, in our culture, to a "loss of capacity to experience for its own sake." Here lies the root of unsatisfactory modes of learning and conceptualizing about the world. It partly explains why the academic community continues to have such a small effect on the massive survival problems of the planet, and why ordinary folks imagine that they can't do anything for themselves, that things are more complicated than they appear to be, that expert knowledge is required to undertake even the most trivial responsibility.

The unremitting dependence of child on parents can, it seems, sometimes wear away at parents' humanity, eventually turning the joy of birth into daily drudgery. Thus it comes to pass that parents grow to dislike and even abuse the children they once welcomed into the world. How is it that parents can give up helping their children gain access to experiences that would help them deal with the world with confidence, understanding and creativity? As these same children become parents, now with built-in limited awareness of children's experiential needs, a deprived culture will tend to develop with serious consequences for both the quality of human development and the quality of environmental development. Child abuse and environmental abuse are evidently different sides of the same 'bad' coin. Hannah Arendt again illuminates a sense of the educational mission needed to counteract these tendencies:

> Education is the point at which we decide whether we love the world enough to assume responsibility for it and by the same token save it from that ruin which, except for renewal, except for the coming of the new and young, would be inevitable. And education, too, is where we decide whether we love our children enough not to expel them from our world and leave them to their own devices, nor to strike from their hands their chance of undertaking something new, something unforeseen by us, but to prepare them in advance for the task of renewing a common world.[16]

What can be done to help children gain knowledge of themselves and their surroundings, so that they will be able to operate effectively, with humanity, in today's world? Beyond their responsibility to provide love, shelter and nourishment, how can parents assist in this task? What is the role of the schools and of nonformal education? How can the interplay of family, community and urban landscape be enhanced by deliberate public policy?

10 *Policy directions*

There is an obligation in this final chapter to surface from immersion in a phenomenology of childhood environments and propose action. Yet the path should be trodden carefully, lest tentative suggestions become solidified answers. Action implies responsibility. We must begin by reminding ourselves of the full scope of childhood-environment issues; we must focus on the principles and policies that should guide action, rather than the actions themselves. These must evolve from each local context.

The approach recorded in this book began with an effort to collaborate with young people and to document aspects of their existing surroundings which they themselves found significant. Only when this phenomenal level of reality had been sensed and codified, were distinctions made between good, bad, and indifferent qualities.

ACCESS TO DIVERSITY

Access and diversity emerge as the most important themes in childhood-environment policy. Playground stereotypes need to be expanded into a vision of children interacting among themselves, with family and community, in every place lived in and used.

The primary justification for diverse environments is that they stimulate and support the development of children within their social heritage and within genetically defined patterns of needs and responses. Collectively, children require an environment with suffi-

cient diversity that their many individual needs are met simultaneously. It must be accessible to all, regardless of ability or disability.
The purpose of design intervention is to increase access and to make
unused or underused environments more diverse.

Access and diversity go hand-in-hand. It makes no sense to improve diversity unless access is equally considered. They must be
considered at every level of decision making, from general policy,
through site design, to day-to-day management. Each level may seem
equally important, but if the policy level is not clear and forceful, improvements on the ground are unlikely to follow.

A common argument against diversity equates it with chaos, or
with presenting the child with an overwhelming number of choices.
But this concern overlooks the way in which patterns of choice are
moderated by access. Diverse landscapes cannot be experienced all-
at-once. They become progressively disclosed, over periods of
time—years in some cases, at many levels of detail, through many
seasons. Spatial sequences become gradually trodden on the ground
and trodden in the mind as structures of memory and experience.

Tunstall provided a clear case of the differences between diversity and chaos. Even in the most chaotic-looking settings, children
created their own order out of the diversity of opportunities—
selecting some and ignoring others. The issue never seemed to be
that children were faced with an overwhelming range of choice. The
more obvious issue was that diversity had been diminished by land
reclamation. Richly-textured, unkempt landscapes had been replaced
with tidy monocultures.

Overgrown railway rights-of-way had become Greenways. Foot
access was still there as before, but much of the rough-ground character has been removed in the rehabilitation process and replaced by
mown grass. On the other hand, a new access opportunity was provided for children to travel much farther afield by bike. The extensive regrading required to construct the Greenways had inevitably
resulted in the disappearance of their former character. But the result
of this initial restructuring did not need to be considered a permanent solution. It could have been followed by a more detailed design
and management phase, conducted in cooperation with the residents, so that the former level of diversity would have been eventually surpassed.

Bedwell in some ways presented a similar situation. Excellent
access existed in the form of traffic-separated residential areas and a
network of bicycle and pedestrian paths. Yet the level of diversity

was limited, as nearly every piece of open space was subject to the homogenizing treatment of the gang-mower. It seemed almost as if the green swatches on the planners' maps had been transferred directly to the ground—with little attention to design for human use. Again, if considered as a first phase of development, a next step could involve residents in intensive diversification.

In Notting Dale, high population density, high-rise housing, high traffic levels and scarcity of land made the prospects for improving access to diversity more challenging. Nonetheless, by working with children in the field, attention was drawn to the following possibilities for improvement:

1. Community use of school grounds and industrial land after hours, at weekends, and during school holidays.

2. Reconstruction of residential streets for community use.

3. Redevelopment of open space around buildings as a social resource, rather than for the sake of appearance alone.

4. Provision of access to areas of unused marginal land such as railway rights-of-way, canalsides, and industrial areas.

5. Physical diversification of local parks and playgrounds, by adding all manner of small-scale objects and natural resources.

Such policies would inevitably mean some areas would take on a rougher, less ordered appearance. Community participation in making such changes would therefore be critical to ensure acceptance.

ADAPTATION TO CHILDREN'S RIGHTS

Room needs to be made for children developmentally, educationally, culturally and legislatively. The right to play and the right to a stimulating, developmentally appropriate environment has been ordained for years in the United Nations Declaration of the Rights of the Child.[1] This does not mean that completely segregated territories are needed. Children develop feelings of territorial possession as they explore, learn, and acquire competence in their use of the outdoors. They also need to see themselves as part of the broader community. Attempts to partition them off will be self-defeating and will inevitably result in unnecessary child-adult conflict.

This is not to say that kids will invade every available space. This is not the issue. Many places simply will remain irrelevant to children's play. (They may be relevant to more formal environmental education or animation—see below. But this is another question. Here we are dealing only with children's informal play.) Most places in this study were lightly populated by children. The principal need was for a welcoming adult attitude in places where young people clearly had a right to be.

City children and adults need to learn to accommodate each others' needs more skillfully. Many play areas would do this if they were located and designed to accommodate the needs of all age groups, including adults. Research for this book uncovered many examples of the antithesis of mutual accommodation: wasted space on housing estates not used by anyone; and at the worst extreme, unimaginative, hard, oppressive spaces that children were forced to inhabit because there was nowhere else to go—particularly in Notting Dale.

Children also need private places where they can escape to do what they please: places around the home, in the corner of parks, in abandoned structures and on wasteland. Ways must be found to accommodate the necessity for children to physically manipulate the environment. Places are needed where stuff can be picked up, thrown about, gathered, jumped on, eaten, kicked, rolled on, climbed into, broken down, dug up, burnt and taken away, without causing offense. Such actions can be interpreted either as expressions of autonomy and proprietorship, or as malicious vandalism. The difference is sometimes obvious and sometimes subtle. If places where physical manipulation can legitimately occur continue to be removed, manipulation will happen in less appropriate places, where the resulting damage will not be so readily tolerated.

Vegetation should be used more frequently in environments used by children. Hedges, thickets, trees and shrubs can be used to define spaces, to encourage (or inhibit) games such as football and to accommodate hide-and-seek and wildlife exploration. Diversity calls for a range of styles from 'rough' to 'manicured.' Nothing less than the whole urban environment should be under consideration: multiuse community spaces, habitats around the home, commercial areas; and above all, neighbourhood streets.

MAKING STREETS LIVABLE

Donald Appleyard's *Livable Streets* (incorporating the pioneering research of Stina Sandels and Charles Zerner)[2] contains examples from several countries of attempts by local communities to make residential streets more habitable. Improvement is achieved by measures such as limiting the flow of through-traffic, reducing speed limits, changing roadway alignments, and giving pedestrians legal priority. The Dutch *Woonerven* (residental precincts) provide the most mature examples of what can be done.[3]

Principal objectives of these efforts are to control the noise, pollution and visual impact of neighbourhood traffic and to reinstate some of the social functions that local streets once enjoyed before the automobile took over. Obviously, children stand to benefit greatly from such actions. Opportunities for street improvement were particularly obvious in corporation housing areas like those in Mill Hill. Traffic levels were moderate, streets were generously laid out and had interesting configurations that already stimulated imaginative play.

Traffic control is the first requirement for making streets livable. Below certain thresholds of vehicles per hour, various levels of child activity on pavement and carriageway become possible. For instance, in games where strings are suspended across the street, play must cease when cars are passing more frequently than once every twenty minutes or so (three or four cars per hour). At somewhere between five and ten cars per hour, utilization of the carriageway as a play-space becomes untenable—depending very much on the average speed of the vehicles and who the drivers are. Residents and tradespeople conversant with the street and its users will keep a much sharper lookout than a fast-moving stranger seeking a shortcut.

Narrower streets also slow vehicles down and increase children's sense of security because the curb is a short jump away. The value of all forms of cul-de-sac is self-evident. Knowing you can't be hit from behind is fundamental to maintaining a sense of security.

The physical relationship of the street to its immediate surroundings is also influential in accommodating children's play. In Mill Hill and Bedwell, streets that worked best were connected to a subsidiary network of 'side,' 'back' and 'front' pathways, back alleys, cul-de-sacs, garage courts and patches of grass that greatly extended the variety of possible games.

Play opportunities on individual streets were enhanced by the number and variety of physical differentiations. Curbs, paving stones, bollards, manhole covers, trees, hedges, doorways, railings, fences, gates, telephone poles, dustbins, overhead wires, painted lines, street drains, posts, letterboxes, benches, parked cars—even litter—influenced the pattern of play. The hilly topography of Mill

Hill was an added influence because it resulted in many more banks, steps and retaining walls around the streets and adjacent buildings. This further increased children's play repertoires, including the use of roller skates and go-carts, and helped perpetuate street-play traditions as part of the local culture.

Streets filled an especially important role in children's loose-knit social structure, by providing a physical threshold a few steps from home for peer contact. Streets and street corners were important meeting places. When traffic density was low and streetscape diversity high, children were drawn to an environment that was extremely well-adapted to their needs.

Seen in this light, the notion of "keeping the kids off the streets" seems highly unrealistic, not to mention undesirable. Street-play is a universal cultural phenomenon which will occur even if traffic levels are high and space differentiation is low. Designated playgrounds can add important play opportunities and attract activity, but they cannot substitute for the immediacy of the street. Streets have always been used for close-to-home play and will surely continue to do so in the future.

The ever-rising costs of running a car probably will mean, as Appleyard suggests, the resurgence of street space as a significant social resource for all ages. If so, it will be more important than ever to ensure that children's needs are to the fore—represented by children themselves taking part in the redesign process and policy formulation. Improved streetscapes need to be integrated into networks of pathways, greenways and urban trails (as in Stoke-on-Trent).[4]

CONSERVATION OF SPECIAL CHILDHOOD PLACES

What is the definition of "special"? Do we mean a place that is special to all children in a particular locale? There was nothing particularly special about commonly-used places such as playgrounds, parks, 'fronts' and 'backs.' 'Special' means something out of the ordinary, a playplace with uncommon characteristics or a feature that gives a locale a particular identity or character: David's old willow tree in Avondale Park, Heather's piece of 'meanwhile' wasteland, Brian's overgrown orchard, Tracy's marlhole, the Brickers, the Grogs, the Dip, Sausage Tunnel, Queenie Pond...all unmistakably special to their coterie of users, most of them not highly valued by adults.

By "conservation" I mean the need to formally recognize and enhance intrinsic values through land-use policy. Not to preserve places intact, necessarily, but to ensure retention of their essential character and, if appropriate, to improve their accessibility. After all, special landmarks and reservations are created because of historic or scientific significance. Why not apply the same procedures to places of childhood significance? Older industrial cities need to see demonstrations of how special landscape features or characteristics can support child development. Decision makers need to be convinced that a rich foundation of childhood experience is more likely to produce environmentally sensitive adults, who, in turn, are more likely to support conservation in the future.

In more densely developed cities, where space is scarce, the same conservationist approach should apply, although the variety and size of environments to choose from may be less, and the competition for space more severe. The challenge is great in an area like Notting Dale. But it is critical not to think of any place as a lost cause. To abandon a community on the assumption that nothing can be done is unforgivable. One can never know what possibilities exist until you go out with the children and look at what is actually important to them.

In the development of new commmunities: New Towns, Expanded Towns, village developments, or run-of-the-mill suburbs, conservation will be hampered early on by the lack of a resident community to work with. Initially, this means that policies will have to be based on experience drawn from adjacent areas, or similar communities elsewhere. Eventually, design opportunities will be greater for the creation of significant conservation and spatial configurations suited to children's needs. A participatory mechanism can be instituted from the moment that families move in.

We must not be naive about democratic procedures in relation to children. Tyranny can arise when special places become the subject of public policy. On the one hand, they remain extremely vulnerable if not identified and made the subject of conservation policy. On the other hand, the very act of identification brings them into a political, decision-making arena, where they may receive little sympathetic support, or even meet with strong disapproval. It is a genuine dilemma. To those who insist that "you can't stop progress for a few kids," the reply has to be that "it is not a few kids...they keep coming year after year...and once a special place is lost, it is lost forever."

Then there is the ethical question raised by delving into children's special places. It can easily be construed as an invasion of privacy. The 'investigator' runs a serious risk of breaking an implied trust, inadvertently betraying secret information to siblings, parents and acquaintances—as happened in this study a couple of times.

Applied to open spaces like Avondale Park or Tunstall Park, a conservation and improvement policy would have to be developed at a fine level of detail to respond to children's individual needs. A classic issue of resource allocation in recreation and leisure planning is the question of how to accommodate a large variety of minority interests economically. The effectiveness of resolution is closely related to the level of specificity at which policy decisions are made. In the case of children, it is often too general.

The important thing is to identify and assess children's values, so that they can be fully represented and considered in their own right—along with other values that enter local land-use decision-making processes. As an initial step, we might think of producing childhood 'turf maps' as a policy statement of existing values. As we saw in Chapter 2, the characteristics of such maps vary considerably from place to place. Although they focus on existing place-values, they can also imply something about missing items. The Mill Hill map suggested a plurality of values distributed throughout the area; the other two maps indicated less choice, more focused, in fewer places. The first type should lead initially to a conservation policy to protect and enhance existing values. The other two types would lead to an examination of 'white areas,' to see how they could be made more attractive.

The methods used to research this book can equally well be used as a policy tool elsewhere, to help children identify important places and decide about changes and additions they would like to see made in working with adults at school, in local planning departments and in youth organizations. It is important to remind ourselves that conservation is but the first phase of policy development: to identify and retain values that already exist. The more comprehensive level of policy must extend beyond a defensive conservationist position. Improvement must be directed towards the bulk of mundane, poor quality environments—a far more challenging task.

Overwhelming significance was given to parks. They were the most popular places to go after school and on weekends; the most common outdoor places to meet friends; and, besides children's own rooms, the most popular places to be alone. Urban parks were a social hot spot. At the same time they were most commonly prohibited by parents. They were also places where child and adult behaviours were most likely to come into conflict.

Parks are highly valued by adults, too, and are likely to become more so in the future—as symbols of certainty in an increasingly unstable world. In the favourite corner of their favourite park, adults can breathe a sigh of relief that the world is still recognizable. For some, parks are natural havens in a synthetic world, the sacred jewels of the urban environment outliving everything else around. They become the timeless repositories of memories of adults' own childhoods, of lovers' meetings; of picnics on Sunday afternoon; of special moments with family and friends, relaxed, playing together disengaged temporarily from the tension of the city. No wonder adults object so strongly to children messing-up parks, disturbing their moments of tranquility. But how can these conflicts be resolved?

One approach would be to broaden the range of park and open space management styles to include 'rough ground' approaches. This would reduce costs by reducing labour intensity; it would improve ecological diversity, and accommodate children's play more appropriately and less visibly. Long grass is a terrific camouflage agent and a good habitat for wildlife. Acres of space in communities like Notting Dale, Stevenage and Stoke-on-Trent are suitable for roughing-up with wild flowers, scrubby bushes, trees, and interesting topography. Such treatment would make them both self-sustaining and child-sustaining.

The indeterminacy of rough ground allows it to become a play-partner, like other forms of creative partnership: actress-audience, potter-clay, photographer-subject, painter-canvas. The exploring/creating child is not making 'art' so much as using the landscape as a medium for understanding the world by continually destructing/reconstructing it. Where is this vital activity to be carried on if every part of the child's environment is spoken for to meet the economic, social and cultural needs of the adult community?

Rough-ground qualities could be built into a space like Avondale Park without too much difficulty. Once the idea was accepted, such areas of official open space could be made to look unofficial. Rip up some of the asphalt, surround it with a sturdy enclosure, add some fertile soil and leave it alone. In other words, make it like a building site: a leaderless, do-it-yourself adventure play area; an anonymous spot for kids and wildlife to colonize together. A remarkable thing about children's hideaways is their small size and scale. Heather's knee-high clubhouse was a few yards from the main thoroughfare of Labroke Grove. Lawrence's willow tree was right next to a new complex of shops and apartment blocks. Packing-case games are played right on the pavement of commercial streets.

There are many public places like Avondale Park, that offer children no more than a routine pattern of activity, obviously not covering the full range of child-development potential. When Notting Dale is fully redeveloped, where will children go to exercise their emotions and creativity? Some of London's open spaces such as Hampstead Heath have rough-ground qualities on a grand scale. The same qualities need to be built into the hearts of residential neighbourhoods.

Qualities of openness, diversity, manipulation, explorability, anonymity and wildness must be planned, but in a nondesigned way. Forget the official stamp of tidy overdesign. Leave it open to the users' own hands and imaginations to define. Think in terms of little bits of adventure-play environment scattered throughout the community, in odd corners, where they will attract young explorers and at the same time be acceptable to parents and neighbours.

In older communities like Tunstall, where land reclamation has already occurred, there is a need to re-emphasise diversity and the proper accommodation of children's play as foils to the fine traditional parks and excellent ballplay facilities. Several of Tunstall's reclamation projects had infact adopted a rough-ground treatment. Scrubby trees were planted in close proximity to each other, with grass left unmown. These new landscapes were used by children for shelter-building games, hide-and-seek, digging and observation of wildlife. Behaviour traces indicated much active use, but little willful damage. Why? It could be that rough ground looks so different that the idea of vandalising it does not arise. A diverse environment offers so many possibilities for positive activity that a desire to 'break the place up' never enters consideration. On the other hand, a lack of diversity makes it impossible for the landscape to accommodate damage. Once the tops of standard trees are broken off, destruction is permanent and final—unless the trees are replaced. Irreversible damage is over in a moment.

Rough ground is both adaptable and resilient. It generates creative interaction and can more easily absorb the messy results. A child breaking off some sticks to make a shelter in a manicured park is likely to engender an immediate reaction from "parkies." In a rough ground area such activity wouldn't even be noticed. An advantage of rough ground is that as time goes on, less and less management is required; whereas, traditional parkscapes need constant care and attention.

The Dutch have developed successful and innovative solutions using native landscape treatments. A study by landscape architect Ian Laurie concluded that there were clear advantages to native planting in the realms of ecology, visual character, relationships to buildings, landscape management and cost. To this list, Allan Ruff, in a further study, added substantial user-benefits, especially for children.[5] Several excellent sources, in the general realm of ecological landscape design and management, indicate that these are not new ideas; indeed, in the case of William Robinson, they go back more than a century.[6]

An understanding of the dynamics of user-landscape interaction lies at the heart of children-environment relations. An emphasis on landscape diversity will lead to the creation of more viable, child-accommodating open spaces—instead of uninviting mown grass and asphalt. We need crossbred landscapes with mature parklike qualities interspersed with rough ground. It is an approach that must be intentionally designed in order to take full advantage of the vagaries of nature.

One purpose of design is to ensure that strong visual identity and sharp visual contrast are built into the environment. 'Identity' is the visual result of ecological 'differentiation' or, in other words, the *figure/ground* of gestalt psychology. Toponymy-inducing elements (like the Brickers, the Sausage Tunnel, Queenie Pond, the Bomb Holes and the Dip) can be provided to help children make connections between landscape, use, and memory. Identity, differentiation and diversity must be created by design and management to give a lasting sense of place. Otherwise there can be no stimulation, no use, and no memory.

URBAN WILDLIFE MANAGEMENT

This is an important extension of roughing-up. Wildlife was not mentioned by most of the children; however, the interest expressed on some of the field trips indicated a lack of wildlife availability, rather than a lack of interest. A major reason for unavailability was the limited habitat. Proper shelter and adequate food sources were not provided by monocultures of mown lawn. By increasing the diversity of urban ecosystems through indigenous landscaping—as promoted by the British Nature Conservancy Council—children will benefit, especially if small-scale wildlife is recognised as an important play-and-learning resource.[7] Research at the Environmental Yard (a redeveloped schoolyard in California, emphasising natural resources) has demonstrated children's keen interest in small creatures such as beetles, ladybirds, spiders, caterpillars, woodlice, butterflies, worms, dragonflies, fish, tadpoles and other pond organisms.[8]

To improve urban wildlife habitats, grass should be allowed to grow tall with all the attendant wild flowers, plants and insects. Areas should be planted and managed as wild, urban woodland. Trees should not be pruned to street-tree standards regardless of their location.

These suggestions should not be construed as a laissez-faire attitude towards landscape management. Quite the contrary, the policy advocated here would require greater management-sensitivity than conventional approaches. The goal is to create a more complex, child orientated, natural resource system in our towns and cities.[9] An indication of success would be measured by periodic bird-sightings and species-counts of insects, mammals, reptiles and aquatic organisms as they became re-established.

The creation of aquatic environments such as ponds and marshes is a particularly important aspect of urban wildlife management. Through careful design, there is no reason why children's needs for exploration and interaction with such environments cannot be accommodated effectively. Fishing for minnows and larger fry is a classic childhood pastime—not to mention feeding ducks. The aim should not be to create highly protected 'nature reserves' with special entry requirements, this would defeat the purpose; but to work with children, to improve habitat conditions throughout the city, wherever suitable opportunities arise.

ADVENTURE PLAYGROUNDS

Adventure playgrounds have been promoted for years as an effective solution to the recreational needs of urban youth.[10] Under guidance from trained leaders, children build their own community and in so-doing build a powerful educational base. Genuine adventure playgrounds usually have no problem attracting children. The problem is that they are difficult to develop, expensive to run, a struggle to sustain, and once in place remain politically vulnerable. Unfortunately, with one exception,[11] almost no systematic studies have been published of how well they work in practice. From the perspective of child development, they appear to be an ideal solution and have been promoted for years as such. Politically, however, they are more contentious. Most parents I spoke to had uninformed, inexperienced or prejudiced conceptions of what adventure playgrounds were. Most of all, they did not have a clear idea about the role of playleaders, referring to them with comments such as "the young men who look after the place."

Furthermore, based on my observations of the adventure playground in Notting Dale and the three accessible to Bedwell children, it was clear that they did not attract all types of children, but were most popular with gregarious children with out-going personalities. Girls mostly used them as social places to hang out, to play games, to fool around and to meet other children. Boys on the other hand (who were usually in the majority), seemed more interested in playing on the huge wooden structures and rope swings that were a common feature of all the sites visited. Girl-users often seemed intimidated by boy-users; on top of which, parental anxieties constrained visits by girls more than boys. To combat this form of inequity would require more diversification of both activity programmes and physical settings than I observed. Even 'clubhouse construction'—normally considered to be the distinguishing activity of genuine adventure playgrounds—was seen on only one of the sites.

The adventure playgrounds I observed clearly catered to those children who were self-motivated to explore the outdoors and whose parents allowed them free range to do so—a self-selected 'elite,' in some ways least in need of the kind of stimulation that adventure playgrounds had to offer. The parents who perceived adventure playgrounds as dirty, dangerous places, most likely had children who would have benefited most, but they did not appear on the scene.

My conclusion is that additional solutions must be found for providing children with comparable levels of social and environmental engagement. In order to approach the same frequency of use as local streets and parks, adventure playgrounds would have to fulfill similar proximity and access conditions, which is clearly impractical in terms of cost. Is there something else that can be done in the local spaces that children frequent that would make them more supportive of child development? What alternatives are there for providing high quality playing and learning experiences that might be easier to initiate and promote at local level?

COMMUNITY ANIMATION

The classic adventure playground playleader is a beautiful example of what has become known as an animator: "one who animates, fills with zest, enlivens and inspires to action...who encourages cooperation, integration and understanding of ourselves, our culture and our surroundings."[12] What if playleaders or animators took an interest in environments beyond the playground. Amongst other things, they could help children make environmental assessments, plans and designs for presentation to the appropriate decision-making bodies. Places of special childhood significance would be identified. Urban trails would be mapped.

An advantage of the term 'animation' is its flexibility. Situations or environments can be 'animated' whereas they can't be grammatically 'play-led.' It is also a sad fact that the term 'play' is not always taken seriously and tends to limit the range of possibilities in some peoples' minds, whereas 'animation' can be applied to almost any creative, interactive situation between adults, children and the places they inhabit. Park keepers, for example, could be trained to 'animate' a more positive, working relationship with children in parks.

More professionals need to be out in the community working collaboratively with *all* children, not just 'problem kids.' Much has to be initiated through schools, because they are the principal channels available for contacting and working with young people. But additional means of contact are also needed. Play-and-learning programmes need to be established in parks, in playgrounds, on greens and in streets, to provide additional bases for environmental animators, trained to connect environmental design, play leadership, the arts, community work and education. Working in teams, they could encompass a broad range of professional expertise, working in many kinds of settings throughout the community, with all manner of materials, especially during the summer months.

Cor Westland and Jane Knight's, *Playing Living Learning*,[13] offers the most comprehensive source of information about these groups and their methods of operation. *Pädagogische Aktion*,[14] based in Munich, is one of the most mature, broadly-based independent groups in Europe—an extraordinarily vital organinization, founded in 1972 by a group of school teachers who had grown impatient with the limitations of their overly didactic role in the state school system. After years of struggle, the group is now almost fully subsidised by the municipality and runs a variety of programs in the 'live' settings of the city: in museums, libraries, parks, playgrounds, squares, streets.... A fleet of seven playbuses, of various sizes and functions, draws on a 'menu' of some thirty programs (circus, film and video, fair, cooperative and traditional games, theatre, etc.) created over the years, and transport them to every corner of the town.

Inter-Action, a London-based British group founded in the 1960s, employs similar 'animation' principles in their community work—much of it related to children. The organization is known for the highly successful City Farm programme that has spread to many cities—and as far as Australia.[15] These, like the German Youth Farms (*Jugenfarmen*), the Netherlands Children's Farms (*Kinderboerderijen*), The Farm, in San Francisco, and many of the Danish adventure playgrounds, use a farmlike animation setting with gardens and animals.

The Notting Dale Urban Studies Centre, London, and the Environmental Resource Centre, Edinburgh, present another form, focusing on urban environmental education. Further forms include the many varieties of adventure playground in different countries; community workshops like the *Erfarenhetsverkstan* (Experience workshop)[16] in Sätra, Sweden; and community arts and environment programs like PLAE, Inc. (Playing and Learning in Adaptable Environments) in Berkeley, California, employing professional community artists and recreation specialists as animators.

Two active groups are based in Bruxelles; one, working under the wing of a private foundation (*Fondation Roi Baudouin*), initiatiates projects through local schools; the other, housed in the francophone Ministry of Education, is a group of community artists (*Service de l'Animation et de la Diffusion Culturelle*) who initiate animation projects in towns and neighborhoods—especially where "guest worker" children live, to help them ease their cultural adjustment *and* keep their indiginous culture alive. A similar group, *Group Ludic*, is based in Paris. Further forms include community schools like Dewson School, Toronto; and museum bases such as the Boston Children's Museum, the Exploratorium in San Francisco and the *Atelier des Enfants* in the *Centre Pompidou*, Paris.[17]

Each type of animation centre provides or has the potential for providing a place that children from the surrounding community can invade and from which animators can invade the surrounding community.

There are many different types of animation organisation, both governmental and nongovernmental, and many ways in which the principles of animation can be put into practice. NUSO (*Nederlandse Unie van Speeltuin Organisaties* Dutch Union of Playground Organisations), a national nongovernment organisation founded in the 1930s, organises and promotes animation programs at local community level through each of its eleven provincial associations. The Danish organisation, SBBU, runs animation programs, staffed by what the Danes call "social pedagogs," in cooperation with many cooperative housing organisations, based at adventure playgrounds and a remarkable variety of community activity centres.

In Vienna, each summer since 1973, *Weiner Kinderfreunde* (Vienna Children's Friends) has run the well-known All-Over-Vienna Holiday Game. In 1984, 350,000 children participated, along with thousands of parents and grandparents. To promote equal access, each child is given a Holiday Passport, explaining how to play the Game, which is introduced in class in every school in the city, towards the end of term. The Game is "stuck together" by stamps which the participants collect at each of the fifty "activity stations" (fire brigades, radio and television stations, libraries, museums, a camp on the banks of the Danube, farms, police stations, stables, and so on) scattered throughout the city—which thereby becomes a fun-filled playing-and-learning environment for the whole summer. (Public transport is free, by the way, during the summer for all young people under nineteen.) Children love to collect the stamps; beyond a certain number, they can send in their passport to receive an invitation to the end-of-game party each September.[18]

Fritid Stockholm (Stockholm Leisure) is an example of a progressive city government organisation which runs programs with all age groups, including children's programs in Stockholm's famous playparks, at school sites and at recreation centres throughout the city, staffed by what the Swedes call "leisure pedagogs." As a government organisation, *Fritid Stockholm* stands alone, to my knowledge, in the degree to which they have developed an explicit set of social/cultural policy goals (democracy, solidarity, security, equality, self-determination and liberation) and related objectives to guide their program offerings.[19]

An advantage of environmental animation is that it can apply to all age groups, not just children. This may make the idea easier to accept, but it also carries the ever-present liability that children will be left aside, because of their lack of political representation. Community animators could be employed by local authorities, although bureaucratic/political constraints might hamper their effectiveness. Attachment to non-statutory bodies removes some of the political vulnerability, but effectiveness still depends on the willingness of local authorities to attend to the needs of their politically unrepresented young citizens.

Community animation is a broad enough concept to cover a range of environmental education, community arts and recreation programming. The examples cited show some of the many ways animation principles can be put into effect to enable residents of all ages to participate more fully in the development of their social and physical environment—their local culture.

Imagine an education system based on life as lived by children, using a variety of urban places, animators and teachers as co-learners. All subject areas would be included in the context of children's own reality, to help them cope with the growing complexity of issues in today's world. If problems like population, pollution, nutrition, housing, employment and world peace are viewed as overwhelming monoliths, a sense of powerlessness and unquestioning acceptance is reinforced. People may take to the streets and create for themselves a short-lived sense of power. Maybe it will capture the media for a few moments. So what? Is this success? Eventually, all democratic problem solving must meet at least two conditions for success: those doing the solving must have had experience of the problem being addressed; and some of those same people must be able to work cooperatively together to find a resolution.

PARTICIPATION

Urban policy must help children gain developmental benefits from their families, their communities and their physical surroundings. People must learn to investigate and resolve the issues of their own life-situations, rather than accept answers only from 'experts.' The mainstream of urban policy making is still dominated by the prescriptions of elite experts, who specify what "ought" to be done on behalf of their clients. Young people, especially, have been so little involved in decision making that their special needs in the urban environment are hardly ever considered. The ability to do this effectively must be rooted in childhood, where a person can learn to explore and understand the phenomenal world—as in traditional cultures, where physical resources and social consequences are more obviously interdependent.

Collective, democratic decision making is not an easy process, especially in our spoon-fed, consumer-oriented culture; it is, however, a skill that can be learned at an early age. Young people need to participate as equal partners in making decisions about their own environmental futures and those of their children yet to come. We can follow Norway's lead here. More than one hundred local municipalities have begun producing Action Plans for Children and Youth, based on three overall goals set by the national government:

1) All policies should be carried out within a social-ecological perspective.

2) Different 'life areas,' such as play, leisure, education, health, social care and family life, should be guided by the same general objectives.

3) Young people must be integrated into society, given responsibilities, and have opportunities to influence their own living conditions.[20]

Although deliberate change is always partially a leap in the dark, social benefits can be more fully guaranteed by first asking good questions—by looking at the world as it *is*, rather than the way it *ought* to be. Existing values must first be assessed. The only way that special childhood places can be identified and conserved, and not forever tidied up, as de Monchaux warns,[21] is through children's genuine participation in the planning process.[22] Changes can be defined in collaboration with residents, and eventually implemented as a series of additions and adjustments (rather than grand gestures of authoritarian design). What *might* eventually be accomplished on the ground depends on local 'controlling factors' such as money, human energy, political influences, organizational capabilities and the community's past history of success or failure.[23] These factors, plus the underlying value placed on the importance of children's participation, will eventually determine the outcome.

The walls of many town halls are papered with good intentions. How can they be turned into positive action? The important thing is to find ways to articulate the variety of local community values, to motivate the apathetic "don't knows," and to explore collectively the options and consequences of action, recognising that local residents are the experts when it comes to managing their own turf.

NOTES AND REFERENCES

Introduction

1   Ward, Colin. *The Child in the City.* London: Architectural Press, 1977.
2   Opie, Iona and Peter. *Children's Games in Street and Playground.* London: Oxford University Press, 1969.
3   Ibid., p.v.
4   Ibid., p.v.
5   Ibid., p.15.
6   Brown, Jane. *The Everywhere Landscape.* London: Wildwood House, 1982.
7   Coles, Robert. *Children of Crisis.* New York: Delta, 1964, Chapter 2: "Observation and Participation."
8   Friere, Paulo. *Pedagogy of the Oppressed.* Harmondsworth, Middlesex: Penguin Books, 1972.
9   Perls, Frederick, Ralph Hefferline and Paul Goodman. *Gestalt Therapy: Excitement and Growth in the Human Personality.* Harmondsworth, Middlesex: Penguin Books, 1973 (first published 1951).
10 Merleau-Ponty, Maurice. *Phenomenology of Perception.* New York: Routledge and Kegan Paul, 1962.
11 Pirsig, Robert M. *Zen and the Art of Motorcycle Maintenance: An Inquiry into Values.* New York: Bantam Books, 1974.
12 Marris, Peter. *Loss and Change.* New York: Bantam Books, 1975.
13 Vickers, Geoffrey. *Freedom in a Rocking Boat.* Harmondsworth, Middlesex: Penguin Books, 1972.
14 Schumacher, E. F. *Small is Beautiful: Economics as if People Mattered.* New York: Harper and Row, 1975.
15 Ward, Colin. *Anarchy in Action.* London: Allen and Unwin, 1973.
16 See Appendix E for addresses.

Playing, learning and place

Pirsig, op.cit., p.233.
Gandhi, Mahatma. Quoted by UNICEF, in *Ideas Forum,* No.12, 1983.

1   Questions of quality

1   Bronfenbrenner, Urie. *The Ecology of Human Development: Experiments by Nature and Design.* Cambridge, Mass: Harvard University Press, 1979.
2   Bill Olkowski must be thanked for this word (so much better than mere 'survival'). I don't know if he or someone else coined it originally.
3   Cobb, Edith (a). *The Ecology of Imagination in Childhood.* New York: Columbia University Press, 1977.
4   Ibid., p.44.
5   Ibid., p.46 and p.48.
6   Ibid., p.47.
7   Pearce, Joseph Chilton. *Magical Child: Rediscovering Nature's Plan for Our Children.* New York: E. P. Dutton, 1977.
8   Ibid., pp.25-28.
9   Huizinga, Johann. *Homo Ludens: A Study of the Play Element in Culture.* Boston: Beacon Books, 1955.
10 Pearce, op.cit., p.26.
11 Wood, Denis. "To Catch the Wind: Kites, Kids and the Environment in Barranquitas, Puerto Rico," 1981 (mimeo), (also published in *Outlook,* 1982, No.45); and "Early Mound Building: Some Notes on Kids' Dirt Play." 1976 (mimeo). Full-length versions of both reports

12 Ibid., *Wind*— p.49.
13 Björklid, Pia. *Children's Outdoor Environment*. (A study of children's outdoor activities on two housing estates from the perspective of environmental and developmental psychology.) Stockholm: Stockholm Institute of Education, 1982.
14 Ibid., p.67.
15 Mead, George H. *Mind, Self, and Society from the Standpoint of a Social Behaviorist*. Chicago: Chicago University Press, 1974.
16 Björklid, op.cit., p.64.
17 Ibid., p.54.
18 Piaget, Jean. "Some Aspects of Operations." In M.W. Piers (Ed), *Play and Development*. New York: W.W. Norton, 1972, p.27; and *To Understand is to Invent: The Future of Education*. New York; Grossman, 1973, p.20.
19 Hart, Roger. *Children's Experience of Place*. New York: Irvington, 1979. In Appendix A, British-born Hart provides a comprehensive review of the theory of childhood and place.
20 Searles, Harold. *The Non-human Environment in Normal Development and Schizophrenia*. New York: International Universities Press, 1959, p.82; discussed in Hart, op.cit., p.412 ff.

21 Useful reviews of existing research are included in:
Björklid, op.cit.
Cohen, Uriel, Ann B. Hill, Carol G. Lane, Tim McGinty and Gary T. Moore. "Recommendations for Child Play Areas." Research Report R79-1, Center for Architecture and Urban Planning Research, University of Wisconsin-Milwaukee, 1979.
Hart, op.cit.
Moore, Robin C. and Donald Young. "Childhood Outdoors: Toward a Social Ecology of the Landscape." In Altman, Irwin and Joachim F. Wohlwill (Eds). *Children and the Environment*. New York: Plenum Press, 1978.
Roberts, Alasdair. *Out to Play: The Middle Years of Childhood*. Aberdeen University Press, 1980, Chapter 4: "Children in Cities."
U.S. Forest Service. *Children, Nature and the Urban Environment: Proceedings of a Symposium-Fair*. Technical Report NE-30, 1977. (For sale by the Superintendent of Documents, U. S. Government Printing Office, Washington, D. C. 20402. Stock no. 001-001-00428-6.) Refer particularly to the contributions of Paul Shepard ("Place and Human Development"), and Martin M. Chemers and Irwin Altman ("Use and Perception of the Environment: Cultural and Developmental Processes").

Key case studies are:
Aiello, James F., Barry Gordon and Thomas J. Farrell. "Description of Children's Outdoor Activities in a Suburban Residential Area." In Moore, Robin C. (Ed). *Man-Environment Interactions Vol 12: Childhood City*. Daniel Carson (general ed.). Milwaukee: Environmental Design Research Association (EDRA), 1974, pp.187-195.
van Andel, Joost. "Effects on children's behavior of physical changes in a Leiden neighborhood." *Children's Environments Quarterly*, 1984/85, 1(4), 46-54.
Becker, Franklin D. "Children's Play in Multifamily Housing." *Environment and Behavior,* 1976, 8(4), 545-574.
Berg, Mary and Elliot A. Medrich. "Children in Four Neighborhoods: The Physical Environment and its Effect on Play and Play Patterns." *Environment and Behavior,* 1980, 12(3), 320-348.
Biel, Anders and Gunilla Torell. "Experience as a Determinant of

Children's Neighbourhood Knowledge." *Göteborg Psychological Reports,* 12(9). University of Göteborg, 1982.

Björklid, op. cit.

Bleeker, Hans and Karel Mulderij. *Kinderen Buiten Spel* Amsterdam: Boom Meppel, 1978. (Includes an action-research, phenomenological investigation of children in urban neighbourhoods. (Dutch)

Brower, Sidney and Penelope Williamson. "Outdoor Recreation as a Function of the Urban Housing Environment." *Environment and Behavior,* 1974, 6(3), 295-345.

Coates, Gary and Ellen Bussard. "Patterns of Children's Spatial Behavior in a Moderate-density Housing Development." In Moore, op.cit. (Milwaukee: EDRA), pp.131-141.

Coates, Gary and Henry Sanoff. "Behavior Mapping: The Ecology of Child Behavior in a Planned Residential Setting." In Mitchell, William (Ed). *Environmental Design: Research and Practice.* Los Angeles: University of California, EDRA3/AR8 Conference Proceedings, 1972, pp.13-2-1 - 13-2-11.

Cohen, Uriel, Tim McGinty and Gary T. Moore. "Case Studies of Child Play Areas and Child Support Facilities." Research Report R78-2, Center for Architecture and Urban Planning Research, University of Wisconsin-Milwaukee, 1978.

Cooper, Clare C. *Easter Hill Village: Some Social Implications of Design.* New York: Free Press, 1975.

Cooper Marcus, C. "Childrens Play Behavior in a Low-rise, Inner-city Housing Development. In Moore, op.cit. (cited under Aiello, above) pp.197-211.

Department of the Environment (DoE). *Children at Play.* London: Her Majesty's Stationary Office, Design Bulletin 27, 1973.

Eubank-Ahrens, Brenda. "The impact of *Woonerven* on children's behavior." *Children's Environments Quarterly,* 1984/85, 1(4), 39-45.

Fanning D.M. "Families in Flats." *British Medical Journal,* 4, 382-386, 1967. This well-known (as yet unreplicated) study compared the health of children living in multistory flats with a comparable sample living in houses, and found that the children in flats had significantly more illness.

Filipovitch, Anthony J. and Kristin Julien. "Children's Drawings of their Home Environment." In Osterberg, Arvid E., Carole P. Tiernan and Robert A. Findlay, (Eds). *Design Research Interactions.* Washington, D.C.: Environmental Design Research Association, 1980.

Francis, Mark. Children's use of open space in Village Homes." *Children's Environments Quarterly,* 1984/85, 1(4), 36-38.

────── and Berta MacDonald. "Children in Village Homes: A Study of Child Ecology with Implications for Design of the Village Homes Playground." Landscape Architecture Program, University of California, Davis, California, 1981.

Gibbons, John and Duncan Stirling. "Aspects of Traffic Separated Housing Layouts." Report prepared by the Architecture Research Unit, University of Edinburgh, published by Stevenage Development Corporation. ND

Hart, op. cit.

Hayward, D. Geoffrey, Marilyn Rothenberg and Robert R. Beasley. "Children's Play and Urban Play Environments: A Comparison of Traditional, Contemporary and Adventure Playground Types. *Environment and Behavior,* 1974, 6(2), 131-168.

Hole, Vere. *Children's Play on Housing Estates.* National Building Studies Research Paper 39. London: Her Majesty's Stationary Office, 1966.

────── and A. Miller. "Children's Play on Housing Estates." *Architect's Journal,* 1966, 143(25), 1529-1536.

Holme, Anthea and Peter Massie. *Children's Play: A Study of Needs and Opportunities*. London: Michael Joseph, 1970. This study is inviting because it included samples from London and Stevenage New Town (as *Childhood's Domain* has). However, as Roberts (op.cit.) points out, their data sources were limited to interviews with mothers (whose knowledge of their children's outdoor behaviour is notoriously limited), and a prescribed checklist completed by children. These reservations aside, some of their comparative findings support some of those reported here, especially criticisms of the Stevenage landscape.

Keller, Suzanne. "Children in New Communities." *Ekistics*, 1978, No.72, 381-383.

Ladd, Florence. "Black Youths View their Environment: Neighborhood Maps." *Environment and Behavior*, 1970, 2(2), 74-99.

Lee, Terence. "Urban Neighbourhood as a Socio-spatial Scheme." *Human Relations*, 1966, no. 21, 241-268.

Lukashok, Alvin K. and Kevin Lynch. "Some Childhood Memories of the City." *American Institute of Planners Journal*, 1956, 22(3), 142-152.

Lynch, Kevin (a) (Ed). *Growing Up in Cities*. (Studies of the Spatial Environment of Adolescence in Cracow, Melbourne, Mexico City, Salta, Toluca and Warsaw.) Cambridge, Mass: MIT Press, 1978.

Mårtensson, Bo. "Observations of Outdoor Activities in some Housing Areas." In *Open Space in Housing Areas*. National Swedish Institute for Building Research, 1972 (Box 1403, S-111 84, Stockholm).

Maurer, Robert and James C. Baxter. "Images of the Neighborhood and City Among Black-, Anglo- and Mexican-American Children. *Environment and Behavior*, 1972, 4(4), 351-388.

Moore, Robin C. "Collaborating with young people to assess their landscape values." *Ekistics*, 1980, (47)281, 128-135.

——— and Young, op. cit.

Muchow, Martha and Hans H. Muchow. *Der Lebenstraum des Grosstadtkindes*. Mit einer Einfuehrung von Juergen Zinnacker, paed. Extra buchverlag (Postfach 295, Bahnhofstrasse 5, D-6140 Bensheim), 2nd. edition, 1980, ISBN 3-921450-58-6. (German)

Muntañola, JosepThornberg and colleagues at the University of Barcelona. See his "Child's Conception of Places to Live in." In Preiser, Wolfgang F.E. (Ed), *Environmental Design Research*, Vol I, Stroudsburg, Pennsylvania: Dowden, Hutchinson and Ross, 1973, pp.178-190; and his *La arquitectura como lugar*. Barcelona: Editorial Gustavo Gili, 1974. (Spanish)

Nicholson, Charles and Harry Marsh. *Children's Outdoor Activities on Three Medium Density Estates*. London: Her Majesty's Stationary Office, 1968.

Payne, R.J. and David R.W. Jones. "Children's Urban Landscapes in Huntington Hills, Calgary. In Suedfeld, Peter and James A. Russell (Eds). *The Behavioral Basis for Design, Book 2* (EDRA 7). Stroudsberg, Pa: Dowden, Hutchinson and Ross, 1977.

Popenoe, David. *The Suburban Environment*. Chicago: University of Chicago Press, 1977.

Sanoff, Henry and John Dickerson. "Mapping Children's Behavior in a Residential Setting. *Journal of Architectural Education*, 1971, 25(4), 98-103.

Setälä, Maija-Leena. "The transmission of childhood culture in an urban neighborhood." *Children's Environments Quarterly*, 1984/85, 1(4), 15-18.

Taishido Study Group. "Three generations of play in Taishido." *Children's Environments Quarterly*, 1984/85, 1(4), 19-28.

van Vliet, Willem. "Neighborhood Evaluations by City and Suburban

Children." *American Planning Association Journal, 1981, 47(4),* 458-466.

White, L.E. "The Outdoor Play of Children Living in Flats. In Proshansky, Harold M., William Ittelson and Leanne Rivlin. *Environmental Psychology.* New York: Holt, Rinehart and Winston, 1970 (1st. Ed.) pp.235-258.

Wood, Denis. "A neighborhood is to hang around in." *Childhood City Quarterly* 1(4), 29-35, Winter 1984/85.

———— "Nothing Doing: Doing Nothing (Mostly) With Kids in the Puerto Rican Highlands," 1985 (mimeo, available from the author at address in Note 11, above). Shortened version published in *Outlook,* No.57, Autumn 1985.

———— op. cit. (Note 11 above).

Zerner, Charles J. "The street Hearth of Play." *Landscape,* 1977, 22(1), 19-30.

22   Cobb, Edith (b). "The Ecology of Imagination in Childhood." In Shepard, Paul and Daniel McKinley (Eds). *The Subversive Science: Essays Toward an Ecology of Man.* Boston: Houghton Mifflin, 1969, pp.123-124.

23   Whitehead, Alfred N. "The Rhythm of Education." (1922). In Talbot, Toby (Ed). *The World of the Child.* New York: Doubleday Anchor Books, 1968, p.298-411.

24   Hodgkin, Robin A. *Born Curious: New Perspectives in Educational Theory.* London: John Wiley and Sons, 1976.

25   Ibid., p.92.

26   Mead, Margaret ("Children, Culture, and Edith Cobb." In U. S. Forest Service, op. cit.), offers some spirited comments on this issue. See also:

Bryant, Peter. *Perception and Understanding in Young Children.* London: Methuen, 1974.

Björklid (op. cit., p.53) reminds us that what Piaget himself claims is that there are certain stages through which an individual must pass; how quickly he passes through these stages, however, is dependent on many factors in the environment in which the individual grows up. She also notes (p.60) Erikson's view that "development is not completed in youth but continues throughout life."

27   Bruner, Jerome S. *Toward a Theory of Instruction.* New York: W. W. Norton, 1968, pp.44-45. Refer also to experiments by Kathy Sylva, Jerome Bruner and Paul Genova reported in:

Bruner, Jerome, Alison Jolly and Kathy Sylva (Eds), *Play: It's Role in Development and Evolution.* Harmondsworth, Middlesex: Penguin, 1976. In Chapter 24, they offer an elegant demonstration of how problem-solving skills can be enhanced through enactive play with loose parts.

28   Hart, op.cit., p.383.

29   Hart, op. cit., quoted by Björklid, op. cit., p.211.

30   Vickers, Geoffrey. *Freedom in a Rocking Boat: Changing Values in an Unstable Society.* Harmondsworth, Middlesex: Penguin Books, 1972.

31   Stone, Christopher D. *Should Trees Have Standing? Toward Legal Rights for Natural Objects.* Los Altos, California: William Kaufmann, 1974.

32   Björklid, op. cit., p.67.

33   Note that each of the four modes are exemplified by the methods used to research this book: *interpersonal* interviews/discussion between researcher and children; *iconic* representations (drawings) of children's favourite places; *enactive* live-experience field trips; and finally, the labourious, largely *semiotic* transformation of raw data, into readable and hopefully useful form.

34 de Bono, Edward. *The Uses of Lateral Thinking*. Harmondsworth, Middlesex: Penguin Books, 1971 (first published 1967).
35 Pirsig, Robert M. *Zen and the Art of Motorcycle Maintenance: An Inquiry into Values*. New York: Bantam Books, 1974, p.114.
36 Bruner, op.cit., p.52.
37 Reilly, Mary (Ed). *Play as Exploratory Learning: Studies of Curiosity Behavior*. Beverly Hills, California: Sage Publications, 1974.
38 Hadfield, J. A. *Childhood and Adolescence*. Harmondsworth, Middlesex: Penguin Books, 1962, pp.61-67.
39 White, Robert W. "Motivation Reconsidered: The Concept of Competence." *Psychological Review*, 1959, 66, 297-333.
40 Scherler, Karl H. "Umwelt als Bewegungsraum." *Sportpadagogik* 1979, 6, 16-25. (German); quoted in Verkerk, Jossie and Sjoerd Rijpma, "Playgrounds: An Emergency Provision?" Municipality of Rotterdam, Department of Sports and Recreation, 1984 (mimeo).
41 Winnicott, D. W. *Playing and Reality*. London: Tavistock Publications, 1971; and New York: Basic Books, 1971. Chapter 7, "The Location of Cultural Experience"(discussed in Hodgkin, op.cit., p.47-48).
42 Hodgkin, op. cit., p.48.
43 Björklid, op. cit., pp.54 and 67.
44 Laing, R. D. *The Politics of Experience*. Harmondsworth, Middlesex: Penguin Books, 1967, pp.28-29.
45 Newson, John and Elizabeth. *Seven Years Old in the Home Environment*. Harmondsworth, Middlesex: Penguin Books, 1978; and with Peter Barnes, *Perspectives on School at Seven Years Old*. London: Allen and Unwin, 1977.
46 Mead, op.cit., p.23.
47 Moore and Young, op.cit.
48 Hart, op.cit., Chapter IV: "Spatial Activity."
49 Tuan, Yi-Fu. *Topophilia* (A study of Environmental Perception, Attitudes, and Values). Englewood Cliffs, N. J.: Prentice Hall, 1974.
50 Lynch, Kevin (b). *Managing the Sense of Region*. Cambridge, Mass: MIT Press, 1976, pp.30-32.
51 Relph, Edward. *Place and Placelessness*. London: Pion, 1976.
52 Boulding, Elise. *Born Remembering*. Wallingford, PA: Pendle Hill, 1975.
    Cooper Marcus, Clare. "Remembrance of Landscapes Past."*Landscape*, 1978, 22(3), 35-43.
    Childhood City Newsletter 14, December 1978, special issue on Environmental Autobiography.
    Hester, Randolph. "A Womb With a View: How Spatial Nostalgia Affects the Designer." *Landscape Architecture*, 69 (5), 475-481, September 1979.
    Lukashok, Alvin and Kevin Lynch. "Some Childhood Memories of the City."*American Institute of Planners Journal*, 38 (2), 108-116, 1972.
    Parr, Albert Eide. "The Child in the City: Urbanity and the Urban Scene." *Landscape*, Spring 1967.
    Perlmutter, Marion, (Ed). *Children's Memory*. New York: Jossey Bass, 1980.
53 Robert Paul Smith's, *Where did you go? Out What did you do? Nothing* (New York: W. W. Norton, 1957; republished San Francisco: Lexikos, 1984), is a particularly noteworthy example. Based on Smith's boyhood in New York state, *"Where did you go?"* contains many gutsy, down-to-earth descriptions of interaction with the environment similar to those reported in *Childhood's Domain*.
54 See Ernest G. Schachtel's well-known essay, "On Memory and Childhood Amnesia" (1947, republished in Talbot, op.cit., Note 23, above), for a wide-ranging discussion of childhood memory in adult life.

55   Cobb (b), op.cit., p.130.
56   A good example is *Talking About Play*, Humberside Playing Fields
      Association, 1982 (14 Market PLace, Howden, Goole, North Humber-
      side, DN14 7BJ) showing how children can contribute to environ-
      mental planning as thoughtful, expert consumers.
57   Björklid, op. cit., p.183.
58   Bronfenbrenner, Urie. "The Origins of Alienation." *Scientific Amer-
      ican*, 231 (2), 53-61, August 1974.
59   Relph, op.cit.
      Berger, John. *Ways of Seeing*. London: BBC; and Harmondsworth,
      Middlesex: Penguin Books, 1972.
      Pawley, Martin. *Private Futures: Causes and Consequences of Comm-
      unity Collapse in the West*. London: Pan Books, 1975.
60   Sennet, Richard. *The Uses of Disorder: Personal Identity and City Life*.
      Harmondsworth, Middlesex: Penguin Books, 1970.
61   Play Board (legal title: Association for Children's Play and Recreation,
      Ltd.) is a membership organization with a broadly defined mission to
      promote opportunities for children's play and leisure time activity,
      sponsor research, and advise and consult with statutory authorities
      and voluntary groups—in pursuit of a general concern with children's
      physical, mental and spiritual wellbeing. Play Board was incorporated
      in May, 1983, and subsumed several pre-existing British play organ-
      izations. It has two regional offices and a head office in Birmingham
      (see Appendix E for address).
62   de Monchaux, Suzanne. *Planning with Children in Mind* (A Notebook
      for Local Planners and Policy Makers on Children in the City Environ-
      ment). Sydney: New South Wales Department of Environment and
      Planning, 1981.
63   Ibid., p.58.
64   Ward, Colin and Anthony Fyson. *Streetwork*. London: Routledge &
      Kegan Paul, 1973. See Appendix E for details of BEE.
65   Bill Olkowski's word again, op.cit. (Note 2).
66   Schumacher, E.F., op.cit. (Intro., Note 14).

2   *Investigation*

1   Cobb (a), op.cit. (Ch.1, Note 3), p.110.
2   A similar emphasis on the outdoors was obtained from the earlier study
     in California, briefly reported in Moore and Young, op.cit. (Ch.1,
     Note 21).
3   As far as I know, the term "turf map" was first used by Jeremy Ander-
     son and Margaret Tindall in "The Concept of Home Range: New Data
     for the Study of Territorial Behavior." In Mitchell, W. J. (Ed). *En-
     vironmental Design: Research and Practice*. Proceedings of the
     EDRA3/AR8 Conference. Los Angeles: University of California, 1972,
     pp.1-1-1-1 - 1-1-7.
4   Lynch (a), op.cit. (Ch.1, Note 21).
5   For the benefit of non-British readers, 'conkers' are the hard, shiney,
     dark brown nuts of the horse chestnut tree *Aesculus hippocast-
     anum*. When playing 'conkers,' each opponent has one suspended
     on a string and each, in turn, tries to break the other's with a
     downward slinglike shot. The winning conker adds the number of
     victories previously held by the broken nut to her/his own—plus
     one—to give a 'fiver,' 'sixer,' etc.; until the winner is, in turn, broken,
     and its score, plus one, is added to the victor. See Opie and Opie,
     op.cit., p.227. Robert Paul Smith, op.cit. (Ch.1, Note 53), p.133 ff, in-
     cludes a wonderful description of "killers, ' the almost identical game
     played in the United States.

Exploring childhood territories

Darling, Frank Fraser. Quoted by Brown in *The Everywhere Landscape*, op.cit. (Intro., Note 6), p.12.
Hodgkin, op.cit. (Ch.1, Note 24), p.38.

3   The flowing terrain

1   Gibbons and Stirling's study of three Stevenage neighbourhoods with full traffic separation, show between 37% and 39% of observed child activity taking place on interior pedestrian pathways (pp.52-53)—a clear vindication of the positive impact of traffic separation. Refer to Note 8, Ch.4, below, for additional sources of related data.

2   Red shale is the pinkish red mineral extracted from coal tips after they have spontaneously combusted. It is used in the Potteries region as a surfacing material.

3   Becker, op. cit. (Ch.1, Note 21), discusses the problems created for children, and others, by elevators and other interior spaces in highrise dwellings.

4   Source of the term, 'loose parts,' is Simon Nicholson's well-known essay, "The Theory of Loose Parts." *Landscape Architecture*, 1971, 62(1), 30-34.

4   Habitats around the home

1   Motivation toward the outdoors varied considerably among the children I worked with. This could have been the result of boring, uninviting settings; or because some children advanced more rapidly to Piaget's period of 'formal operations'—playing in their own minds rather than with their material surroundings. In other words, some children graduated earlier than others from primary experience, moved towards secondary sources of learning, and switched more attention towards parents, teachers, each other, and the indoor 'work' settings of home and school.

2   'Docker' (1892): 'Dock cases' in which you are retained by the prisoner in the dock (Unabridged O.E.D.). The Opies (op.cit., p.62) note an early reference (1622) to 'tick' or 'prison-base.'

3   The Opies recorded 'crab tiggy,' ibid., p.69.

4   Similar ball games were recorded by the Opies, but not ones with these particular names.

5   The Opies discuss 'wall-to-wall' and other ball/wall games (ibid., p.126 ff.), but not "wally."

6   The Opies discuss door-knocking and other pranks under the rubric "Truth, Dare, Promise, or Opinion" (ibid., p.263 ff.), accompanied by their usual fascinating historical anecdotes.

7   Department of the Environment (DoE), op.cit. (Ch.1, Note 21), values recorded on pp.18-20 are quoted in Moore and Young, op.cit. (Ch.1, Note 21). They show that between 23% and 41% of observed activity occured in garage courts and miscellaneous paved areas in five out of six sites surveyed (Table 8, p.116).

8   The Oldham figures are included in the same Table 8, referred to in Note 7, above. Refer also to Moore and Young's Table 7 for six additional sets of behaviour-mapping data. Eight of the total of twelve sets of British and American data, contained in the two tables, indicate impressive amounts of sidewalk, pavement and street play (between a quarter and a half of total observed outdoor activity). Several other studies, cited under Ch.1, Note 21, contain additional evidence: Brower and Williamson, in their Baltimore observations, found a

marked focus on street activity. Becker found between 22% and 38% of child activity on pathways (more than in other locations) in four multifamily housing developments (p.564). Francis' behaviour map shows 44% activity taking place on streets and pathways in Village Homes. Holme and Massie's mothers reported 21% of Stevenage children and 64% of Southwark children "usually play on the street." Finally, Gibbons and Stirling's data indicate a dramatic contrast between the amount of child activity observed on streets in traffic-separated compared to nonseparated neighbourhoods (17%-18% and 48%, respectively) in Stevenage New Town (pp.52-53).

9   Zerner, op.cit. (Ch.1, Note 21).
10 The Opies recorded "queenie-eye-o-coco" without the "eye," but that's the way Carole spelt it on her drawing.
11 For more details of these ancient favourites, see the Opies, p.86 ("shadow tick"); p.291 ("queenie-o-co-co"); p.194 ("sly fox"); p.276 ("pop stars"); p.110 ("stuck in the mud"); p.81 ("off-ground tick") and p.74 ("ball tick").
12 The Opies include examples of "Coloured Birds" and "Coloured Eggs" as guessing games (p.288), but not "coloured cars."

5   Parks and playgrounds

1   Wood, Denis. "Free the Children! Down with Playgrounds!" *McGill Journal of Education*, 1977, 12(2), 227-243.
2   In Holme and Massie, only 5% of Stevenage mothers reported that their children played in the recreation grounds (in contrast, 64% reported garden play and 21% reported street play, p.140, Table 2). Of the behaviour-mapping studies reported in Moore and Young (op. cit., Ch1. Note 21, pp.114-116, Tables 7 & 8), Sanoff and Dickerson, Auslander et al, Department of the Environment and Cooper Marcus recorded only 2% - 15% of activity occuring in playgrounds. Andel (op. cit., Ch.1, Note 21) reported 4% of activity, and still only 15% after site improvements had been carried out, on the playground in his research area (p.52, Fig.9). Becker's study (op. cit., Ch1. Note 21) showed an average of 15% playground use in four lowrise, multifamily developments in New York state (p.562, Table 7). Francis (op. cit., Ch.1, Note 21) mapped only 4% of outdoor activity on the Village Homes playground (p.37, Fig.2).
3   Moderate-to-high levels of playground use were recorded in two of the studies reported in Moore and Young (op. cit., Ch.1, Note 21): Dresel 42% (p.115, Table 7), and Hole and Miller 23% (p.116, Table 8). Becker (op. cit., Ch.1, Note 21) recorded some high values, 36% - 40%, on four lowrise, multifamily developments (p.562, Table 7).
4   Also recorded by the Opies, op. cit., p.273.

6   Greens

1   'Queen Anne' was the London version of Stoke-on-Trent's 'queenie-o-co-co' (played by Carole in Ch.4). See the Opies for further details, ibid., p.292.
2   See the Opies for many alternative names and variations of this game, ibid., p.90.
3   Fifty-fifty' appears to be a variation of the chasing game of 'block' recorded by the Opies, ibid., p.160.

7   Rough ground and abandoned places

1   Even though "messing around," "nothing," "mucking about," etc., are terms that kids use constantly to describe everyday activities, they rarely appear as research categories. A valuable exception is Denis Wood's "Nothing Doing: Doing Nothing (Mostly) With Kids in the

Puerto Rican Highlands," op.cit. (Ch.1, Note 21). Based on what the kids he worked with had to say, he distinguishes four main categories: "Got to," "Doing something," "Doing nothing" and "Nothing to do."

2   The German organisation, *Deutscher Werkbund* (Alexandraweg 26, Ernst-Lugwig-Haus, 61 Darmstadt, West Germany), have published a fascinating special issue of their journal, *Werkbund Material* 80/2, devoted to the topic (I am grateful to Wolfgang Zacharias for bring it to my attention).

3   In truth, the place name, Grogs, was rooted in pottery industry jargon. *Grog* is previously burnt, pulverised pottery, used as an additive to open up the pores of the clay in the manufacture of fire bricks (Unabridged O.E.D.). Perhaps it had been processed at the Grogs at one time. The pottery fragments picked up by Chris and Paul actually looked like the usual *shraff* found on any pottery tip in Stoke-on-Trent.

4   For the benefit of non-British readers, Guy Fawkes was the fellow who tried to blow up the House of Lords on November 5, 1605, in a Catholic plot to assassinate King James 1. The "gunpowder plot" failed. Fawkes was caught red-handed, taken to the Tower of London and beheaded. To commemorate the event, effigies known as "guys" are paraded on street corners for weeks before the "fifth," to collect "firework money," then burned on bonfires (constructed weeks ahead, too, and sometimes prematurely burned) in backyards, parks and vacant land. "November 5th." is an indelible date to every British child—almost as much as December 25th.

5   *Marlhole* was the local term for a surface clay *marl* mine. Some of these workings became gigantic holes in the ground, much larger than Tracy's modest example. Marl is actually used for the manufacture of earthenware products such as glazed drainage pipes. The famed Wedgewood and Spode china is made from much finer clay imported from Cornwall.

6   *Shraff* is a term that applies to the large amount of imperfect pieces of pottery and china thrown out by the factories. The word is a corruption of the Anglo-Indian *saraf*: an expert detector of bad coin. More generally, it means the separation of the genuine article from rubbish (Unabridged O.E.D.). In colonial times, pottery exports to India were apparently accompanied by the import of this Potteries term.

Conserving and creating childhood domains

United Nations Declaration of the Rights of the Child, Article Seven, Paragraph Three.

8   Hidden dimensions

1   Broadly speaking, *Tom Tiddler's Ground* means a disputed territory, a no-man's-land (*niemansland*), a place where any consideration may be readily gained (Unabridged O.E.D.). It is also a children's 'sanctuary' game, first recorded over 150 years ago. Children gather along a line or around a circle drawn on the ground indicating 'Tom Tiddler's Ground' and dare each other to rush in to 'pick up gold and silver' without being tagged by 'Tom,' who has to stay in his 'ground.' See Opie and Opie, op.cit., p.83 ff., for many fascinating scholarly details.

2   White, op.cit. (Ch.1, Note 21), documented similar repressions and hostilities between children and adults in his housing estate study.

3   In fact, a Community Centre was constructed by the community on the Edward Woods Estate, in the late 1970s. It surely helped ameliorate

some of the Estate's worst problems (see the *Bulletin for Environmental Education*, No.117, January 1981, for further details).

4   Royal Society for the Prevention of Accidents. *Road Accident Statistics*. Birmingham: RSPA, 1978.
Holme and Massie, op. cit. (Ch1., Note 21), emphasise traffic as the main reason why Southwark children received more territorial parental restrictions than did Stevenage children.

5   Hart, op.cit. (Ch.1, Note 21), Chapter IV.

6   Björklid Ch. i 1 and Holme and Massie pp.143-150 (both op.cit. Ch.1, Note 21).

7   For a study of (North American) child-environment-friendship variables, see Vliet, Willem van. "The Environmental Context of Children's Friendships." In Osterberg, Arvid, Carole Tiernan and Robert Findlay (Eds). *Design Research Interactions*. Washington DC: Environmental Design Research Association, 1981.

9   *Environmental change*

1   See the discussion in Roberts, op.cit. (Ch.1, Note 21), p.43 ff., in reference to Holme and Massie's, op.cit. (Ch.1, Note 21), Southwark and Stevenage data (p.140). Roberts observes that the crowded streets of Southwark seemed to encourage the playing of traditional games. He comments on the lack of play-supporting passages, alcoves and staircases in Stevenage and the absence of ball-bouncing games, that Holme and Massie also noted. They describe play in Stevenage's open spaces as "passive" and "home-orientated" (more Stevenage than Southwark children spent more of their leisure time indoors "sitting about"). Stevenage mothers controlled their children's play behaviour more closely and were more anxious about prowlers. Southwark children were left more to their own devices out on the crowded (and therefore socially-safer) streets. Roberts concludes that the planned environment of Stevenage was associated with both the absence of play and a different, more passive style of play. He suggests that these differences may be the result of the oral link to the children's past being broken by so many young families moving, en-masse, to a new environment. The young are then left overdependent on their parents and teachers, instead of learning through child-to-child interaction with older children, and become "rootless at an early age" (p.44). He notes Gladys Kendon's similar conclusion in *Children of the New Estate* (London: Methuen, 1954).

2   For details of the California interview data, see Moore, op.cit. (Ch.1, Note 21).

3   See Schachtel, op.cit. (Ch.1, Note 54), for helpful insights on this issue. Also see his *Metamorphosis: On the Development of Effect Perception and Memory*. New York: Basic Books, 1959.

4   For a full discussion of the dynamics of property damage see the illuminating volume edited by Colin Ward: *Vandalism*. London: Architectural Press, 1973.

5   Seabrook, Jeremy. *What Went Wrong*. London: Victor Gollancz, 1978.

6   Giovanni Battista Piranesi (1720-1778). Italian architect, known for his brilliantly executed engravings of *Vedute* (topographical views) and architectural *capricci* (imaginary compositions) of classical antiquity. The latter capture wonderfully, and accurately, a sense of the gradual reclamation of cultural artifacts by nature. (See Wilton-Ely, John. *Piranesi*. London: Thames and Hudson, 1978.)

7   Whitmore, Ken, has written a 90-minute radio play, *Watch the Forest Grow* (Harvey Unna & Stephen Durbridge, Ltd, London, agents), which beautifully draws the listener into the turmoil of social changes taking place in the Potteries since the late 1960s, including the tensions between the generations resulting from their varied perceptions

of the renewing landscape. The title of the play is a reference the *Forest Park*, reclaimed from a hundred acres of exausted mine workings within a stone's throw of Hanley centre, and the site of some of the action in the play. "It's a flamin' slagheap with a green tea cosy on...put there by me and a few thousand other mugs" says Horace, a retired miner. "It's the great merry-go-round of nature, dad...starting the forest all over again," says Doreen, his daughter. "We don't want no flamin' trees falling down and turning to coal again. They'll be sending some poor sods down to dig it up again." Horace retorts.

8   Lynch, Kevin. *What Time Is This Place?* Cambridge, Mass: MIT Press, 1972, includes a discussion of the Stoke-on-Trent land reclamation issue (pp.12-16).

9   J.B. Jackson's stimulating title essay in the *The Necessity for Ruins* (Amherst, Mass: University of Massachusetts Press, 1980), raises a number of related issues in the North American context.

10   Seabrook, op.cit.

11   Sennet, op.cit. (Ch.1, Note 60).

12   Arendt, Hannah. *Between Past and Future: Eight Exercises in Political Thought.* New York: Viking Press, 1954; revised edition, 1968, pp.192-93.
     See also Peter Marris' *Loss and Change* (Garden City, New York: Doubleday/Archor Books, 1975), especially Chapter 1: "The Conservative Impulse," for a useful discussion of the psycho-social dynamics of change.

13   Vickers, op. cit. (Intro., Note 13), presents a particularly useful discussion related to this issue.

14   'Polysemy' or 'polysemic' refers to something with many meanings, as opposed to 'ambiguity' which means something that is unclear. I am grateful to Denis Wood for pointing to the difference and suggesting the additional term.

15   Schumacher, op. cit. (Intro., Note 14).

16   Arendt, op.cit., p.196.

10   *Policy directions*

1   See Gross, Beatrice and Ronald (Eds). *The Children's Rights Movement*, New York: Anchor Books, 1977, for a history of the U. N. Declaration (pp.333-339). The effort began in 1923 with a five-point Declaration drafted by the International Union for Child Welfare. The broader history goes back even further. Jean-Jacques Rousseau (1762) called for a "charter of childhood" (Talbot, op.cit. [Ch.1, Note 23], p.355) George Bernard Shaw (1914) wanted a "'Juvenile Magna Carta'...by way of including children in the Constitution" (ibid. p.376). The current U. N. Declaration was adopted by the General Assembly in 1959. There is a current (1985) initiative to upgrade the existing Declaration (which has no real influence) to become a *Convention* which is binding once a country has ratified it. Refer also to the 1979 "Declaration of the Child's Right to Play," drafted by an international consultation of the International Association for the Child's Right to Play (address App.E).
     For the most global, well-documented, carefully articulated statement, see Elise Boulding's *Children's Rights and the Wheel of Life* (New Brunswick, New Jersey: Transaction Books, 1979).
     Refer to the quarterly, *International Children's Rights Monitor* (address App.E), for continuing documentation of issues in the broad area of children's rights.

2   Appleyard, Donald. *Livable Streets.* Berkeley, California: University of California Press, 1981.
     Sandels, Stina. *Children in Traffic.* London: Paul Elek, 1968.
     Zerner, op.cit. (Ch.1, Note 21).

3   Appleyard, op.cit., pp.249-251 and 306-309. See also:
    Eubank-Ahrens, Brenda. "The impact of *Woonerven* on children's
    behavior." *Children's Environments Quarterly*, 1984/85, 1(4), 39-45.
    Moore, Robin C. "Streets as Playgrounds." In Vernez-Moudon, Anne
    (Ed.). *Streets as Public Property*. New York: Van Nostrand Reinhold
    (in press).
4   City of Stoke-on-Trent, Environmental Services Department (P.O. Box
    207, Unity House, Hanley, Stoke-on-Trent ST1 4QL, England) has
    publicity material. See the *Bulletin for Environmental Education*
    (BEE) for a continuing source of up-to-date information (address Ap-
    pendix E).
5   Laurie, Ian. "Return of the Dutch Natives." *Landscape Architecture*,
    1974, 65(5), 410-413.
    Ruff, Allan R. "Holland and the Ecological Landscapes." University of
    Manchester, Department of Town and Country Planning, 1979.
6   Laurie, Ian (Ed). *Nature in Cities*. New York: Wiley and Sons, 1979,
    contains useful information from European and American sources.
    Refer particularly to the contribution by Owen Manning, "Designing
    for Nature in Cities."
    Fairbrother, Nan. *The Nature of Landscape Design*. London: Architec-
    tural Press, 1974. An invaluable source relating to the principles of
    ecological landscape design and management.
    Robinson, W. *The Wild Garden*. London: John Murray, 1956 (16th Edi-
    tion, edited by Roy Hay; originally published 1885; republished,
    1983, by Century Publishing, London, in association with Capabilities
    Books, Deer Park, Wisconsin). An extraordinarily stimulating source
    of ideas for naturalistic, indigenous landscape design.
7   A series of marvellous posters illustrating wildlife in various urban
    habitats is available from the Nature Conservancy Council (address
    App.E).
    The Ecological Parks Trust is another organisation promoting new
    forms of more ecologically viable urban landscapes—the William Cur-
    tis Ecological Park, Tower Bridge, London, for example (address
    App.E).
8   Moore, Robin C. "Learning from the Yard." In Paul F. Wilkinson (Ed).
    Innovation in Play Environments. London: Croom Helm, 1980.
9   *Childhood City Quarterly*, 1982, 9(2), special issue on Urban
    Wildlands, is another useful source.
10 For classic descriptions refer to:
    Balmforth, Nick and Wendy Nelson. *Jubilee Street: Pebble Mill's Guide
    to Adventure Play*. London: British Broadcasting Corporation, 1978;
    Lambert, Jack and Jenny Pearson. *Adventure Playgrounds*. Harmond-
    sworth, Middlesex: Penguin Books, 1974;
    Bengtsson, Arvid. *Adventure Playgrounds*. New York: Praeger, 1972;
    Benjamin, Joe. *Grounds for Play*. London: National Council for Social
    Service, Bedford Square Press, 1974.
    Allen of Hurtwood, Lady Marjorie. *Planning for Play*. Cambridge,
    Mass: MIT Press, 1968.
11 Hayward, D.G., M. Rothenburg and R.R. Beasley. "Children's Play and
    Urban Playground Environments: A Comparison of Traditional, Con-
    temporary and Adventure Playground Types." *Environment and
    Behavior*, 1974, 6(2), 131-168.
12 Quoted from PLAE, Inc.'s Summer Program brochure: Berkeley,
    California, 1985 (address App.E).
13 Westland, Cor, and Jane Knight. *Playing Living Learning*. State Col-
    lege, Pa: Venture Publishing, 1982.
14 Addresses of all groups and organisations can be found in App.E.
15 Eliott, Christine. "Growing in the City: Employment, Education and
    Recreation in Australian City Farms and Community Gardens." Social

Impacts Publications, PO Box 390, Milsons Point, New South Wales 2061, 1983.

16 ''The Experience Workshop: An experimental neighborhood workshop in the Stockholm suburb of Sätra.'' ND. Available from Stockholm Department of Planning and Building Control, Information Section, PO Box 8314, S-104, Stockholm, Sweden.

17 Details of these and other 'action centres' may be found in *Childhood City Newsletter*, special issues on Participation Projects, Programs and Organizations (No. 23, Spring 1981) and City Farms (No. 26, Winter 1981-82).
   Also refer to Westland and Knight, op.cit.

18 I am grateful to Veronica Kothbauer, Press Officer for *Osterreichische Kinderfreunde* (the national parent body), for supplying this information.

19 Nilsson, Nic. ''The Political Programme for Leisure in the City of Stockholm—and its Implementation.'' In *Leisure: Politics, Planning and People*. Leisure Studies Association Conference Proceedings, 1985.

20 Hongrø, Knut. ''Children and Youth Plans in Municipal Planning: Some Norwegian Experiences.'' Play 2000: Perspectives on Pedagogy and Planning Conference, Munich, July, 1983. (The author, former Senior Executive Officer, Ministry of Culture, State Office for Youth and Sports, can be contacted at Lerkeven 7A, N - 1404 Siggerud, Norway).

21 de Monchaux, Suzanne. *Planning with Children in Mind* (A Notebook for Local Planners and Policy Makers on Children in the City Environment). Sydney: New South Wales Department of Environment and Planning, 1981, pp.66-68.

22 Details of many participation techniques that can be used by adults working with children are described in:
   Berkeley Youth Downtown Planning Team. ''Berkeley Youth Downtown Planning Project: Findings and Recommendations.'' Berkeley: Moore Iacofano Goltsman (1824, Fourth Street, Berkeley, CA 94710, USA), 1985.
   Childhood City Quarterly, double issue 9 (4)/10(1), 1982-83.
   Comité pour le développement de l'espace pour le jeu (CODEJ, address Appendix E). ''Participation des enfants et des jeunes á la transformation de leur environnement.'' (descriptions, in French, of ten case studies), 1984.
   Francis, Mark. ''Designing Landscapes with Community Participation and Behavioral Research.'' *Landscape Architectural Forum*. 3(2), 14-21, 1982.
   Jeavons, Sally. ''Small people on big estates.'' *Childhood City Quarterly* 1(4), 55-60, Winter 1984/85.
   Joseph, Stephen, John Howes and Justin Cooke. *Up Your Street: An environmental action guide for young people*. London: Youth Environmental Action (address Appendix E), 1981.
   Norton, Michael. *Planning your Environment*, 1976; and Simonon, Lin. *Making Playgrounds*, 1981. Resource Packs, published by Community Service Volunteers, 237 Pentonville Road, London N1 9NJ.
   For a general theoretical statement regarding community partication in planning and design, see Iacofano, Daniel S. ''Participatory Decision Making: Some Directions for Evaluating Theory and Practice.'' In Klein, Stephan, Richard Wener and Shelia Lehman (Eds.). *Environmental Change / Social Change* (EDRA 16 Conference Proceedings). Washington, D.C.: Environmental Design Research Association, 1985.

23 A good example of this kind of local policy approach is described in Andrews, Sean and Ciaran O'Connor. *Space for Play*. Dublin: Comhchairdeas, 1980.

APPENDICES

A   *Notes on method*

The study evolved in stages. For purposes of comparison, I knew I needed sites that would contrast with each other physically and historically. They had to be urban—I was interested in urban childhood. The three sites were not chosen systematically, against a pre-established list of criteria. They were places I knew already, that offered the kind of contrasts I was looking for. In Stoke-on-Trent and Notting Dale, I had already worked with the community and therefore had good grassroots contacts. Their important contribution was to identify local schools having sympathetic head teachers. In Stevenage New Town I approached the Corporation's Office of Community Relations for the same assistance.

The local go-betweens made initial contact with head teachers and explained the bare bones of what I needed. A face-to-face meeting then followed, with the successful result that each school granted me "permission" to proceed. The head teacher, in turn, introduced me to sympathetic classroom teachers willing to release some of their children for the interview and drawing exercises. From that point on, the formal procedure (already developed in the earlier Californian study) was used.

Using classroom attendance rolls, a sample of study participants was developed, spread evenly across the 9-12 age range and split 50/50 by sex. A quiet working spot was found in the school (corner of the library, art room, lunch room) with tabletops or floor area to work on.

Five or six children at a time came to complete the drawing exercise. They spread out as much as possible in the work space to prevent them "copying" from each other. Each worked with an 18" × 24" piece of white cartridge paper, a black, medium-point, marker pen and a set of coloured wax crayons. At the start of the exercise the children were asked: "Can you please make me a map or drawing of all your favourite places—where you go after school or at weekends, including the summer—around your home, in the neighbourhood where you live."

I emphasised that whatever they put down in drawings or words was just fine. I reassured them that the exercise had nothing to do with their normal classroom work and that it was not going to be "marked." I said I was interested in learning from them and that a drawing was an easy way to start. Most children cooperated well and completed the task with genuine interest. There were no refusals.

Once the exercise was underway, and interesting looking things began to appear on paper, I went from child to child and discussed the contents of their drawings. I wanted to make sure I understood what was being drawn. For future reference, I added my own notes in light pencil. Children took from twenty minutes to an hour to complete the task. As each neared the point of completion, I verified that they had not forgotten anything.

The same day or next day, the children returned one-by-one for short personal interviews. These lasted between fifteen and twenty minutes. Children like Tracy expressed intense interest in this part of the study. "Are we going to do any more 'paper questions'?" she asked. "I like them."

The field trips were a further, and essential, method for understanding significant details and for appreciating individual differences between the children. The field trip selection procedure was based on the results of drawings and interviews. One-in-four children were chosen as 'experts' from whom I felt I could learn the most on trips around their territories. A couple of reserve candidates were selected in case of illness.

A note, on school stationary, signed by the head teacher, went home to the parents of each of the field-trip children explaining the purpose of the research project. It let the parents know that I would be in touch to seek their permission to go out with their child. Follow-up contact was made by telephone or by means of a house call. Either an appointment was made or sometimes the field trip took place at the time of the house call.

An interview was scheduled with the parent(s), preferably following immediately after the trip (for the sake of continuity and to save time).

The field trips were the most informative and fascinating part of the project. They took place either after school or on weekends. I brought the child's drawing along (rolled-up, projecting from a small knapsack) as a kind of geographic checklist. Most often more ground was covered on the trip than was shown on the drawing. Having the drawing with me, incidentally, also assured the parent(s) of my legitimacy. It was like a ticket of admission.

Field trips lasted anywhere from twenty minutes to two-and-a-half hours, and some of them could have gone on longer still. The crucial thing was to make sure the child took the lead (and did not look to me to do it) and that the trip was conducted at their own pace.

Sometimes children asked if they could bring a "best friend" along. This usually posed a difficult decision. In the past it had sometimes meant that the best friend took the lead and in essence conducted a trip through *their* territory instead of the chosen child's. Alternatively, the chosen child would spend part of the trip introducing the special features of her/his territory to the supposed best friend (such a case occurred in Mill Hill), instead of them interacting together in their shared territory. When the question of "best friend" came up before a trip I probed whether the other child was "really" a best friend or not. Genuine best friends had nearly always been mentioned in the interview or during the drawing exercise. In genuine cases, they added enormously to the meaning of the trip and the richness of results (Jill and Lesley in Mill Hill were a good example). There was one three-person trip (twin girls and their brother in Bedwell) that worked fine. Occasionally a group of friends were encountered while a trip was underway—Brian's bicycle friends were a good example—in all cases it was a valuable experience.

Recording devices consisted of two 35mm cameras (colour and black-and-white) and a small (6" × 8") spiral-bound notebook and retractable lead pencil. I wore a jacket with a large pocket that I could slip the notebook into when using the cameras (slung around my shoulders). As the trip progressed, key words were scribbled down that would later prompt my memory about each 'play episode' when I came to write up the trip.

Where possible, photographs were taken without interrupting the flow of the trip. However, to obtain good results, for the majority of photographs I had to ask the child, "Could you do that again please, so I can get a good picture" (usually twice: for colour and black-and-white). I briefed each child about photography at the beginning of the trip (and obtained a signed release from parents). There was always a danger that the photography would interrupt the flow. Especially when a 'best friend' came along, it could easily interfere with the children's interactions. Photography had to be quick and right first time to avoid becoming too dominant.

Back home, the interview with parent(s) lasted between fifteen and forty-five minutes. Interviews were usually with the mother. Occasionally I succeeded in talking to both parents. No interviews occurred with the father alone. They were impossible to schedule. Fathers were simply not at home enough. About one-in-four parents expressed strong personal interest in the study and wanted to extend discussion of issues raised by the interview questions. In nearly all these cases, as one might expect, the child was drawn into the discussion by the parent(s). Their interest in the study and encouragement of their child's participation indicated a higher level of awareness and intrafamily communication concerning outdoor play.

In the majority of cases, however, parents did not encourage their child's participation, so that s/he went off to do something else; or they actively discouraged participaton, feeling that the discussion was private "adult business." The dynamics of family democracy were fascinating and worthy of future study. Occasionally, the purpose of the interview itself was misperceived. At the conclusion of the interview with Paul's parents, I asked (as always) whether they had any questions for me. "Well, obviously we want to know how he did relative to other children," Paul's father asked. He clearly thought I had been conducting some kind of school test. But Paul had the last word. "Don't forget to look at my trolley," he sneaked in. As I left, he fetched a homemade go-cart from the garage and proudly displayed it. He had obviously understood the true purpose of the visit.

As soon as possible after the trip and parent interview, I wrote up a detailed narrative account based on my cryptic notes. The best situation for this was to sit in my car or a local café and do the rough write-up. This was not always possible because weekend trips were scheduled back-to-back. Write-ups done the same evening, or at the latest, first thing the next day, were still satisfactory. Left longer than that, essential details began to fade, or they would become distorted, or would be confused with the details of other trips. The creation of these 'trip accounts' had to be very disciplined, but the payoff was substantial. The accounts included a summary of each trip listing the places, pathways, people, objects and activities encountered. Sketches of significant physical features and spaces were also added.

Two 'data books' were assembled (one each for field-trip and non-field-trip children), organized by individual child and subdivided by study site.

The contents of the drawings were coded using a set of categories developed in the Californian phase of the project (with the eventual aim of making cross-cultural comparisons) and tabulated with computer.

A key assumption in relation to the drawings was that they were a valid representation of each child's most vividly recalled favourite places, and that together they represented a valid 'turf map' for each study site. Obviously, the drawings demonstrated a wide range of graphic skill on the part of the authors. A second important assumption, therefore, was that these differences cancelled each other out across the whole sample.

Interviews were coded using a two-step procedure for the open-ended questions; first, categories were established, based on frequency of mention; second, responses were coded according to these categories. The results were tabulated with desk calculator.

It is interesting to note, once again, the difference between interview and drawing responses. The number of *places* mentioned in the interviews (193 "after school" and 126 "at weekends") were far fewer, and focused on far fewer 'place elements,' than those contained in the drawings (723 total). The graphic data were therefore much richer than the verbal data. The drawings contained a larger variety and a greater number of elements, and provided more substantial insights into the physical attributes of place, than did the interviews. The interviews were essential, however, for investigating the *social* and *psychological* 'hidden dimensions' of places.

The comparison of results from graphic and verbal sources points to the importance of using several methods of investigation. Rough-ground places for instance were represented in the drawings by indicators such as trees, ponds, shrubs, topography, dirt/sand, holes and hills. In other words, the drawings provided a means for representing significant place elements. They enabled broad territories to be differentiated, that verbally may have been represented by a single word. On the other hand, precisely because of their verbal limitation, the interviews highlighted the most significant general categories that were less likely to show up as single entities in the drawings. The use of both methods in conjunction with each other, helped extend understanding more than if one method alone had been used. For example, few mentions of playgrounds were made in the interviews, but they appeared (as pieces of equipment) in 65 percent of the drawings. The strong visual identity of the brightly-coloured individual pieces of equipment may have made them an obvious thing to draw. The reason they were not mentioned verbally was the fact that most well-used playgrounds were located in parks. Verbally, children recalled them as part of the "park."

Results from the drawings and interviews began to suggest chapter topics for the book. Copies of the field trip accounts and interviews were cut up and reshuffled according to these topics. In one case ("The flowing terrain") the cut-up account suggested a chapter topic. For the most part, however, the account data was used to guide and elaborate the development of subtopics in chapters already defined by the numerical data from drawings and interviews.

The foregoing describes the specific methods. But there was another level of methodology, another more personal realm of interpretation: the realm of researcher-as-laboratory. Just as a group of sculptors with blocks of marble will produce as many pieces of sculpture, so researchers, especially those chipping away at the social/physical systems where things—including the researchers' own perceptions— are in a constant state of flux, will produce varied results.

Think of oneself in relation to a river system. In the course of time the mainstream alters course, sporadically overflows its banks, and occasionally turns into a widespread flood. But the ongoing system seems stable. Someone navigating the river for the first time would be interested mostly in the main course. Tributaries might be explored, but only to a limited degree. Some would turn out to be more interesting than others.

In this analogy, methodology and knowledge acquisition are inseparable. The system reflects different factors and their variable effectiveness. The unknown is represented by the terrain yet to be acted upon...yet as the rain falls on this ground and forms rivulets, tributaries and main course, there is no clear dividing line between known and unknown, between present and future states. There is only a variable degree of awareness. Known and unknown mutually define each other. The infinite extension of the unknown is felt with greater clarity the more one progresses toward it.

Sometimes the known/unknown interface is as clear and as sharp as a rocky canyon. Huge hunks of unknown on each side, hard and impenetrable. We hurry through; there is no point in stopping. But in more alterable landscapes the river takes up new knowledge and assimilates it into the system. This is where awareness is most open to influence. Putting oneself at the interface to be "taken up," disposed between known and unknown, learning from the everchanging interaction of thought and experience.

The mood of the river changes; some days calm, smoothly flowing. Everything looks in order at last. But it is a mirage, the result of looking at a small time interval of the larger system. Next day there is a raging flood; our epistemology is in ruins. The river takes hold of great chunks of the landscape and redeposits them in completely new places, building new layers on the known/unknown terrain, to be worked away afresh in new cycles yet to come.

To have knowledge of the river and its ways of working one must throw oneself into it. But not into a torrent, to be drowned and lost forever. On calm days it is easy to swim around, to gain confidence, to briefly wallow in the illusion that you are master/mistress of the situation and to encounter other researching swimmers. But wait until another storm erupts. Plunge in. Be carried along, half-following your own way, half-following the river's way, to the limits of your capacity for understanding. A greater torrent will overwhelm, a lesser torrent will not stretch deductive capacities to their limit.

There is an affective dimension to people-environment research—a search for analogies to set one's efforts into a larger context. Self and method seem inseparable in the interpretation of results, in their communication, in the evolution of an epistemology and in eventual environmental reconstruction based, in part, on them. These are the inseparable elements of a system for studying the behaviour of one's own species in an environment subject to both intentional and unintentional change.

Mention rates of place elements from children's drawings, in rank order [2]

Place elements		Number of mentions	Mention rate
1	Lawns	68	.71
2	Playgrounds/school yards	62	.65
3	Child's own home	49	.51
4	Local park	38	.40
5	Single trees	35	.36
6	Streets	33	.34
7	Pavements	29	.30
8	Other dwellings	28	.29
9	Fences	27	.28
10	Friends' homes	24	.25
11	Footpaths	23	.24
12	Swimming pools	18	.19
13	Sports fields	17	.18
14	Flowers	16	.17
15	Misc. built structures	16	.17
16	Ponds/lakes	15	.16
17	Shrubs	14	.15
18	Child's school	12	.13
19	Child's friends	12	.13
20	Traffic	11	.11
21	Bridges	11	.11
22	Self portrait	10	.10
23	Topography	10	.10
24	Dirt/sand	10	.10
25	Tree clusters	9	.09
26	Homesite yard/garden	9	.09
27	Hills	8	.08
28	Asphalt/concrete	8	.08
29	Climatic conditions	8	.08
30	Car parks	6	.06
31	Climbing trees	6	.06
32	Woodland	6	.06
33	Abandoned buildings	6	.06
34	Wild birds/insects	5	.05
35	Cul de sacs	5	.05
36	Culverted stream	4	,04
37	Shops	4	,04
38	Tall grass/leaves/weeds	4	,04
39	Cats/dogs	4	,04
40	Building interiors	3	.03
41	Shopping centres	3	.03
42	Community buildings	3	.03
43	Vegetable gardens	3	.03
44	Rocks	3	.03
45	Streams	3	.03
46	Wild animals	3	.03
47	Child's relatives/other adults	3	.03
48	Railway lines	2	.02
49	Bus stop	2	.02
50	Forts/clubhouses/camps	2	.02
51	Sports courts	2	.02
52	Vacant building sites	2	.02

Table 1 continued

Place elements		Number of mentions	Mention rate
53	Fruiting trees	2	.02
54	Neighbours/babysitters' homes	1	.01
55	Secret/hiding places	1	.01
56	Tree houses	1	.01
57	Tree swings	1	.01
58	Fish/aquatic life	1	.01
59	Child's siblings	1	.01
60	Churches	1	.01

N = 96

[1] All percentages have been rounded to the nearest whole number, hence totals may not equal 100.

[2] Mention rate is the number of mentions in a given category, divided by the number of drawings. In Table 1, since there were almost 100 drawings, the mention rates and numbers of mentions have almost identical values. Mention rate becomes useful when collapsing categories, as in Table 2.

2   *Aggregated mention rates for 18 classes of place element, from children's drawings, by study site*

Class of place element	Notting Dale No.	Notting Dale Rate	Bedwell No.	Bedwell Rate	Mill Hill No.	Mill Hill Rate
Homesites						
Child's home	15		11		23	
Friends'/relatives' homes	6		5		13	
Neighbours'/babysitters' homes	1		—		—	
Other dwellings	11		6		11	
Yard/front steps	—		—		9	
Gardens	—		1		2	
Average rate 1.19	33	.97	23	.82	58	1.71
Open spaces						
Local park	17		11		10	
Playgrounds/school yard/play equipment	26		17		19	
Vacant land	—		—		2	
Parking area	2		—		4	
Average rate 1.12	45	1.32	28	1.0	35	1.03
Vegetation (N)						
Single trees	10		9		16	
Fruiting trees	—		1		1	
Tree clusters	3		3		3	
Shrubs	1		6		7	
Tall grasses/dead leaves	—		3		1	
Flowers	8		4		4	
Climbing trees	3		—		3	
Tree swing	1		—		—	
Average .91	26	.76	26	.93	35	1.03

Table 2 continued

	Mention rate					
	Notting Dale		Bedwell		Mill Hill	
Class of place element	No.	Rate	No.	Rate	No.	Rate
Natural ground surfaces (N)						
Dirt/sand/gravel	1		4		5	
Rocks	—		3		—	
Lawns	23		19		26	
Average .84	24	.71	26	.93	31	.91
Pathways and associated spaces						
Footpaths/alleys/shortcuts	—		4		19	
Pavements/'fronts'	6		10		13	
Cul de sacs/driveways	1		—		4	
Bus stops	1		—		1	
Railway lines	1		—		1	
Bridges/tunnels	2		3		6	
Average .75	11	.32	17	.61	44	1.29
Sports facilities						
Swimming pools	6		3		9	
Sports fields	8		3		6	
Sports court	1		—		1	
Average .39	15	.44	6	.21	16	.47
Nonresidential buildings						
School	1		7		4	
Community buidings	3		—		—	
Church	1		—		—	
Misc. built structures	2		7		7	
Average .33	7	.21	14	.50	11	.32
Macro-landscape features (N)						
Hills	—		2		6	
Topography	1		2		7	
Climatic conditions	2		3		3	
Woodland	—		5		1	
Average .33	3	.09	12	.43	17	.50
Fences	5	.15	9	.32	13	.38
Average .28						
People						
Self portrait	3		1		6	
Child's friends	5		2		5	
Child's parents	—		—		—	
Child's siblings	—		—		1	
Child's relatives/other adults	3		—		—	
Average .27	11	.32	3	.11	12	.35
Through streets	6	.18	7	.25	20	.59
Average .24						
Aquatic features (N)						
Stream	1		—		2	
Culverted stream	—		3		1	
Pond/lake	1		7		7	
Average .23	2	.06	10	.36	10	.29

Table 2 continued

Class of place element	Notting Dale No.	Notting Dale Rate	Bedwell No.	Bedwell Rate	Mill Hill No.	Mill Hill Rate
Animals (N)						
Cats and dogs	2		—		2	
Fish/aquatic organisms	—		1		—	
Wild animals	—		3		—	
Wild birds/insects	1		2		2	
Average .14	3	.09	6	.21	4	.12
Traffic	6	.18	—	—	5	.15
Average .11						
Child-made/appropriated places						
Forts/club houses	1		1		—	
Abandoned buildings/structures	3		—		3	
Secret/hiding places	—		1		—	
Tree houses	1		—		—	
Average .10	5	.15	2	.07	3	.09
Asphalt/concrete ground surface	5	.15	3	.12	—	—
Average .08						
Commercial facilities						
Local shops	1		1		2	
Shopping centre	—		3		—	
Average .07	1	.03	4	.14	2	.06
Building interiors	—	—	3	.11	—	—
Average .03						
Aggregated natural elements (N)	58	1.71	80	2.86	97	2.85
Average 2.47						
Total, all elements	208	6.11	199	7.10	316	9.29

N = 96

C   Tables for children's interviews

3   **Favourite places to go after school and on weekends**

	After School		Weekends	
Favourite Places	No.	%	No.	%
Home and Homesite				
Own home/own room	14		3	
Own garden/own yard	3		—	
Garage/shed	2		—	
Relatives home	2		15	
Friend's home	15		7	
Friend's garden/yard	5		—	
	41	21	25	19
Streets and Associated Space				
Streets	18		3	
Fronts/grass areas	11		1	
Backs/alleyways/mews	3		1	
Around the flats	3		—	
Garage courts	2		—	
	37	19	5	4
Formal/Official Open Space				
Parks	43		20	
Fairlands Park	5		11	
Playground/play area/swings	12		5	
Adventure playground	7		4	
Sports ground/playing field	4		1	
	71	37	41	32
Informal/Unofficial Open Space				
Fields/rough ground/farmland	21		8	
Abandoned places/construction sites	8		7	
	29	15	15	11
Commercial Areas				
Shops	5		1	
Town centre	3		8	
Another town	—		4	
	8	4	13	10
Institutions/Community Facilities				
Swimming pool	3		10	
Youth club	1		—	
Horse stables/riding	1		3	
Church	—		2	
Football match	—		6	
Pictures	—		4	
Dancing classes/disco	—		1	
	5	3	26	20
Nonspecific				
Anywhere/outside	3	1	1	1
Other				
Nonlocal recreation areas/ countryside/seaside/fishing place	—	—	4	3
Total	194	100	130	100

N = 96

Favourite Activities	Mentions			
	After School		Weekends	
	No.	%	No.	%
General Outdoor Play and Games				
Playing/games	62		31	
Playing on grass/in trees/in woods	4		6	
Gymnast	2		1	
	68	36	38	22
Playing on Equipment	26	14	18	10
Ball Play/Ball Games	20	10	12	7
Adventure Play				
Climbing trees/climbing about/ climbing fences	15		8	
Water play/fishing/boating/ canoeing/swimming/paddling	10		20	
Collecting things/conkers/ birds eggs/newting/firewood	5		10	
Adventure playground	4		7	
Tarzan swing/tyre swing	4		—	
Throwing things/at trees/ at birds/into ponds	4		1	
Making fires	1		—	
Making camps	2		1	
Playing in sand	2		1	
Setting-off fireworks	1		—	
Setting-up bike ramp	1		—	
Animal play/feeding ducks	1		6	
	50	26	54	31
Mobile Play				
Walking	5		6	
Biking	6		6	
Go-carting/horse riding/roller-skating/cross-country running	3		3	
	14	7	14	8
Spectator/Formal Events				
Shopping/eating out	1		15	
Watching football matches	—		4	
Going to the pictures	—		2	
Other	3		1	
	4	2	22	13
Activities Inside Home				
Watching television	5		5	
Helping parents/relatives	—		9	
Reading/writing/drawing	3		1	
Playing around	2		—	
	10	5	15	9
Total	192	100	173	100

N = 96

Places where children went to meet other children and to be alone

	Mentions			
	To meet other children		To be alone	
Places	No.	%	No.	%
Home and Homesite				
Own home/own room	—		51	
Own garden/own yard	—		4	
Garage/shed	—		3	
Relatives home	—		—	
Friend's home	14		2	
Friend's garden/yard	—		—	
	14	11	60	59
Streets and Associated Space				
Streets	14		5	
Fronts/grass areas	7		2	
Backs/alleyways/mews	2		2	
Around the flats	6		2	
Garage courts	—		2	
	29	23	13	13
Formal/Official Open Space				
Parks	35		14	
Fairlands Park	7		—	
Playground/play area/swings	8		3	
Adventure playground	2		1	
Sports ground/playing field	—		1	
	52	41	19	19
Informal/Unofficial Open Space				
Fields/rough ground/farmland	10		—	
Abandoned places/construction sites	5		—	
	15	12	—	—
Commercial Areas				
Shops	2		—	
Town centre	4		—	
Another town	—		—	
	6	5	—	—
Institutions/Community Facilities				
Swimming pool	1		—	
Youth club	—		—	
Horse stables/riding	—		—	
Church	—		—	
Football match	1		—	
Pictures	—		—	
Dancing classes/disco	2		—	
	4	3	—	—
Nonspecific				
Anywhere/outside	7	5	5	5
Other				
Climb tree/secret place	—	—	4	4
Total	127	100	101	100
	(Don't need to/never want to:1) (Don't know:2)		(Don't need to/never want to:6) (Never get a chance [siblings]:4)	

N = 96	n = 93 for resposes tabulated	n = 86 for responses tabulated

6　*How children travelled to favourite places after school and on weekends*

How children travelled	Mentions			
	After School		Weekends	
	No.	%	No.	%
Walk	90	93	66	64
Bike	6	6	9	9
Car	1	1	13	13
Public transport	—	—	15	14
Total	97	100	103	100

N = 96

7　*Frequency of bicycle use by children*

Bicycle use	Children	
	No.	%
Did not have use of bicycle	36	38
Every day	10	10
Some days	24	25
Weekends only	14	15
Almost never	4	4
Bicycle was broken	8	8
Total	96	100

N = 96

8   *Territorial limits: places prohibited by parents and farthest places travelled to by children*

Territorial limits	Mentions			
	Places prohibited by parents		Farthest place travelled to by child	
	No.	%	No.	%
Nonspecific—loosely defined (e.g., everywhere)	20	13	3	2
Nonspecific—tightly defined (e.g., not far)	11	7	2	1
Within neighbourhood Not beyond street/to school only/local shops/not on road with bike/not off the estate/not out of neighbourhood/to friends or relatives house	14	9	10	8
Parks and Open Space	21	14	14	12
Adventure Playgrounds	13	9	3	2
Other Specific Places Lakes/canals/swimming pools	8		9	
Marlholes	6		—	
Abandoned places	3		1	
Other landmarks	4		6	
	21	24	16	13
Across main road/other geographic boundaries	13	9	—	—
Another neighbourhood	2	1	8	7
Shopping centre/town centre	13	9	29	24
Next town/another town	4	3	25	21
Out into the country	—	—	2	1
Entertainment places Discos/footballmatches/funfairs/other notorious places	10	7	1	1
Buses/trains/Underground	8	5	8	7
Total	150	100	121	100

N = 96

9   *Amount of time each day children spent watching television*

Amount of time each day	Children	
	No.	%
None	—	—
One hour or less	14	15
One to two hours	20	21
Two to three hours	27	28
More than three hours	35	36
Total	96	100

N = 96

10   *Reasons why children were not allowed to go to certain places* [1]

Reasons why	Mentions	
	No.	%
Traffic	25	33
Physical hazards (other than traffic) Water/heights/unsafe buildings	18	24
Social Threat Strangers/other kids/adolescents	17	23
Social disaproval	1	1
Get too dirty	6	8
Too far/Get lost	4	5
Too dark/Scary	4	5
Total	75	100

[1]In response to the question: "Why?"—following the child's response to the question: "Are there places your parents won't allow you to go?" N = 96

What children especially liked about the outdoors [1]

What children liked	Mentions	
	No.	%
Better than indoors/being out	5	5
Playing	7	8
Playing with friends/people	13	14
Playing with stuff/with things/ more things to do/always something to do	15	16
More space to play/more room	8	9
Football	3	3
Riding bikes/horses/go-carts	5	5
Climbing trees/climbing fences	4	4
Nature Animals/birds/conker trees/frogs/cats/dogs	9	10
Specific Places Pictures/sweet shop/hut/yard/pen/swings/hide-and-seek fence/crates	10	11
Sensory Qualities Microclimate/snow/sun/colours	12	13
It's good for you	2	2
Total	93	100

(Nothing/don't know: 42 = 44% children and 31% total mentions)

[1] In response to the question: ''What is it about the outdoors you especially like?'' N = 96, n = 54 for resposes tabulated

What children disliked	Mentions	
	No.	%
Rough kids/ruffians/big boys/violence	14	27
People who complain/who chase you away/ who boss you around	5	10
Too many people/other children/too many bikes	3	6
Having to stay in/go out	2	4
Park too far away	1	2
Swings facing the wrong way	1	2
Too many rats	1	2
Sensory aspects Getting hurt/bumpy road/metal play equipment/too noisy/vertigo in flats/ smelly/getting dirty/falling over/scary	9	18
Microclimate/seasons Winter/too hot/too cold/rain/sleet/snow/ gets dark too early	15	29
Total	51	100

(Nothing/don't know: 61 = 63% children and 54% total mentions)

[1]In response to the question: "What is it about the outdoors you especially dislike?" N = 96, n = 35 resposes tabulated

13   *What children wanted added or changed to the outdoors* [1]

Changes or additions	Mentions	
	No.	%
New fixed resources Football stadium/outdoor pool/new pool/new play equipment in flats/new playground/make an adventure playground/make a park in our area/put equipment in the Dip/slides on hills/round-a-bout in square/hut/tree camp/hut to camp in/more swings/airplanes in field/banks for go-carts/swings/climbing frame	24	29
New natural resources Better conker trees/plant trees/flowers/lakes/grow trees/make forest/grass/pool/change garden	13	16
Animals Home for stray cats and dogs/squirrels/more pigeons	13	16
Organizational change No time limit on swings/get rid of cars on the street/open pool more often/no more wars/allow ball games around the flats/keep big boys out of the Canyon/bring library nearer/keep older kids out of the park/let kids play on roof of the garages/change it (Greenway) back to what it used to be/leave it as it is	12	14
Adjustments to existing resources Fix bike/put grass in park/bigger diving boards/proper football pitch with grass and football posts/more stuff in the park/make street smooth for roller-skating/make pavement wider	7	8
Changes to people Get rid of nasty people/make people be kind/get rid of bad kids/make caretakers let us play games	7	8
Climatic changes Summer all year/stop rain/not too hot/sunny all the time	4	5
Personal freedom Be able to go to Knebworth House on my own/be allowed to ride on motor bike/be allowed to go to the Dip	3	4
Total	83	100

(Don't know: 42 = 44% children and 34% total mentions. Prefer indoors:1, Everything is okay:2)

[1]In response to the question: "What would you like to see added or changed to the outdoors?" N = 96, n = 54 for respeses tabulated

D

Play objects and places encountered or referred to on field trips

Abandoned
  brickworks (Brickers)
Abandoned garden
Abandoned house
Abandoned orchard
Abandoned studio
Acorns
Adventure
  playgrounds
Asbestos cement roof
Ash paths
Asphalt surfaces

Back gardens
'Backs'
Backyards
Backyard gates
Balls
Bandstand
Baskets
Bee nests
"Beehive"
Beetles
Benches
Berries
Big pipe
Big slide
Bikes
Birds
Birds nests
Bird table
Blackberries
Blackberry patches
Blackberry places
Bluebells
Board games
Boats
Bollards
Bonfire materials
Bonfire places
Bricks
Brick walls
Brick paving
Bridges
Brushwood
Broken glass
Brook
Broken pottery
Burned pigeon hut
Bushes
Butterflies
Button

Camps
Cardboard boxes
Cardboard rolls
Car parks
Caves
Chainlink fences
Chalk
China plates

Chrysanthemums
Cinema
Cliffs
Climbing walls
Clock towers
Coal
Coats
Concrete-block wall
Concrete edging
Concrete shelter
Concrete transition
  structure
Conkers
Conker places
Conker trees
Conservatory
Corrugated steel
  sheets
Cricket bat
Cul-de-sac streets
Cul-de-sac 'green'
Cup of tea
Curved, steep path

Dams
Dead leaves
Debris
Derelict building
Dirt mound
Dirt path
Dirt slides
Ditch
Dogs
Domestic furniture
Door bells
Dragonflies
Drainage structures
Ducks

Electric torch
Electrical switchgear
Electrical transformer
Estate grounds

Fallen tree
Farm buildings
Fences
Fields
Fires
Fire brigades
Fire works
Fish
Fishing nets
Flagpole
Flat mound
Flights of steps
Flowers
Formal flower garden
Freshwater shrimp
Frogs
Front gate

'Fronts'
Fruit

Gap between garages
Gap between railings
Garages
Garage court
Gate
Go-carts
Goldfish
Grass
Grasshoppers
Grassy banks
Grassy path
Grasses
Grass seeds
'Greens'
Greenways
Guard dog
Gymnast bars

Handrails
Hard-standing
Hawthorn bushes
Hawthorn hedge
Head winding gear
Hedges
Hole in fence
Horses

Industrial junk
Insects
Inspection chamber

'Jerker'
Jetty

Kerbs

Ladybirds
Lakes
Lampposts
Lawns
Leaves
Lily pads
Lizards
Loft
Lookouts in trees
Long grass

Machine parts
Marlholes
Marlhole ponds
"Matchstick"
Maze
"Meteorite"
Mews
Milkcrates
Mice
Miscellaneous junk
Model boats

Monuments
"Mossy" grass
Mud
Museum exhibits
Mushrooms
Music shell

Neighbour's dog
Newts
Nursery school
  entrance

Oil drums
Old bed sheets
Old box
Old bike wheels
Old car seats
Old car tyres
Old chairs
Old houses
Old garages
Old railway engine
wheels
Old safe
Old setees
Old stove
Old tin cans
Ornaments (china)
Ornamental pool
Outhouses
Overgrown front
  garden

Paddling pools
Parks
Park boundary fence
Parked cars
Parked van
Park keeper's house
Park shelter
Patch of grass
Patch of lawn
Paths
Pavements
Paving stones
Pigeon loft
Pigeons
Piles of cut grass
Piles of leaves
Pipe
Plants
Planting beds
Plastic bottle
Plastic milk crates
Plastic mouldings
Plates (china)
Play equipment
Playgrounds
Playing fields
Playpark materials
Playpark structures
Playpark swing ropes
Ponds
Pond water

Pools of water
Posts
Potato crisp bag
Pottery fragments
Power ball
Primroses
Privet hedges
Pub
Puppet show

Rabbits
Rabbit hutches
Radio-controlled boats
Radio-controlled
planes
Red shale
Refuse tip
Reject toilet bowls
Remains of bush
Retaining walls
Rhododendron buds
Rhododendron
  bushes
Rhododendron
  "tunnels"
Roads
Rockeries
"Rocket"
Rocket ship
Rocks
Rocks and water
Rock-sided channel
Rock strata
Roller-coaster place
Roller skates
Roof girder
Roof terrace
Rooms
Ropes
Rose gardens
Rosehips
Round-the-block
Running water

Sand
Sandpit
Sandy patch
Sandbox
School grounds
Seeds
Seesaws
Sheds
Shopping carts
Shops
Shortcuts
"Shotties"
Schraff
Schrubs
Skipping ropes
Slides
Slopes
Small fishing net
Snowberries
Spiders

Squirrels
Steep bank
Steps
Sticks
Stinging nettles
Stones
Stone walls
Streets
Street lights
Street signs
Street trees
Subsidence area
  (Bomb Holes)
Subways
Sunken area (Dip)
Swans
Swimming baths
Swing rope
Swings
Sycamore seeds
Sycamore trees

Tadpoles
Tall grass
Tar patch
Telephones
Telephone wires
Tennis courts
"Tiddlers"
Toads
Toadstools
Top of bank
Top of gate
Topography
Toy cars
Town centres
Transport containers
Trees
Tree bark
Tree branches
Trollies
Tunnels

Vacant land

Walls
Water
Waterfall
Water beetles
Water rats
Water shrimp
Water spiders sic
Weeds
Weeping willows
Wheat
Wild grasses
Wildflowers
Wild animals
Windows
Wishing wells
"Witches' hats"
Wood
Woodland
Worms
Wrecked tractor

E

Organizations working on behalf of children's play, environmental education and children's rights

INTERNATIONAL ORGANIZATIONS

*Association for Childhood Education
International*
3615 Wisconsin Avenue N.W.
Washington, D.C. 20016, U.S.A.

Defense for Children International
P.O. Box 359
CH-1211, Geveve 4, Switzerland.

Environment Liaison Centre
P.O. Box 72461, Nairobi, Kenya.

*Environmental Design Research
Association* (EDRA)
L'Enfant Plaza Station
P.O. Box 23129
Washington, D.C. 20024, U.S.A.

Ekistics
24 Strat Syndesmou
Athens 136, Greece.

*European Leisure and Recreation
Association (ELRA)*
Seefeldstrasse 8
8022 Zurich, Switzerland.

*International Association for People
and their Physical Surroundings*
(IAPS)
School of Architecture, Kingston
Polytechnic Kingston-Upon-Thames
Surrey KT 1 2QJ, England.

*International Association for the
Child's Right to Play*
Playboard
Britannia House
50 Great Charles Street
Birmingham B3 2LP, England.

International Catholic Child Bureau
65, rue de Lausanne
1202 Geneva, Switzerland.

International Children's Centre
Chateau de Longchamp
Carrefour de Longchamp
Bois de Boulogne
75016 Paris, France.

International Cooperative Alliance
11 Upper Grosvenor Street
London W1X 9PA, England.

*International Council for
Children's Play*
Institute for Special Education
State University of Groningen
Onde Boteringestraat 1
9712 GA Groningen, Netherlands.

*International Council for
Environment and Development*
10 Percy Street
London W1P ORO, England.

*International Council on Health,
Physical Education and Recreation*
1201 Sixteenth Street N.W.
Washington, D.C. 20036, U.S.A.

*International Falcon Movement—
Socialist Educational International*
13 Place du Samedi
1000 Brussels, Belgium.

*International Federation of
Pedestrians*
Passage, 61-111
2511 The Hague, Netherlands.

International Rehabilitation
432 Park Avenue South
New York, N.Y. 10016, U.S.A.

*International Union for Child
Welfare*
Post Box 41
1211 Geneva, Switzerland.

*International Union of Family
Organizations*
28, Place Saint-Georges
75009 Paris, France.

*International Youth Federation for
Environmental Studies and Conservation*
10, Rue Prosper Merimée
67100 Strasbourg, France;
and
Klostermolle, Klostermollevej 48,
DK-8660 Skanderborg, Denmark.

*Latin American Leisure and Recrea-
tion Association* (ALITAR)
P.O. Box 3659, Hato Rey
San Juan, Puerto Rico 00919.

*UNEP (United Nations Environment
Program*
P.O. Box 30552, Nairobi, Kenya.

UNICEF
Palais des Nations
1211 Geneve 10, Switzerland.

UNICEF
866 UN Plaza
New York, NY 10017.

UNESCO
7 Place de Fontenoy
75700 Paris, France.

World Assembly of Youth
Ved Bellahøj 4
2700 Bronshøj, Denmark

*World Association of Girl Guides and
Girl Scouts*
132 Ebury Street
Westminster, London SW1W 9QQ,
England.

*World Leisure and Recreation
Association*
113 Tabaret Hall
University of Ottowa
Ontario, K1N 6N5 Canada.

*World Organization for Early
Childhood Education, OMEP*
International Headquarters
81 Irving Place
New York, N.Y. 10003, U.S.A.

World Scouting Association
Baden-Powell House
Queens Gate, London SW7, England.

NATIONAL ORGANIZATIONS

Argentina
IPA-Argentina
Arenales 3742-3 °B
1425 Buenos Aires
Argentina.

Australia
*Blue Folk Community Arts
Association*
P.O. Box 46
Higgins, ACT 2615 Australia.

Community Activity Centres Network
34 Liverpool Street
Sydney, NSW 2000 Australia.

*Out of School Child Care and
Activites Association (OSCCAA)*
Graylands Teachers College
Mimosa Avenue
Graylands, 6010 W. Australia.

IPA-Australia
8/183 Kooyong Road
Torak, Victoria 3142, Australia.

Austria
*Osterreichische Kinderfreunde
Wiener Kinderfreunde*
Albertgasse 23
1081 Vienna, Austria.

IPA-Austria
Laaerbergstrasse, 36/5/30
1100 Vienna, Austria.

Belgium
IPA-Belgium
Rijborgstraat 12
9790 Wortegem-Petegem, Belgium.

*Nationale Dienst voor
Openiuchtleven*
National Service for Openair Life
Spastraat 32
1040 Brussels, Belgium.

Notre Quartier au Jour le Jour
(Our Neighbourhood Day-by-Day)
Fondation Roi Baudouin
44 Pachecolaan
1000 Brussels, Belgium.

Met Open Oog Op Weg (Walking
Around With Your Eyes Open)
Koning Boudewijn Stichting
44 Pachecolaan
1000 Brussels, Belgium.

*Service de l'Animation et de la
Diffusion Culturelle*
(Animation Service)
Ministere de l'Education Nationale et
de la Culture Francaise
Galerie Ravenstein 4
1000 Bruxelles, Belgium.

Canada
Adventure Education Concept
427 Bloor Street
West Toronto, Ontario, M5S 1X7
Canada.

*Canadian Associatian of Toy
Libraries*
50 Quebec Avenue, Apt.1207
Toronto, Ontario M6P 4B4, Canada.

*Canadian Council on
Children and Youth*
and *IPA-Canada*
2211 Riverside Drive, Suite 11
Ottawa, Ontario K1H 7X5, Canada.

*Children's Environments
Advisory Service*
Central Mortgage and Housing Cor-
poration
Ottawa, Ontario K1A OP7, Canada.

*Canadian Parks and Recreation
Association*
333 River Road, Vanier City
Ottawa, Ontario K1L 8B9, Canada.

Children's Play Resource Centre
1811 West 16th Avenue
Vancouver, British Columbia
V6J 2M3, Canada.

Sports and Games Cooperative
18 Bedale Drive
Ottawa, Ontario K2H 5M1, Canada.

Denmark
Danish Playground Association
and *IPA-Denmark*
Virkfeltet 2
2700 Brönshöj, Denmark.

Socialt Bolig Byggeris
Ungdomsklubber (SBBU)
Langhusvej 89
2700 Brønshöj, Denmark.

England

Better Britain Competition
Bennyrigg Nature Conservancy
Council
P.O. Box 6, Godwin House, George
Street, Huntington, Cambs. PE18 6BU,
England.

Children's House Society
31 Tooley Street
London SE1, England.

*Council for Environmental
Conservation* (CoEnCo)
29 Grenville Street
London EC1N 8AX, England.

Community Service Volunteers
237 Pentonville Road
London N1 9NJ, England.

Council of Environmental Education
School of Education
University of Reading
Reading, Berks RG1 5AQ, England.

Fair Play fof Children
17 Bradford Road
Lewes, East Sussex, England.

Ecological Parks Trust
The Linnean Society
Burlington House
Piccadilly, London W1V 0LQ,
England.

*Handicapped Adventure Playground
Association*
Fulham Palace, Bishops Avenue
London SW6 6EA, England.

IPA-England
54 Dawlish Avenue, Weeping Cross
Stafford ST17 OEU, England.

*Inter-Action Trust Limited and
National Federation of City Farms*
15 Wilkin Street
London NW5 3NG, England.

Kidsline
10A St. Georges Square
London, England.

National Playbus Association
St. Thomas Church, St. Thomas
Street Bristol BSI, England.

National Playing Fields Association
25 Ovington Square
London SW3 1LQ, England

*Nature Conservancy Council
Interpretive Branch*
Attingham Park
Shrewsbury, Salop SY4 4TW, England.

Notting Dale Urban Studies Centre
189 Freston Road
London W10 6TH, England.

Out of School Alliance
Oxford House, Darbyshire Street
Bethnal Green
London E2 6HG, England.

*Play Board (Association for
Children's Play and Recreation, Ltd.)*
Britannia House
50 Great Charles Street
Birmingham B3 2LP, England.

Playeducation
97 Dale Street
Lancaster LA1 3AP, England.

Save the Children Fund
17 Grove Lane
London SE5 8RD, England.

Scrap Project
29-30 Arlington Way
London EC1, England.

Seeds for Self-Sufficiency
Save the Children Fund
157 Clapham Road
London SW9 OPT, England.

*Streetwork/Bulletin for
Environmental Education* (BEE)
189 Freston Road
London W10 6TH, England.

*Toy Library Association
of the United Kingdom*
Seabrook House, Wyllyotts Manor
Darkes Lane, Potters Bar
Hertsfordshire EN6 2HL, England.

Youth Environmental Action (YEA)
173 Archway Road
London N6 5BL, England.

Finland

IPA-Finland
Tuulimyllynkuja 1
29200 Harjavalta, Finland.

Mannerheimin Lastensuojeluliitto
Mannerheim League for Child Welfare
Postilokero 143
00531 Helsinki 53, Finland.

France

*Association des Amis des
Journées Arc-en-Ciel*
B.P. 5066, 31033 Toulouse-Cedex,
France.

*Association Francaise pour
l'Education par le Jeu*
19 avenue Mozart
75016 Paris, France.

*Comité pour le Développement de
l'Espace pour le Jeu* (CODEJ)
18 rue Chatillion
75014 Paris, France.

Group Ludic
49 rue Alexandre Dumas
75011 Paris, France.

IPA-France
18 quai de Béthune
75004 Paris, France.

German Federal Republic
*Bund der Jugenfarmen und Ak-
jtivspielplatze*
(Youth Farms)
1 Elsental 3
D 7000 Stuttgart 80
German Federal Republic.

IPA-West Germany
Arbeiterwohlfahrt Bundesverband
Postfach 1149, 5300 Bonn 1
German Federal Republic.

Pädagogische Aktion
(Animation Group)
Schellingstrasse 109a
8000 München 40
German Federal Republic.

Greece
IPA-Greece
4 Kouma Street
Larissa, Greece.

Playstreets
Ministry of Physical Planning Housing
and the Environment Department of
Playstreets
2 Panormou Street
Athens, Greece.

Hong Kong
IPA-Hong Kong
P.E. Section, KSO Ed
Kowloon Government Offices, 7th.
Floor
405 Nathan Road
Kowloon, Hong Kong.

India
Bal Bhavan Society
Kotla Road
New Delhi-2, India.

IPA-India
Nehru Bal Samiti, E/63 NDSE Part 1
New Delhi 110049, India.

*National Institute of Public Coopera-
tion and Child Development*
(NIPCCD)
5, Siri Institutional Area, Hauz Khas
New Delhi 110016, India.

Israel
*Association for the Advancement of
Play in Israel*
and *IPA-Israel*
Nordau 81
Herzlia
Israel.

Italy
*Comitato italiano per il gioci in-
fantile*
vis Jervis 24
10015 Ivrea, Torino, Italy.

Japan
Group Orizi
1-31-21 Diazawa, Setagaya-ku
Tokyo 155, Japan.

IPA-Japan
1-25-3 Kyodo, Setagaya-ku
Tokyo 156, Japan.

Taishido Study Group
Kodomo no Asobi to Machi
Kenkyukai
2-9-3- Taishido, Setagaya-ku
Tokyo 154, Japan.

Malta
IPA-Malta
103 Gunlayer Street
Floriana, Malta.

Netherlands
IPA-Netherlands
c/o Rotterdam City, Sports and Recreation Department
Weena 760
3014 DA Rotterdam, Netherlands.

Kinderboerderijen
(Children's Farms)
Instituut voor Natuurbeschermings-
educatie
Plantage Middenlaan 41
1018 DC Amsterdam, Netherlands.

*Nederlandse Unie van Speel-
tuinorganisaties* (NUSO)
Nieuwe Herengracht 119
1011 SB Amsterdam, Netherlands.

*Service for School and Children's
Gardens*
Leidsestraatweg 77
2594 BB The Hague, Netherlands.

Stichting Ruimte
Weena 732, P.O. 20732
Rotterdam, Netherlands.

Stichting Recreatie
Statenplein 1
The Hague, Netherlands.

Stichting Speel-o-theek
Sarphatipark 79-81
1073 CT Amsterdam, Netherlands.

Woonerven
(Residential Precincts)
Royal Dutch Touring Club (ANWB)
Wassenaarseweg 220
2 609 BA The Hague, Netherlands.

New Zealand
IPA-New Zealand
159 Highgate
Dunedin, New Zealand.

*New Zealand Council for Recreation
and Sport*
P.O. Box 5122
Wellington, New Zealand.

Norway
IPA-Norway
Lerkeveien 7A
1404 Siggerud, Norway.

*Norwegian Institute of Urban and
Regional Research*
(Research reports on children and en-
vironment)
Post Box 322 Blindern
Oslo 3, Norway.

Norwegian Ministry of Culture
State Office of Youth and Sports
Postbox 8172 Dep.
Oslo 1, Norway.

Jondal Soknerad
(Pedagogical Play Centre)
5627 Jondal in Hardanger, Norway.

Scotland
Environmental Resource Centre
Old Broughton School
MacDonald Road
Edinburgh EH7 4LO, Scotland.

Children's Scrap Centre
16 Burgess Street
Leith, Edinburgh, Scotland.

IPA-Scotland
5 Jubilee Gardens
Milton of Balgonie
Fife KY7 6QF, Scotland.

Play Resource Unit
School of Community Studies
Moray House College of Education
Holyrood Road, Edinburgh EH8 8AQ,
Scotland.

Sweden
Barnmiljöradet
Children's Environments Council
Box 22106
104 22 Stockholm, Sweden.

Erfarenhetsverkstan
(Experience Workshop)
Box 3055, 127 03 Skärholmen
Sätra, Sweden.

Fritid Stockholm
Stockholm Leisure
Box 195, 101 22 Stockholm, Sweden.

Hyresgästernas Riksforbund
Swedish Tenants Association
Box 7515
103 92 Stockholm, Sweden.

IPA-Sweden
Skogslöparvägen 24
163 60 Stockholm, Sweden.

Stockholm Institute of Education
Department of Educational Research
Box 34103
100 26 Stockholm, Sweden.

Togo
*l'Association des Educateurs pour la
Santé d'Afrique, de Madagascar et de
l'Ile Maurice*
B.P. 2021, Lomé, Togo.

United States
*American Association for
Leisure and Recreation*
1900 Association Drive
Reston, Va. 22091, U.S.A.

Architects-in-Schools
Educational Futures Inc.
Box 13507 Philadelphia, Pa. 19101,
U.S.A.

*American Association for the
Anthropological Study of Play*
Box 297 Alamo, Ca. 94507, U.S.A.

Children's Environments Quarterly
Centre for Human Environments
Graduate Centre, C.U.N.Y.
33 West 42nd Street
New York, N.Y. 10036, U.S.A.

City Building Education Programs
235 South Westgate Avenue
Los Angeles, C.A. 90049, U.S.A.

The Farm/Crossroads Community
1499 Potrero Avenue
San Francisco, C.A. 94110, U.S.A.

IPA-U.S.A.
1700 North Lilac Drive
Golden Valley, M.N. 55422, U.S.A.

*National Assocation for Education of
Young Children*
1834 Connecticut Avenue, N.W.
Washington, D.C. 20009, U.S.A.

PLAE, Inc. (Playing and Learning in
Adaptable Environments)
1824 Fourth Street
Berkeley, C.A. 94710, U.S.A.

Playground Clearing House
26 Buckwalter Road
Phoenixville, P.A. 19460, U.S.A.

Childhood's Domain

INDEX

abandoned places, 160-91, 195
  brickworks, 189-90
  definition of qualities, 162
  houses, 182, 188
  industrial buildings, 188, 189-90
  old garages, 181-2, 185, 187
  orchard, 168, 239
  marlholes,
  parental anxiety about, 162, 108
  parents perception of, 222-3
  powerhouse, 190
  school building ("studio"),
    185-7
  weighbridge, 190
  youth club, 182
  see also Bomb Holes, Brickers,
    Grogs, marlholes
access
  to diversity, 51, 80, **234-6**
  to diversity in Tunstall, 205
  as essential ingredient, 157
  restrictions on, 200-1
  see also barriers, boundaries,
    restrictions
accidents
  and risk-taking, 72
Action Plans for Children and Youth
  (Norway), 251
adults
  conflict with, 102, 140, 179, 187,
    188, 199-200, 204; as
    neighbours, 199-200
  as friends, 127, 181
  relations with in parks, 127-8
  see also parents
adventure play, **48-50**, 227
adventure playgrounds, 48-50,
    132-7
  animals on, 88
  Chris' comments about, 137
  Danish, 248, 249
  evaluation of, 52
  as furthest place travelled to, 203
  parents attitude towards, 136,
    246-7
  policy towards, 246-7
  as prohibited places, 201
  in Stevenage, 132
  trees on, 132, 137
  see also Holland Park Venture
    Sausage Tunnel, 229
air play, 9

alleys, 44, 91-4
  see also backs, mews
Anarchy in Action (Ward), xviii
animals
  as play objects,45,78,80
  bees, 168
  beetles, 90, 245
  birds, 45, 78, 119, 123, 124, 176
  cats, 169, 176
  caterpillars, 90, 245
  on Danish adventure playgrounds,
    248
  dogs, 144, 149, 172, 176
  dragonflies, 115, 254
  ducks, 120
  fish, 80, 115, 123, 149, 153, 173,
    245
  frogs, 80, 153, 173, 174, 203
  goldfish, 115
  grasshoppers, 90, 173, 176,
  horses, 119
    importance of facilities for, 88
  ladybirds, 90, 168, 176, 187, 245
  lizards, 176
  minnows, 173, 245
  mice, 176
  myna birds, 119, 213
  newts, 50, 173, 225
  pigeons, 86, 119, 176
  rabbits, 176
  shrimp (freshwater), 154
  spiders, 176, 245
  squirrels, 170
  swans, 126, 210
  tadpoles, 173, 225, 245
  tiddlers, 123, 149, 153
  toads, 225
  wasps, 2
  water beetles, 173
  water lice, 154
  water spiders, 173
  wood lice, 245
  worms, 154, 245
  see also fishing, parks, urban
    wildlife
animation, **247-51**
  policy towards, 52
  see also playleaders, social
    pedagogs
annual holidays, 216
apples as play objects, 169
Appleyard, Donald, xix, 237, 239
appreciation, see environmental
  appreciation

aquatic features
mentioned in drawings, 44
in parks, 80, 114, 115
see also lakes, ponds, pools
archaeology as play theme, 2, 76, 226
Arendt, Hannah, 231, 233
asphalt
low score for, 46
to play on, 139
used for ball games, 129
assimilation / accommodation, 11, 18
Aston, as furthest place travelled to, 203
Atelier d'Enfants (France), 249
Australia, City Farms, 248
Austria, *Weiner Kinderfreunde*, 249
Avondale Park, 32, 112, 130-1, 243
as destination, 209
flower beds in, 120
large amount of asphalt in, 129
need for play leadership in, 128
park keepers in, 127
reasons for high level of use, 132
roughing-up policy for, 243
traditional play equipment in, 112
trees in, 120, 129

Bachelard, Gaston, 19
backs, 91-4
on Mill Hill turf map, 36
as play places, 59, 68
see also alleys, mews
ball games
as favourite activity, 47-8
in Mill Hill backs, 92-3
balustrades, 47
see also fences, railings
banks
children's comments about, 222
grassy, 74, 116, 139, 144, 155, 158
see also hills, slopes
barriers to experience, 14, 70
canals, 205
consideration in planning, 205
fences and railings, 70, 138
housing estate boundaries, 203-4
industrial zones, 205
rail lines, 205
roads, 132, 205, 209
see also access, boundaries, restrictions
base (den, docker)
backyard entrance as, 92

letterbox as, 76
Bedwell, 24
access to diversity, 235
adventure playground use, 50, 246
Dip, 142-4
fields, 141-2
fronts, 97-102
garage courts, 102
Guy Fawkes fires, effect of, 165-6
lack of traffic mentions, 46
natural environment elements, 42
neighbourhood boundaries, effect of, 204
pathways, 40, 80
pedestrian movement, 58-59
traffic-separated routes, 59-60, 62, 65
tree-play issues, 99-100
turf map, 33-6, 38-40
weekend trips, 215
see also Fairlands Park
bees as play objects, 168
beetles as play objects, 90
Belgium
Fondation Roi Baudouin, 249
Service de l'Animation et de la Diffusion Culturelle, 249
benches as play objects, 47, 107
Berger, John, 21
best friends, 104, 182
duet, 57
mentions of in drawings, 46
Between Past and Future (Arendt), 231, 233
bicycles, 63-7, 104
access to diversity with, 235
conflict with pedestrians, 65
free-range use of, 66, 209
furthest place travelled to with, 203
hazards on major roads, 66
in Holland Park, 65
in Little Park, 155, 158
in multistory housing, difficulties with, 64
'occasional' trips to lakes with, 65
'occasional' trips to town centres with, 201
ownership, 64
riding, low mention of, 48
riding through water, 123
scrambler bikes, 74
sensory character of, 66

as macro landscape feature, 42
maze in, 124
orangery in, 124
rose garden in, 124
on turf map, 32
Venture in, 112, 132, 136, 137
watching tennis in, 124
Holme, Anthea, 209
hologram (as metaphor), 8
homes / homesites, 40, 43-4, 48
architecture, play value of, 84
child's own, 40, 41
of friends, 40, 41
as haven, 82
other than child's, 40, 41
push-pull of in relation to outdoors, 84
transition spaces in, 84
Homo Ludens (Huizinger), 9
horses, 119
horse riding, **67-8**
as mobile activity, 48
need for places for, 221
housing authority management
negative effect on play, 90-1, 204
housing conditions, 196-7
Huizinger, Johann, 9
huts, child-built, 134
see also camps, clubhouses,
hiding places, lookouts
Hyde Park, weekend trips to, 216

Iacofano, Daniel, xix
iconic mode of playing and learning,
12, 21
imaginative play, 2
individual differences; masked by
results, 44
industrial zones; as access barriers,
205
Inter-Action, 248
interiors
low score for, 46
shown in drawings, 31
International Association for the
Child's Right to Play (IPA), xix
interpersonal mode of playing and
learning, 12, **16**
interracial conflict, 182
interviews
with children, 24
results of, 43
islands; in lake, 120, 124

Jackson, Inge, xx
junk, attitude towards, 174

Kidsgrove; as 'occassional'
destination, 201
Kittredge, Lucia, xix
Knebworth House; as furthest place
travelled to, 203
Knight, Jane, xix, 248
Knypersley; as 'occasional'
destination, 201

ladybirds, 90, 168
Laing, R.D., 16
lakes
by Burslem Greenway, 149
in Fairlands Park, 44-5, 120,
122-3
as furthest place travelled to, 203
in Glenn's marlhole, 177
as 'occasional' places, 65
in Tunstall Park, 45, 120, 123-4
see also aquatic features, ponds,
pools, Rudyard Lake, Stanley
Lake, Westport Lakes
lampposts as play objects, 47, 74,
100-2, 104
landscape management issues, 245
landscape perceptions
of parents, 221-4
child-parent differences, 222-4
landscape reclamation
conflicting values in, 222-224
as perceived by children, 223, 225
policy issues of, 221-33, 243-5
Land Use Consultants, xx
language aptitude, 195-7
"lateral drift," 15
lateral thought, 15
Laurie, Ian, 244
lawns / mown grass
associated with street play, 44
as favourite places, 40-1
fenced-in in Notting Dale, 94
as play places, 47, 90, 95, 97, 116,
141
as roundabout, 97
unused in parks, 34, 129
watching sports from, 124
wind-swept, 114
see also grass, grassy patches,
slopes (grassy)
leaves
as play objects, 72, 80, 92, 116,
117, 120, 123, 141, 158, 168

raking, with park keepers, 127
legality of child-made places, 46
legends of childhood landscapes
  Bomb Holes, 75
  dinosaur print, 76
  tractor in marlhole, 174
  see also stories
leisure pedagogs, *see* animation,
  playleaders, social pedagogs
Lerup, Lars, xviii
letterboxes as play objects, 66, 76
libraries, public
  as animation sites, 248, 249
  need for access to, 221
  nonuse of, 214
  use of, 214, 228
Lintell, Mark, xx
Little, Brian, xix
Little Park, 150-8
Livable Streets (Appleyard), 237
live experience, value of, 21
London mainline stations, 203
lookouts, 74, 76, 100, 119, 147, 148,
  169, 172, 222
  see also camps, clubhouses,
  hiding places, huts
loose parts, **78-80**
  balls as, 97
  in clubhouses, 85, 86
  for cockshy, 165
  excavated on Greenway, 227
  to fish with, 123, 154
  in Glenn's marlhole, 176-82
  in Heather's old garage, 181-2
  on housing estates, 204
  on the Grogs
  see also animals, found objects,
  vegetation
Loss and Change (Marris), xviii
Lustick, Marlene, xix
Lynch, Kevin, xix, 19, 229

macro-landscape features, 42
Magical Child (Chilton Pearce), 8
major roads as access barriers, 205
mainline stations, London, 203
Marat Farm, 162, **168-70**
"Marat's toffee," 170
marbles, *see* shottie
marlholes
  as forbidden places, 210
  as play places, 80, 173-81,
  189-90, 225
  as special places, 224

Marris, Peter, xviii
marshes, policy towards, 245
Massachusetts Institute of
  Technology, xix
Massie, Peter, 209
Mead, George Herbert, 10, 12
Mead, Margaret, 12, 16
memorable environments,
  effects of, 21
  and figure / ground relationships,
  244
  lack of adults in, 47
  of parents, 197, 205, 223
  of parks, 128-9
Merleau-Ponty, Maurice, xviii
methodology, **29-31**
mews, 94
  see also alleys, backs
microclimate
  of Avondale Park, 132
  of back alleys in Mill Hill, 92
  children's perception of, 220-221
  of the Dip, 144
  of Edward Woods Estate, 4, 144
  of Heather's 'meanwhile' sanctuary, 167
  of Heather's old garage, 182
  of the Little Park, 157
  of mews in Notting Dale, 94
  need for design of, 221
  of school grounds, 140, 144
  of Tracy's marlhole, 176
microcomputers, potential of, 21
milieu, 195-8
milkcrates as play objects, 78, 134
Mill Hill, 24
  access to diversity, 80, 90
  adventure play, opportunities for,
  191
  backs, 91-4
  fronts, 94-7
  front garden play, 89
  Guy Fawkes Fires, effect of,
  165-6
  homesites, 42
  Little Park, 150-8
  natural environment elements,
  42
  natural resources, access to, 90
  parks; diversity of, 114-19
  pathways, 40, 70, 80
  pedestrian movement, 59
  pets, places for, 86
  physical diversity, 81

traffic-separated routes, 60, 62-3,
65
roller skating, 68
sheds and garages, 84
stable environment, effect of, 216
street improvements, op-
portunities for, 238
street play traditions, 239
go-carting, 68-9
traditional games; richness of, 219
turf map, 36, 39-40, 241
see also Tunstall, Tunstall Park
Milne, A.A., 19
Minister for Children's Play (British),
22
missing items in drawing and
interview data, 44-7
mobile play, 47, 56-74
modes of acquiring and representing
experience, definitions of, 12
de Monchaux, Suzanne, 22, 252
monuments as play objects
bird table, 116
Castle, 116
Clock Tower, 117
"meteorite," 117
old railway engine wheels,
228-9
moss as play place, 155
mounds of clay, 190
Mow Cop as 'occasional'
destination, 201
mud, 154
as "Marat's toffee," 170
museums
as animation sites, 248, 249
use of, 213, 228
mushrooms as play objects, 197
myna birds as play objects, 119, 213

National Endowment for the Arts
(USA), xix
native landscape treatment
Dutch approach, 244
user benefits, 244
natural environment
children's comments about, 124
elements in drawings, 42
need for on adventure
playgrounds, 137
w̶ ᵘ ᵈd by children, 220
natural ground surfaces, 40, 43
Nature Conservency Council
(British), 245

negotiation of territorial limits,
203-5, 208-10, 212
neighbours, 199
Netherlands
children's farms, 248
native landscaping, 244
NUSO, 249
Newson, John and Elizabeth, 16
New South Wales Government, 22
newts as play objects, 50, 173, 225
niemansländ, 162
Norway; Action Plans for Children
and Youth, 251
Notting Dale, 2, 24
access to diversity, 236
adventure play, opportunities for,
191
adventure playground use, 50, 246
Commonwealth Institute, 214
development character, 219
housing authority; effect on play,
90-1
lack of aquatic features, 44
Lancaster Club, 214
mews, 94
natural environment elements, 42
open space, 42
pedestrian movement, 58-9
play space, lack of, 90
rough ground areas, 167-8
roughing-up policy, 242
school grounds, 138
social diversity, 81
special places, 240
swimming pool, 213
traffic-separated routes, 62-3
turf map, 32, 38-40
underused space for sport, 149
weekend trips, 215, 216
see also Avondale Park, Holland
Park, St. Mark's Park
Notting Dale Urban Studies Centre,
xx, 248
NUSO (Netherlands), 249
nuts as play objects, 76

occasional range
definition of, 17-18
and public transport, 217
town centres in, 201
oil drums as play objects, 80, 164
Oldham, study of play in, 104
open space, 40, 44
formal / official, 42-4

304

informal / unofficial, 42-4
Opie, Iona and Peter, xiv-xvi
orangery, 124
orchard (old) as play place, 168, 239
    see also woodland
outdoor-indoor differences in
    drawings, 31

Padägogische Aktion (Germany),
    248
paddling pools
    see pools
parents
    and abandoned places, 162
    anxiety of, 80, 187, 198, 201,
        205-8
    attitude towards education, 196
    children's dependence, effect of,
        233
    control of homesite play by, 88-9
    fears of, 205-8
    influences of, 4, 196
    low score for, 47
    methodological issues with, 210
    mother-father differences, 210-2
    negotiation of territorial limits,
        203-5, 212
    perceptions of environmental
        change, 221-4
    and territorial autonomy, 227
    weekend trips with, 215-6
    working, 198
parks, 40, 41, 42, 108-32
    adult attitudes towards, 110, 242
    animals in, 115, 119-20
    as animation sites, 248
    Burslem Park, 114
    child-adult relations in, 127-8,
        223
    comparative sizes of, 129
    concerts in, 128
    as destinations, 210
    diversity in Victorian, 114
    edible landscapes in, 120
    formal gardens in, 126
    as furthest place travelled to, 203
    hiding places in, 117, 119
    lack of adventure play in, 227
    lakes in, 120-4
    management issues in, 123, 242
    as places to be alone, 126
    as places to heighten environmen-
        tal awareness, 126
    as places for picnics, 212

as playgrounds, 114-19
policy towards, 51, 242
as prohibited places, 201
social value of, 128-9
sports in, 124
trees in, 120
vandalism in, 128
park benches; use by horse riders,
    68
park keepers, 119, 124, **127-28**, 158
    absence of in Little Park, 157
    in Avondale Park, 127
    need for female, 128
    Simon's definitions of, 127
    in Tunstall Park, 127
participation
    of children in decision making,
        226
    of children in research, 20
    policy towards, 52, 251-2
pathways, 40, 43, 48, **58-63**
    hidden paths, 70
    in Stevenage, 214
pavements
    mention in drawings, 40, 41
    as play places, 48, 97-8, 102, 104,
        106, 195
paving stones as play objects, 72
Pawley, Martin, 21
Pearce, Joseph Chilton, 7-9, 12
Pedagogy of the Oppressed (Friere),
    xviii
pedestrian networks, 58-63
pedestrian subways, bicycle use in,
    66
Perls, Frederick, xviii
permission, negotiation of, 18
people, low score for, 46
personality, 194-5
pets
    birds, 86
    cats, 45, 86
    dogs, 45, 86
    pigeons, 86
    places for, 86-8
    rabbits, 86
Phenomenology of Perception
    (Merleau-Ponty), xviii
Piaget, Jean, 8, 10, 11, 12, 14, 16
Piccadilly as play place, 203
picnics, 2
pigeons as play objects, 86, 119, 172
Pin Green, 203
pipe, water, 153, 158

public transport, 216-7
   see also buses, Underground
   (London), trains
pubs as undesirable places, 207
puppet shows, 128
purity
   and disorder, 230-2
   of urban environments, 21
putt, 124

Queenie Pond, 225, 239, 244

railings as play objects, 72, 74
railway lines as barriers, 36, 205
range
   development, 18
   frequented, 17-18, 40
   growth, 18
   habitual, 17, 40
   occasional, 17-18, 40
redevelopment zones as play places,
   182-91
red shale, 59, 68
refuse tips as play places, 76,
   179-81
Reilly, Mary, 15
Relph, Edward, 19, 21
remembrance of childhood play
   places, 19-20
research methods, 24-9, 268-72
   as policy tool, 241
resource management of greens,
   158
restrictions on children
   by adults other than parents, 102,
   204
   on housing estates, 90-1, 94, 204
   lack of in marlholes, 176
   by parents, 90-1, 108, 191, 197,
   200-1
   in parks, 120
   on school grounds, 140
   by Stevenage landuse pattern, 191
   see also access, barriers,
   boundaries
rhododendron
   buds as play objects, 78
   bushes as hiding places, 117-9
rights of the child, *see* UN Declaration of
rill in Little Park, 154, 158
   see also brooks, Scotia Brook,
   streams
roads as barriers, 36

Robinson Crusoe playgrounds
   (Switzerland and Germany), 50
Robinson, William, 244
rockeries, 114, 123
rocks
   outcroppings as play objects, 177
   as play objects, 78, 122
roller skating, 48, 68-9, 98, 104,
   187, 239
   need for good surface, 221
rootedness, 19
rope swings, 134, 182, 199, 246
rosebay willowherb (fireweed), 92,
   167, 189
rose gardens as play places, 116, 124
rosehips as play objects, 76
rough ground, 160-81
   animals in, 90
   definition of qualities, 162,
   242-5
   as favourite place, 42
   play potential of, 242
   policy towards, 242-5
   on turf maps, 36
   and vandalism, 243-4
Rousseau, Jean Jacques, 19
rubbish tips; *see* refuse tips
Rudyard Lake as furthest place
   travelled to, 65, 203
Ruff, Allan, 244
rural-urban contrasts, 197

St. Mark's Park, 110
safe (old, steel), as play object, 189
safety issues in play environments,
   208
sand
   box, 139
   patch (Little Park), 155
   pile, 191
   pit, 111
Sandels, Stina, 237
San Francisco, Farm, 248
Satre, Jean-Paul, 230
Sausage Tunnel, 229, 239, 244
SBBU (Denmark), 249
Scherler, Karl, 15
   communicative function, 16
school sites / yards / grounds, 34, 40,
   41, **138-41**, 144-6
   out-of-school use, 140-1
school trips
   to Commonwealth Institute, 215
   to nature reserve, 215

schools; role in environmental
  education, 233
Schumacher, E.F., xviii, 23, 232
Scotia Brook, 80, 123, 152, 158
Scotland
  Environmental Resource Centre,
    248
scrap
  projects, 181
  scavenging by children, 179-81
scrap pieces of wood as play
  objects, *see* sticks
scrap pottery as play objects,
  163-4, 176, 179, 227
  see also shraff
Seabrook, Jeremy, 228, 230
Searles, Harold, 10
secret places, *see* hiding places
seeds as play objects, 76, 94
seesaw, 188
semiotic mode of learning, 12
sense of enclosure as essential
  ingredient, 157
sense of place, 245
Sennett, Richard, 21, 230
*Service de l'Animation et de la
  Diffusion Culturelle* (Belgium),
  249
"sewer," 149
sewer pipes, as play objects, 50, 170,
  172
sex differences
  on adventure playgrounds, 246
  issues related to environmental
    planning, 211-2
  in negotiating territorial limits,
    208
  in parental control, 208
  in perceptions of mothers and
    fathers, 211
  in spatial behaviour, 204, 205
  in watching football matches, 213
sheds, 84-6, 189
  see also garages
Shepherd's Bush Market, 201
shopping, 47
shopping areas as play places, 34, 45
shopping trollies as play objects, 109
shops
  favourite types, 46
  local, 45
  toy-and-hobby, 46
shotties, 179
shraff, 176

shrimp (freshwater), 154
shrubs, *see* bushes
siblings, low score for, 47
Siggers, Trevor, xx
Simmons, Maureen, xix
slides
  grass / cardboard, 155, 158
  milkcrate, 78
  see also play equipment (slides)
slopes, grassy, 74, 119, 152, 155, 170
  see also banks, hills
Small is Beautiful (Schumacher),
  xviii, 232
Smith, Robert Paul, 19
snowberries as play objects, 78
socialisation, definition of, 16
social pedagogs, 249
  see also animation, play leaders
sound of stones on asbestos cement,
  190
special trips, 212-5
special places; conservation policy
  for, 239-41
sports
  fields, 148-50
  putt, 124
  tennis, 124, 144
  watching, 124
squatters, 184
squirrels as play objects, 170
Stanley Lake as furthest place
  travelled to, 203
steps as play places, 74, 117
Stevenage
  cycleways, 63
  development style, 218-9
  museum, 213
  pathways, 214
  restrictions of landuse pattern,
    191, 236
  roughing-up policy, 242
  town centre, 201
  walking tradition, 59
Stevenage Development
  Corporation, xx
sticks as play objects, 80, 158, 164,
  204
stinging nettles, 168, 169
Stoke-on-Trent
  roughing-up policy, 242
  urban trails, 239
Stone, Christopher, 14
stones as play objects, 165, 170, 177,
  190

stories, 195
  see also legends of childhood
    landscape
stove (old) as play object, 185
strangers, fear of, 197, 201, 205, 207, 210
streams, 34
  child-made, 155
  see also brooks, rill, Scotia Brook
streets
  as animation sites, 248
  and associated spaces, 44, 238-9
  cul-de-sac / deadend, 59, 94, 100, 104
  furniture; effect on play, 238
  livable, 237-9
  mentioned in drawings, 40, 41
  parents' comments about, 223
  as places for mobile play, 48
  as play places, 44, 100, 104-7
  play tradition in, 239
  policy towards, 51, 237-9
  as a social resource, 239
  use after school, 44
street people, 184, 186
streetside architecture, 106-7
street signs as play objects, 95
Streetwork (Ward and Fyson), xix, 22
string as play object, 84, 204
study sites, 24-50
  existing conditions in, 218-9
substations as play places, 109, 190
subways (pedestrian) as play places, 66, 195
swans as play objects, 126, 210
Sweden
  Experience Workshop, 248
  Fritid Stockholm, 250
swimming
  pools, 32, 44, 201, 213
  at weekends, 50
swings
  conflict with park keepers, 127
  giant tyre, 134
  in Little Park, 158
  on pipe, 212
  rope, 134, 182
  tree, 88, 199
  see also Tarzan (swings)
symbolic mode of learning, 12
symbolic / semiotic mode of learning, 14

tar patch as play object, 173
Tarzan, 88
  swings, 112, 113, 116, 134
teenage gangs, 184
telephone wires as play objects, 104
television
  effect of, 195, 197, **198-9**
  frequency of mention, 48
tennis, 124
terra ludens, 9, 14
territorial autonomy, 227
territorial range, 17-19
  effect of traffic-separated routes, 60
  limits of, 200-5
  parental restrictions on, 197
  negotiation of with parents, 203-5
throwing stones, 50
tiddlers, *see* fish
tightrope, 150
time
  homework, 198
  household chores, 198
  television, 198-9
  on use of space, 95
  weekday / weekend differences, 44
tin cans as play objects, 165
toadstools as play objects, 78
"To Catch the Wind" (Wood), 9
Tom Tiddlers Ground, 195
topography, **74-6**
  and bicyles, 66
  and bike wheels, 80
  and car tyres, 80
  effect on play, 238-9
  as essential ingredient, 157
  and go-carts, 68-9
  see also banks, cliffs, hills, mounds, slopes
toponymy, 225-6
topophilia, 19
town centres, 201-3
  as destinations, 210
  see also commercial areas
Town and Country Planning Association, xx
traditional games, *see* games
Trafalgar Square as play place, 203
traffic
  effect on street play, 238
  fear of, 205, 207
  lack of in Bedwell, 46
  low score for, 46

walls as play objects, 42, 72, 92, 97, 107, 142
walking, 48
   tradition in Stevenage, 59
Ward, Colin, xiii, xviii, xx, 22
wasps, 2
wasteland, 2
water
   parental fears about, 208
   play, 44, 50, 122, 123, 149, 150, 154, 174
   wanted by children, 220
   see also aquatic features, brooks, lakes, ponds, pools, streams, waterfalls, Westport Lakes
waterfalls, 114, 122, 123
water features, see aquatic features, brooks, lakes, ponds, pools, streams, water, waterfalls, Westport Lakes
water lice, 154
water rats as play objects, 80
Ways of Seeing (Berger), 21
Webb, Chris, xx
weekend visits, 215-6
'wedge' methodology, 29-30
Weiner Kinderfreunde (Austria), 249
   All-over-Vienna game, 249
Westland, Cor, 248
Westport Lakes
   access barriers to, 70
   as destination, 210
   as furthest place travelled to, 203
Westway, 63
What Time is this Place? (Lynch), 229
What Went Wrong? (Seabrook), 228
wheat as play object, 203
wildlife, see urban wildlife
willow trees, 75, 80, 120, 129, 195, 239, 243
window shopping, 201
wind-tunnel effect, 4
Winnicott, D.W., 12, 16
White, Robert, 15
Whitehead, Alfred North, 11
wishing wells, 214
Wong, Herb, xix
Wood, Denis, xix, 9
wood; pieces of to build with, 191
Woods Estate, see Edward Woods Estate
woodland, 34, 132, 170, 197
   see also orchard (abandoned)

Woonerven (residential precincts), 238
Wordsworth, William, 19
workingmen's club, 197
worms as play objects, 154

yards (and gardens) as play places, 88-91
Young, Donald, xviii, xix
youth clubs, use of, 214
Youth Farms (Germany), 248
youth organizations as a means of access, 215

Zazie dans le Metro (Queneau), 56
Zen and the Art of Motorcycle Maintenance (Pirsig), xviii
Zerner, Charles, 104, 237